Lundy & Irish Sea Pilot

Land's End to Portpatrick

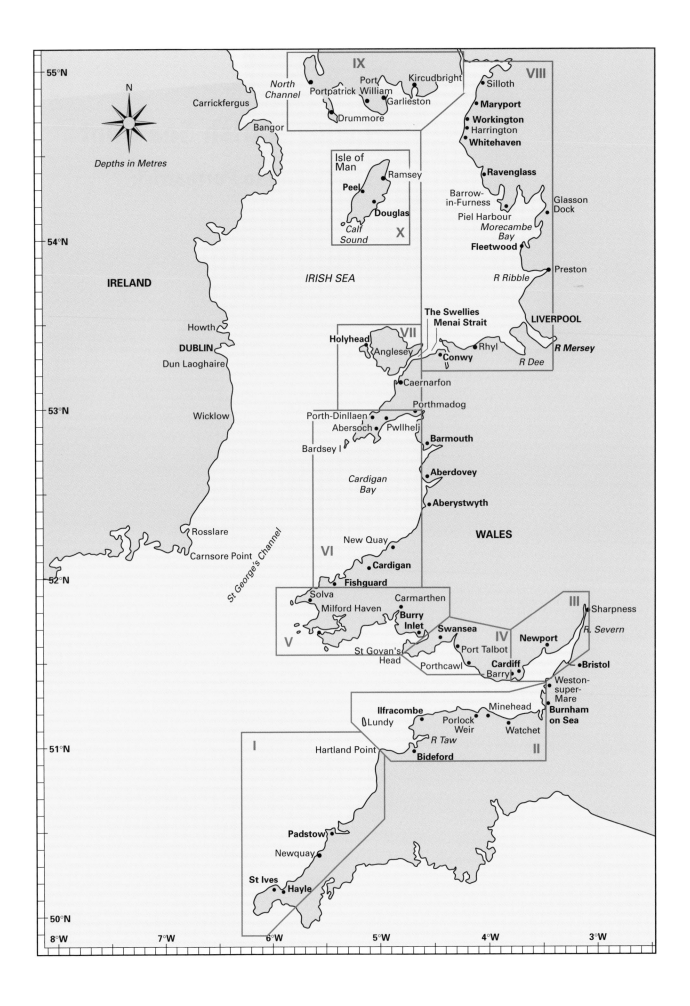

Lundy & Irish Sea Pilot

Land's End to Portpatrick

DAVID TAYLOR

Imray Laurie Norie & Wilson Ltd
St Ives Cambridgeshire England

Published by
Imray, Laurie, Norie & Wilson Ltd
Wych House, St Ives, Cambridgeshire, PE27 5BT,
England
☎ 01480 462114 *Fax* 01480 496109
E-mail ilnw@imray.com
www.imray.com
2001

1st Edition 1994
2nd edition 2001

© David Taylor 2001

British Library Cataloguing in Publication Data.
A catalogue record for this book is available from the British Library.

ISBN 0 85288 448 6

CAUTION
Whilst every care has been taken to ensure accuracy, neither the Publishers nor the Author will hold themselves responsible for errors, omissions or alterations in this publication. They will at all times be grateful to receive information which tends to the improvement of the work.

CORRECTIONAL SUPPLEMENTS
This pilot book will be amended at intervals by the issue of correctional supplements. These are published on the internet at our web site www.imray.com and may be downloaded free of charge. Printed copies are also available on request from the publishers at the above address.

PLANS
The plans in this guide are not to be used for navigation. They are designed to support the text and should always be used with navigational charts.

The last input of technical information was October 2001.

Printed in Great Britain by
Butler and Tanner, Frome, Somerset

Contents

Preface

Most of my cruising years have been spent experiencing the delights and tribulations of the Irish Sea, St George's Channel and the Celtic Sea, and I have long been aware of the lack of a good yachtsman's cruising guide to the area.

The current volume incorporates an updated version of the guide to the Bristol Channel first published in 1988. My original idea was to produce a guide covering Lundy, Fastnet and the Irish Sea, and it was initially decided to subdivide the area into three manageable volumes.

I have always believed that an author of cruising guides should be prepared to visit by sea at least once, and more often if possible, every harbour and anchorage covered by the volume. The logistics of carrying this out, since my cruising is limited by the weather and by other demands on my time, have meant that the planned second volume has taken longer to prepare than anticipated. During this time Imray, Laurie, Norie & Wilson have taken over the publishing of the Irish Cruising Club sailing directions, so it seemed a good time to reconsider the original proposal. The publishers suggested that as the Bristol Channel cruising guide was now five years old, it would make good sense to incorporate an updated version of it into a single volume covering the coast from Land's End to Portpatrick.

I trust that the end result will be useful in highlighting the delights and lessening the tribulations of sailing this gratifying cruising area.

David Taylor
Madoc Yacht Club
Porthmadog, Gwynedd 1994

On a personal note, I am currently between boats. Having sold my Snowgoose catamaran I am well underway with the construction of a Grainger 480 catamaran at the Weaver Boatyard, Northwich, Cheshire. Working on the revision of this volume has helped maintain my enthusiasm for getting back to sea and revisiting many of my favourite harbours and anchorages. I sincerely hope that this revised volume will similarly enthuse and encourage yachtsmen to visit the harbours and anchorages of this rewarding cruising area.

David Taylor
Cheshire 2001

Acknowledgements

My thanks go to all who have helped me with this publication. To my sailing friends who have lent documents and added their own useful comments, to those who have sailed the region with me, and to the local yachtsmen, harbourmasters and fishermen who have made useful comments. To Willie Wilson and the staff at Imray, Laurie, Norie & Wilson, Debbie Stapleford and Elaine Sharples for their amiability and tolerance. The sea level sketches were drawn by Lucy Wilson and the index compiled by Liz Cook My thanks to you all.

Preface to the second edition

In the seven years since the first edition of this book was published there has been a marked increase in demand for yachting facilities. New marinas have been established to meet the demand for moorings and existing harbours have been improved to increase accommodation and to make them more attractive to visitors. Work was obviously needed to bring the pilot up-to-date and I was delighted when the publishers informed me that they wanted to upgrade the old black and white to a full colour version. I feel that the addition of the excellent aerial photographs from Patrick Roach have given a new dimension to the appreciation of the harbours and marinas, whilst, of course, retaining the essential pilot book requirement of views from seaward.

Introduction

This volume has been prepared as a cruising guide for yachtsmen, and is intended to be read in conjunction with the relevant Admiralty and/or Imray charts.

General description

This cruising guide covers a diversity of sailing grounds. For the most part the coast is subject to prevailing winds, and the harbours and anchorages are often isolated and limited in their times of access. Harbour approaches can be difficult, and many are impossible in heavy weather. There are few marina facilities, although these are increasing. The result is a challenging cruising area with the added factor of strong tidal streams which demand careful passage planning.

The Bristol Channel is a formidable cruising area, with its strong tidal streams and ocean swells, and yet it is rich in nautical history and in its variety of scenery, from the rugged Cornish cliffs to the gentle wooded slopes of the River Cleddau.

The Welsh coast for the most part has less strong tidal streams than the Bristol Channel, but it includes Jack and Ramsey Sounds, Bardsey Sound and the Swellies, where notoriously strong currents demand the greatest care from the yachtsman. The delightful scenery extends from the gentle resorts of the Gower and Cardigan Bay to the sheltered cruising grounds of the Menai Straits, with their Snowdonian backdrop.

The harbours of the northwest coast of England have declined along with the old industrial base of the region, as alternative forms of transport have been established and the fishing trade has diminished. The introduction of new marinas along this coast and the improvement of harbours to provide amenities for yachtsmen are indicative of the increasing demand for such facilities.

The Isle of Man not only provides an excellent cruising ground in its own right but is also, by virtue of its position, a useful resting point for yachtsmen crossing the Irish Sea.

The harbours of the southern coast of Scotland which are covered by this guide are for the most part small and limited in their times of access, but offer the reward of the gentle scenic beauty that is characteristic of this part of the country.

Equipment for yachts

The physical characteristics and nature of the area make a good reliable engine a prerequisite for successful cruising. Good fuel and water capacity will facilitate passage planning. To explore the area fully it will be an advantage to have a yacht that can take the ground; the harbours and anchorages where a yacht may stay afloat are in the minority. Good ground tackle is essential for cruising the area, and a reliable depth sounder will prove its worth.

Plans and sketch maps

These have been prepared by the author, some based on available charts, others based on his personal survey. Some of the harbours, anchorages and facilities will be subject to man-made or natural change, and the plans should be used with prudence.

Waypoints

Waypoints have been included in this volume for most harbours. They have been given close to harbour entrances so as to be of the greatest possible benefit, but it is essential that the navigator check the waypoint position in relation to his line of approach in order to avoid any possible dangers.

Meteorological

The weather of the region is very variable, and it is difficult to summarise because of the frequent day-to-day changes.

Winds Predominantly from the southwest and west throughout the summer months; more variable in spring, when winds from the northeast and east are fairly frequent. Gales are infrequent in the summer months, but when they occur they are more likely to be severe in the exposed areas such as the approaches to the Bristol Channel. In the more sheltered areas gales are likely to be less severe and of shorter duration. The most frequent directions for gales are from the southwest and west.

Fog On the whole, fog and poor visibility are not common in the area. Sea fog occurs on an average of 2 to 3 days a month in the southern part of the area, decreasing to 1 to 2 days a month further north, and being more frequent in the earlier months. The fog may persist for as long as 2 to 3 days, although the average duration is only from 6 to 10 hours.

Precipitation and temperature May and June are usually the driest months, although September can be relatively dry for the time of year. July and August are generally the warmest months, with a mean air temperature of 16°C.

Weather forecasts

Forecasts for the region are readily available from a variety of sources.

BBC Radio 4

England and Scotland 198, 720kHz, 92·4–94·6MHz; Wales and N Ireland 92·4–96·1 or 103·5–104·9MHz.

Storm warnings All channels at the first available programme junction after receipt. After the first news bulletin after receipt. Gale warnings for all United Kingdom fcst areas, including Trafalgar.

Weather bulletins All channels at 0048, 0535. All channels at 1754 . Gale warnings in force, synopsis, 24h fcst for United Kingdom fcst areas. Reports from selected observation stations.

BBC Radio Cymru/Wales

NE Wales 657[1]; (All) Wales 882[1], Mid Wales 1125kHz[1]. 92·4–94·6MHz[2], 96·8MHz[2], 103·5–105MHz[2].

1. Bcsts as BBC Radio Wales.
2. Bcsts as BBC Radio Cymru, from over 40 transmission sites with power outputs ranging from 0·3 to 250kW).

Storm warnings All stations. On receipt. Severe weather (snow, gales etc) warnings for coastal (and inland) area of Wales.

Weather bulletins All weather broadcasts cover coastal (and inland) area of Wales.

657, 882, 1125kHz in English
Mon–Fri at 0658, 0758, 0903 LT. Sat 0903 LT. Sun 0859 LT. General fcst, synopsis for that day, live from National Weather Centre for Wales.

At 1259 LT. Mon–Fri 1734 LT. Sat, Sun 1759 LT. General fcst, synopsis for that afternoon and night, live from National Weather Centre for Wales.

Mon–Fri at 1000–1100 LT. Sat 0600, 0700, 0800, 1000, 1100 LT. Sun 0700, 0800, 1000 LT. Brief weather summary and fcst, after news bulletin, for that day.

Mon–Fri at 1200, 1400, 1500 LT. Sat 1200 LT. Sun 1500 LT. Brief weather summary and fcst, after news bulletin, for that afternoon and night.

Mon–Fri at 1600, 1700, 1800, 1900, 2000, 2100, 2200 LT. Sat 1700[1] LT. Sun 1700, 2000 LT.

1. Bcsts may start up to 4 mins late.

Brief weather summary and fcst, after news bulletin, for that night and following day.

92·4M–94·6, 96·8MHz, 103·5–105MHz in Welsh.
Mon–Fri at 0601, 0728, 07758, 0824, 1759 LT. General fcst, synopsis.

Mon–Fri at 0900, 1000, 1100 LT. Sat 0700, 0800, 0900 LT. Sun 0700, 0800, 0900, 1100 LT. Brief weather summary and fcst, after news bulletin for that day.

Mon–Fri at 1200, 1300, 1315, 1400, 1500 LT. Sat 1200, 1300. Sun 1300 LT. Brief weather summary and fcst, after news bulletin for that afternoon and night.

Mon–Fri at 1600, 2000 LT. Sat 1700, 1800 LT. Sun 1600, 1700, 1800 2200 LT. Brief summary and fcst, after news bulletin for that night and following day.

Falmouth (Coastguard MRCC)

VHF Ch 23 *or* 86 from CG District.

Storm warnings on receipt and at the following bcsts until cancelled 0140, 0540, 0940, 1340, 1740, 2140.

Weather bulletins at 0140, 0540, 0940, 1340, 1740, 2140. Inshore fcst for local area.
0940, 2140. Shipping fcst: gale warnings, synopsis, 24h fcst for areas Plymouth, Lundy, Fastnet and Sole.
1 Oct–31 Mar at 0950, 2150. Winter fishing fleet fcst:

3 day fcst for areas Plymouth, Shannon, Fastnet, Sole and Finisterre.

Navigational warnings on receipt and at the following bcsts until cancelled 0140, 0540, 0940, 1340, 1740, 2140.

Submarine/Gunnery Exercises at 0140, 0540, 0940, 1340, 1740, 2140. Bcst after any storm warnings, weather messages and navigational warnings.

Swansea (Coastguard MRCC)

VHF Ch 10, 23, 73, 84, 86 from CG District.

Storm wanrings on receipt and at the following bcsts until cancelled 0005, 0405, 0805, 1205, 1605, 2005. Gale warnings for areas Lundy, Irish Sea and Fastnet.

Weather bulletins from 0005, 0405, 0805, 1205, 1605, 2005. Inshore fcst for local area.
0805, 2005. Shipping fcst: gale warnings, synopsis, 24h fcst for areas Lundy, Irish Sea and Fastnet.

Navigational warnings on receipt and at the following bcsts until cancelled at 0005, 0405, 0805, 1205, 1605, 2005.

Milford Haven (Coastguard MRSC)

VHF Ch 84 *or* 86 from CG District.

Storm warnings on receipt and at the following bcsts until cancelled 0335, 0735, 1135, 1535, 1935, 2335. Gale warnings for areas Lundy, Irish Sea and Fastnet.

Weather bulletins at 0335, 0735, 1135, 1535, 1935, 2335. Inshore fcst for local areas.
0735, 1935 Shipping fcst: gale warnings, synopsis, 24h Fcst for areas Lundy, Irish Sea and Fastnet.

Navigational warnings on receipt and at the following bcsts until cancelled 0335, 0735, 1135, 1535, 1935, 2335.

Holyhead (Coastguard MRSC)

VHF Ch 73, 84 from CG District.

Storm warnings on receipt and at the following bcsts until cancelled 0235, 0635, 1035, 1435, 1835, 2235. For area Irish Sea.

Weather bulletins at 0235, 0635, 1035, 1435, 1835, 2235. Inshore fcst for local area.
Great Orme at 0635, 1835. Shipping fcst: gale warnings, synopsis, 24h fcst for area Irish Sea.

Navigational warnings on receipt and at the following bcsts until cancelled 0235, 0635, 1035, 1435, 1835, 2235.

Liverpool (Coastguard MRSC)

VHF Ch 10, 73, 86 from CG District.

Storm warnings on receipt and at the following bcsts until cancelled 0210, 0610, 1010, 1410, 1810, 2210. Gale warnings for areas Irish Sea and Malin.

Weather bulletins at 0210, 0610, 1010, 1410, 1810, 2210. Inshore fcst for local area.
1010, 2210. Shipping Fcst: Gale warnings, synopsis, 24h fcst for areas Irish Sea and Malin.

Navigational warnings on receipt and at the following bcsts until cancelled 0210, 0610, 1010, 1410, 1810, 2210.

Clyde (Coastguard MRCC)

VHF Ch 10, 23, 73, 84, 86 from CG District.

Storm warnings on receipt and at the following bcsts until cancelled 0020, 0420, 0820, 1220, 1620, 2020.

Weather bulletins at 0020, 0420, 0820, 1220, 1620, 2020. Inshore fcst for local area.
0820, 2020. Shipping fcst: gale warnings, synopsis, 24h fcst for area Malin.

Navigational warnings on receipt and at the following bcsts until cancelled 0020, 0420, 0820, 1220, 1620, 2020, request. Information on military firing practice exercises, when required.

Submarine/Gunnery Exercises at 0020, 0420, 0820, 1220, 1620, 2020. Bcsts after any storm warnings, weather bulletins and navigational warnings; SUBFACTS will cover any planned submarine activity for the following 24h.

Dublin (Coastguard MRCC)
VHF Dublin Ch 83; Wicklow Head Ch 87; Rosslare Ch 23 and Mine Head Ch 83.
Storm warnings All channels on receipt and 0033, 0633, 1233, 1833 after announcement on Ch 16. Gale warnings for Irish coastal waters up to 30 miles offshore and the Irish Sea.
Weather bulletins All channels 0103, 0403, 0703, 1003, 1303, 1603, 1903, 2203. Gale warnings, synopsis and 24h fcst for Irish coastal waters up to 30 miles offshore and the Irish Sea.
Navigational warnings All channels at 0033, 0433, 0833, 1233, 1633, 2033. For the E, SE, S and SW coasts of Ireland and approaches.

Coast radio stations

Falmouth (Coastguard MRCC)
Note This station does not accept public correspondence; accepting distress, urgent and safety traffic only.
RT (MF) Transmits and receives on 2182 (H24), 2226, 2670kHz.
VHF Transmits and receives on Ch 16 (H24), 10, 67, 73.

Swansea (Coastguard MRCC)
Note This station does not accept public correspondence; accepting distress, urgent and safety traffic only.
RT (MF) Transmits and receives on 2182kHz (H24).
VHF Transmits and receives on Ch 16 (H24), 10, 67, 73, 23, 84, 86.

Milford Haven (Coastguard MRSC)
Note This station does not accept public correspondence; accepting distress, urgent and safety traffic only.
RT (MF) Transmits and receives on 2182 (H24), 1767kHz.
VHF Transmits and receives on Ch 16 (H24), 10, 67, 73, 23, 84, 86.

Holyhead (Coastguard MRSC)
Note This station does not accept public correspondence; accepting distress, urgent and safety traffic only.
RT (MF) Transmits and receives on 2182 (H24), 1880kHz.
VHF Ch 16 (H24), 10, 67, 73.

Liverpool (Coastguard MRSC)
Note This station does not accept public correspondence; accepting distress, urgent and safety traffic only.
RT (MF) Transmits and receives on 2182kHz (H24).
VHF Ch 16 (H24), 10, 67, 73.

Clyde (Coastguard MRCC)
Note This station does not accept public correspondence; accepting distress, urgent and safety traffic only.
RT (MF) Transmits and receives on 2182 (H24), 1883kHz.
VHF Ch 16 (H24), 10, 23, 67, 73, 84, 86.

Dublin (Coastguard MRCC)
VHF Antenna located at:

	VHF Ch	
Dublin	16, 67, 83	53°23'N 6°04'W
Wicklow Head	16, 67, 87	52°58'N 6°00'W
Rosslare	16, 23, 67	52°15'N 6°20'W
Mine Head	16, 67, 83	52°00'N 7°35'W

Traffic lists on working channels at 0103, 0503 and every odd H+03 (0903–2303)

Marinecall Automatic telephone weather service with recorded forecasts updated twice daily. For the southwest (Lyme Regis to Hartland Point) ☎ 0891 500 458, for the Bristol Channel (Hartland Point to St David's Head) ☎ 0891 500 459, for Wales (St David's Head to Great Ormes Head) ☎ 0891 500 460 and for the north Irish Sea ☎ 0891 500 461.

Navtex Transmissions on a common frequency of 518kHz can be received by radio teleprinter or purpose-built receiver. Weather messages for the area broadcast at 0700 and 1900 UT from Niton, and at 0620 and 1820 UT from Portpatrick. Gale warnings are broadcast on receipt and are repeated at scheduled times.

Radiobeacons

The majority of radiobeacons have ceased operation, a few having been replaced by the Differential Global Positioning System (DGPS). Aero radiobeacons have not been affected by changes.
Lizard Lt 306kHz – On trial
Nash Point 309·5kHz 100M – On trial
Point Lynas 297·5kHz 100M – On trial
Aero radiobeacons
Penzance Heliport *PH* 333kHz 15M 50°07'·67N 5°31'·00W
Cardiff *CDF* 388·5kHz 20M 51°23'·57N 3°20'·23W
Swansea *SWN* 320·5kHz 15M 51°36'·10N 4°03'·88W
Ronaldsway, Isle of Man *RWY* 359kHz 20M 54°05'·15N 4°36'·45W
St Mawgan *SM* 356kHz 20M 50°26'·51N 4°59'·36W
Blackpool *BPL* 420kHz 15M 53°46'·17N 2°59'·3W
St Mary's, Isles of Scilly *STM* 321kHz 15M 49°54'·82N 6°17'·43W
Aberporth *AP* 370·5kHz 20M 52°06'·92N 4°33'·57W
Killiney *KLY* 378kHz 50M 53°16'·17N 6°06'·33W
Dublin Rush *RSH* 326kHz 30M 53°30'·73N

List of major lights

Bishop Rock Fl(2)15s44m24M Horn Mo(N)90s Partially obscured 204°-211°, obscured 211°-233°, 236°-259°. Racon
Peninnis Head Fl.20s36m17M 231°-vis-117°, partially obscured 048°-083° within 5M. F.R lights on TV tower 1·7M N
Round Island Fl.10s55m24M Horn(4)60s 021°-vis-288° Racon
Seven Stones LtV Fl(3)30s12m25M Horn(3)60s Racon
Longships Iso.WR.10s35m18/14M Horn 10s 189°-R-208°-R(unintens)-307°-R-327°-W-189° F.R on radio mast 4·9M NE
Pendeen Fl(4)15s59m16M Horn 20s 042°-vis-240°; in the bay between Gurnard Head and Pendeen, it shows to the coast

Godrevy Island Fl.WR.10s37m12/9M 022°-W-101°-R-145°-W-272° 4F.R(vert) shown on radio mast 6·5M ESE

Trevose Head Fl.7·5s62m21M Horn(2)30s Storm signals. R Lt on radio mast 180m ESE. F.R on mast 4·7M SSE

Hartland Point Fl(6)15s37m25M Horn 60s

Instow Ldg Lts 118° *Front* Oc.6s22m15M 104·5°-vis-131·5° F.R on radio masts 4M NNW. F.R occas lights on Heanton Punchardon church 2·75M NNE *Rear* 427m from front Oc.10s38m15M 103°-vis-133°

Lundy I Near N Point Fl.15s48m17M 009°-vis-285° Southeast Point Fl.5s53m15M Horn 25s 170°-vis-073°

Bull Point Fl(3)10s54m20M Obscd by high ground from shore-056° F.R.48m12M 058°-vis-096°

Lynmouth Foreland Fl(4)15s67m18M 083°-vis-275°

Watchet W breakwater head Oc.G.3s9m9M

Burnham-on-Sea entrance Fl.7·5s7m12M 074°-vis-164°

    Dir Lt 076° DirF.WRG.4m12-10M 071°-G-075°-W-077°-R-081°

East Usk Fl(2)WRG.10s11m15-11M 284°-W-290°-R-017°-W-037°-G-115°-W-120° Oc.WRG.10s10m11-9M 081°-G-022°-W-024°-R-028°

Portishead Point Q(3)10s9m16M Horn 20s 060°-vis-262°

Black Nore Point Fl(2)10s11m17M 044°-vis-243° Obscured by Sand Point when bearing less than 049°

Flatholm LtHo SE Point Fl(3)WR.10s50m15/12M 106°-R-140°-W-151°-R-203°-W-106°

Monkstone Rock Fl.5s13m12M

Barry W breakwater head Fl.2·5s12m10M

Wenvoe Aero Q.365m12M Obstruction

Breaksea LtF Fl.15s11m12M Horn(2)30s F riding light Racon

Nash Point Fl(2)WR.15s56m21/16M 280°-R-290°-W-100°-R-120°-W-128°

Mumbles Head Fl(4)20s35m15M Horn(3)60s

Caldey Island Fl(3)WR.20s65m13/9M 173°-R-212°-W-088°-R-102°

St Anne's Head Fl.WR.5s48m18-14M Horn(2)60s 233°-W-247°-R-285°-R(intens)-314°-R-332°-W-131° partially obscd between 124°-129° Radar scanner 7m SW

Skokholm Island Fl.WR.10s54m18/15M 301°-W-154°-R-301° partially obscured between 226°-258°

The Smalls Fl(3)15s36m25M Horn(2)60s Racon F.R.33m13M 253°-vis-285° over Hats and Barrels Rock

South Bishop Fl.5s44m16M Horn(3)45s Also shown at night in reduced visibility only Racon

Strumble Head Fl(4)15s45m26M 038°-vis-257°

Fishguard N breakwater Fl.G.4·5s18m13M Bell(1)8s

New Quay Fl.WRG.3s12m8/5M 135°-W-252°-G-295° Mo(AP)R 129m occas on aerodrome Identification beacon 9·7M SW

Aberaeron Fl(3)G.10s6M 050°-vis-243°

Aberystwyth S breakwater head Fl(2)WG.10s12m10M 030°-G-053°-W-210° 4F.R(vert) on radio tower 2·8M S

St Tudwal's West Island Fl.WR.15s46m14/10M 349°-W-169°-R-221°-W-243°-R-259°-W-293°-R-349° Obscured by East Island 211°-231°

Bardsey Island Fl(5)15s39m26M Horn Mo(N)45s Obscured by Bardsey Island 198°-250° and in Tremadoc Bay when bearing less than 260°

Llanddwyn Island Fl.WR.2·5s12m7/4M 280°-R-W-120°

South Stack Fl.10s60m24M Horn 30s Obscured to northward by North Stack and may also be obscured in Penrhos Bay by the high land of Penrhyn Mawr, but is visible over the land from the southward when in line with Rhoscolyn Beacon

Holyhead harbour breakwater head Fl(3)G.10s21m14M Siren 20s F.R on chimney 2M SSE

The Skerries Fl(2)10s36m22M Horn(2)20s Racon F.R.26m16M 231°-vis-254°

Lynas Point Oc.10s39m20M Horn 45s 109°-vis-315°

Trwyn Du Fl.5s19m12M Bell(1)30s 101°-vis-023° but partially obscd 019°-023° F.R on radio mast 2M SW, R Lt on radio mast 3·3M W

Bar LtF Fl.5s10m12M Horn(2)20s Racon

Formby LtF Iso.4s11m6M

Crosby LtF Oc.5s11m8M

Walney Island Fl.15s21m23M 122°-obscd-127° when within 3M of shore

St Bees Head Fl(2)20s102m18M Obscd-340°-shore-F.R lights on tower 14·6M SSE

Whitehaven west pier head Fl.G.5s16m13M

N pier head 2F.R(vert)8m9M

Workington S pier Fl.5s11m8M Siren 20s

Silloth, East Cote F.G.15m12M 046°-vis-058°, intens 052°

Hestan Island E end Fl(2)10s42m9M

Little Ross LtHo Fl(5)50m12M Obscured in Wigton bay when bearing more than 103°

Mull of Galloway SE end Fl.20s99m28M 182°-vis-105° 3F.R on radio mast 16M ENE

Crammag Head Fl.10s35m18M

Killantringan Black head Fl(2)15s49m25M F.R lights on radio masts 3·6M N

Corsewall Pt Fl(5)30s34m22M 027°-vis-257° R Lts on tower 1·9M E

Isle of Man

Calf of Man Fl.15s93m26M Horn 45s 274°-vis-190°

Chicken Rk Fl.5s38m13M Horn 60s

Port St Mary, Alfred Pier head Oc.R.10s8m6M

Langness. Dreswick Point Fl(2)30s23m12M

Ramsey S pier head Q.R.8m10M

N Pier head Q.G.9m10M

Douglas Head Fl.10s32m24M Reduced range shore-220° Obscured when bearing more than 037° F.R lights on radio masts 1 and 3M W

Maughold Head Fl(3)30s65m21M

Point of Ayre Fl(4)20s32m19M Horn(3)60s Racon Fog Det Lt UQ vis 148°

Peel Oc.R.7s8m5M 156°-vis-249°

VHF direction-finding service

This service is for emergency use only. Each VHF direction-finding station is remotely controlled by an HM Coastguard Maritime Rescue Coordination Centre (MRCC) or Maritime Rescue Sub-Centre (MRSC). Watch is kept on Ch 16. Ship transmits on Ch 16 (distress only) or Ch 67 so that the station can determine its bearing. Ship's bearing from the station is transmitted on Ch 16 (distress only) or Ch 67.

St Ann's Head RG Controlled by MRSC Milford Haven

Great Ormes Head RG Controlled by MRSC Holyhead

Walney Island RG Controlled by MRSC Liverpool

Snaefell RG Controlled by MRSC Liverpool
Hartland RG Controlled by MRCC Swansea
Land's End Controlled by MRCC Falmouth
St Mary's, Isles of Scilly RG Controlled by MRCC Falmouth
Trevose Head RG Controlled by MRCC Falmouth

CHART SYMBOLS

The following symbols are used on the plans, and are shown in magenta

- Visitors' moorings
- Visitors' berths
- Yacht marina
- Yacht berth
- Public landing
- Slipway for small craft
- Water tap
- Fuel
- Gas
- Public telephone
- Customs
- Chandlery
- Public house, inn, bar
- Restaurant
- Yacht or sailing club
- Toilets
- Public car park
- Parking for boats/trailers
- Launderette
- Caravan site
- Camping site
- Nature reserve
- Harbour master
- Post office

TABLE OF NAVIGABLE DISTANCES (IN NAUTICAL MILES)

	Longships LtHo	Padstow	Ilfracombe	Cardiff	Swansea	Dale	Fishguard	Pwllheli	Holyhead	Conwy	Fleetwood	Port St Mary	Ramsey	Maryport	Isle of Withorn
Padstow	47														
Ilfracombe	90	53													
Cardiff	133	97	42												
Swansea	113	77	26	44											
Dale	107	69	52	89	57										
Fishguard	136	86	82	116	87	35									
Pwllheli	187	149	133	167	138	86	57								
Holyhead	210	172	156	190	161	109	83	56							
Conwy	222	184	168	202	173	121	97	70	36						
Fleetwood	283	245	229	263	234	182	155	128	73	53					
Port St Mary	251	213	197	231	202	150	125	98	46	58	62				
Ramsey	272	234	218	252	223	171	144	117	64	67	55	28			
Maryport	305	267	251	285	256	204	179	152	94	89	59	63	40		
Isle of Whithorn	295	257	241	275	246	194	166	139	86	87	69	46	23	30	
Portpatrick	295	257	241	275	246	194	166	139	94	105	97	52	44	65	36

Pilotage

I. Land's End to Hartland Point

Land's End

Land's End peninsula is a 100-metre-high plateau with low rolling hills and 60-metre-high granite cliffs facing the sea. There are traffic separation zones to the west of the peninsula. In unsettled weather Land's End should be rounded to the west of the Longships Reef. In fair weather Longships Passage can be used. Tidal streams can run strongly in the area (maximum 2½ knots at springs, 1¼ knots at neaps); the north stream begins at HW Dover, the south stream at HW Dover −0510.

Longships Passage

A ½-mile-wide passage between Land's End and Kettle's Bottom which may be used in settled weather. Kettle's Bottom, a rock which is only just covered at MHWS and can always be identified by broken water, and Shark's Fin rock (dries 3·4m ½ mile NNW of Kettle's Bottom) are left to seaward. The Brisons, two rocky islets ½ mile southwest of Cape Cornwall, lead the passage, with the highest part of the north (high) Brison bearing 001° and open to the west of the south (low) Brison.

Sennen Cove

An attractive drying fishing harbour lying at the south end of Whitesand Bay. A stone breakwater gives limited protection to the harbour; the approach is fully exposed to the Atlantic and there are off-lying dangers. Anchorage is available 100m north of the harbour in 5m sand only in the most settled conditions or offshore winds.

Whitesand Bay

Anchorage can be obtained off the centre of the bay in offshore winds. Rocks extend from the shore at the north and south ends of the bay, which is exposed to the Atlantic swells.

The Brisons

Two steep-sided rocky islets (27 and 22m) ½ mile southwest of Cape Cornwall; connected to the mainland by a rocky shallow reef, parts of which dry to 1·8m.

Cape Cornwall

A steep cliffed point (85m high) with a coastguard lookout hut and a disused chimney marking the site of the abandoned Cape Cornwall tin mine on its summit. There is a radio mast (red lights) 2½ miles to the ESE and a TV mast 2 miles to the ENE.

St Ives

⊕ 50°13'·4N 5°27'·9W ½M NE of St Ives Head
Population 10,052 (1981)
Local High Water is Dover −0605
Charts Admiralty *1149, 1168*; Imray *C7*

General

A picturesque drying harbour busy with fishing vessels and pleasure craft. The narrow streets and granite-paved lanes of the town provide a haven for artists, and visitors flood to the resort in the holiday season. The harbour was formed by the building of a stone pier in 1770, becoming Cornwall's biggest pilchard port over the following century. Facilities are fair and the town offers a good range of shops.

Warning

The harbour can be entered for 2½ hours either side of HW, although the visitors' moorings can only be reached within 2 hours of HW. The harbour dries to firm sand and has approximately 4·5m at MHWS at the harbour entrance. The harbour entrance is wide and does not prevent the swell from entering with strong onshore winds. If such winds are forecast, shelter can be found in nearby Hayle.

Approaching St Ives, with green buoy marking former jetty in the foreground

St Ives   *PRPA/Patrick Roach*

ST IVES BAY

Depths in Metres

5°30'W

White

23   20

Stones
Q
Bell Whis
BY

50°15'N

Red

The
Stones

20

20

16   Godrevy
Island
Fl.WR.10s37m
12/9M

23

26   17

26

White

50

See plan
St Ives   15
Head

100 St
Ives   13

Carracks   13

7   10

Carbis Bay   See plan   .70

50

Knills Mont   50
166   50

150   150

100   50   N

HAYLE

0   1   2

Nautical Miles

Entrance to St Ives harbour

Approach

By day Enter St Ives Bay between St Ives Head and Godrevy Island with its off-lying rocks. To clear the rocks off St Ives Head, Knills Monument (166m) should be kept open of the Tregenna Castle Hotel (conspicuous, to the south of the town) on a course of approximately 195°. A green buoy marks the end of a ruined stone jetty, which is submerged at HW and must be left to starboard.

By night The harbour can be reached using the following lights:

Pendeen Fl(4)15s59m16M Horn 20s
Godrevy Island Fl.WR.10s37m12/9M
St Ives east pier 2F.G(vert)8m5M
St Ives west pier 2F.R(vert)5m3M

Anchorage in the approach

Anchor in 5m sand 2 cables ESE of harbour entrance in settled weather.

Entrance

Between the two stone piers forming the harbour.

Moorings

Six visitors' moorings are provided, marked by white buoys. These are on the west side of the harbour in front of Woolworth's (four-storey beige building fronting the harbour).

Berths

It is possible to berth along the north side of the west pier, but this is untenable if any swell enters the harbour.

Harbourmaster

At north end of east pier.

Charges

There are harbour charges.

Facilities

Fuel From tankers (only occasionally).
Water Three taps on west pier.
Slip Northwest corner of harbour.
Provisions Good range of shops in the town.
Showers At limited times at the sailing club; see harbourmaster.
Post office Main post office on High Street.
Gas Calor Gas and *Camping Gaz* from P. N. Harvey, High Street. Only *Calor Gas* from Bennet's, behind former lifeboat house.
Chandlery Limited chandlery available from United Cooperative Fishermen's Association, on the harbour.
Refuse disposal Litter bins around the harbour.

Hayle

⊕ 50°12'·3N 5°26'·0W ½M N of harbour entrance
Population 6,179 (1981)
Local High Water is Dover –0605
Charts Admiralty *1149, 1168*; Imray *C7*

General

Formerly a busy port exporting copper and tin. The closure of a large foundry in the town in 1904 started its decline. The drying harbour is now used by a small fishing fleet. Although strong onshore winds make entrance impossible, the harbour itself is well protected and is the place to head for if bad weather is forecast.

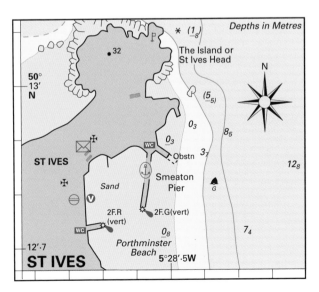

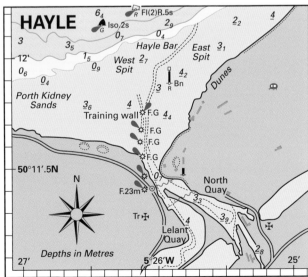

Warning

The harbour should not be approached in strong onshore winds. In more settled conditions, approach should ideally be made one hour before HW, although the harbour can be entered for 2 hours either side of HW. There is approximately 5m at the harbour entrance at MHWS.

Approach

By day Enter St Ives Bay between St Ives Head and Godrevy Island with its off-lying rocks.

By night A night approach and entrance are not advised.

Anchorage in the approach

Anchorage here in 5m sand is only possible in the most settled weather. A more suitable anchorage in which to wait for the tide can be found in Carbis Bay 1 mile southeast of St Ives, avoiding the Carracks to the north of Carbis Bay.

Entrance

The green conical buoy to the north of the line of posts marking the training wall must be identified and all should be left approximately 30m to starboard. The church on the hillside is conspicuous and an approach on a bearing of 180° will lead to the channel.

When alongside the training wall make for the timber-boarded house and the larger white house above and behind. Turn to port alongside the houses, keeping all red buoys and the posts marking the central island to port. Enter the channel with the warehouse building on the east side.

Berthing

Along west side of channel at vacant place on quay or alongside fishing boat.

Harbourmaster

At entrance to berthing channel.

Charges

There are harbour charges.

Facilities

Fuel From filling station just out of town centre on the road to Redruth.

Water Tap near harbourmaster's office.

Provisions Adequate shops for everyday requirements in the town centre.

Post office In Foundry Square.

Camping Gaz and paraffin Biggleston's, on road facing the quay.

Godrevy Point

The Stones are three groups of dangerous drying rocks lying between ¾ mile and 1½ miles northwest of Godrevy Point. A north cardinal whistle and bell buoy marks their seaward extremity. The area abounds with overfalls and should be passed to the northwest of the buoy in all but the most settled conditions. There is an inshore passage between Godrevy Island and Godrevy Point which can be

Godrevy Island, looking NE

used in calm conditions, care being taken to avoid Bessack Rock 1 mile SSW of Godrevy Island.

Portreath

⊕ 50°16'·2N 5°18'·1W ½M NW of harbour entrance
Local High Water is Dover –0600
Charts Admiralty *1149*; Imray *C7*

General

In 1760 the building of the pier at Portreath formed a harbour to serve the local copper and tin mines. Coasters continued to visit the harbour until the 1960s, when a housing estate was built on the land surrounding the harbour. Portreath is now a small holiday resort with limited facilities for yachtsmen.

Warning

The harbour can only be entered for 2 hours either side of HW and should not be attempted in strong onshore winds. In these conditions the swell can find its way into the harbour. The harbour dries to a firm bottom of sand and small stones.

Approach

By day The monument on Carn Brea (221m), 3 miles to the southeast of Portreath, is conspicuous. A mast (red lights 401m) is ¾ mile southeast of the monument. These indicate the approach to Portreath from seaward when they are in alignment. Approaching from the south, Gull Rock should be passed to seaward. The white 8-metre-high daymark on the headland at an elevation of 37m to the north of the harbour entrance is also conspicuous.

Entrance to Portreath

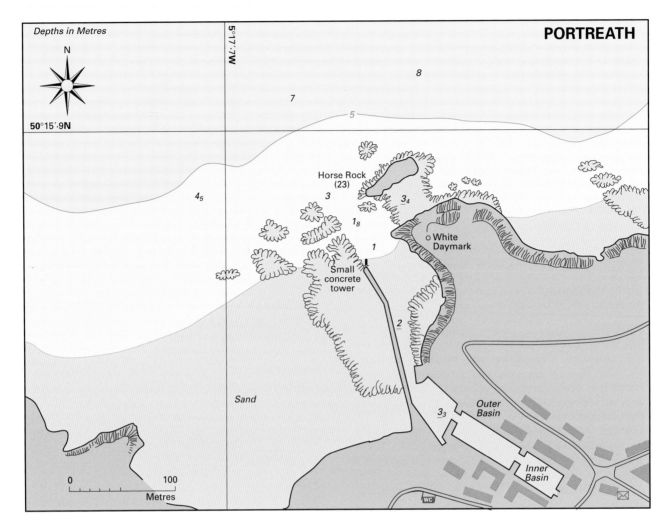

By night A night approach and entrance should not be attempted.

Entrance

A small concrete tower marks the end of the stone pier. Approach should be made with the northeast face of the pier just open, leaving Horse Rock to the northeast. Keep close to the pier until into the turning basin, then pass through the central opening into the outer harbour.

Berthing

Alongside the wall in the outer harbour. There is a shortage of fixed ladders, and the harbour bottom is some 4m below the top of the harbour wall.

Harbourmaster

An officer of the Portreath Harbour Association will visit the boat. Charges are levied.

Facilities

Slip In southeast corner of inner harbour.
Fuel From filling station on the road to Redruth just beyond the post office.
Provisions Small shopping centre close to the harbour.
Post office By the shopping centre.

Trevaunance Cove

The location of three former harbours, the last destroyed in 1934. Temporary anchorage may be had in 5m sand, although the bay is open from the west through north to northeast and subject to the Atlantic swells.

Bawden Rocks

Two islets 1 mile north of St Agnes Head.

Ligger or Perran Bay

Anchoring or fishing is prohibited in an area extending for 3 miles seaward of the bay, owing to the presence of scientific instruments and cables. Two orange buoys are moored in the bay.

The Gannel

A narrow picturesque creek suitable for shallow draught craft, drying almost completely to firm sand. Entrance is through Crantock Bay, leaving The Goose, a rock to the west of Pentire Point East, to the north. Approach should not be made in strong onshore winds, although good shelter is to be found further up the creek. Enter up to 1½ hours either side of HW, keeping ½ cable from the south shore of Pentire Point East, then moving close to the north shore when halfway into the bay, until the entrance to the creek opens. There is a wooden

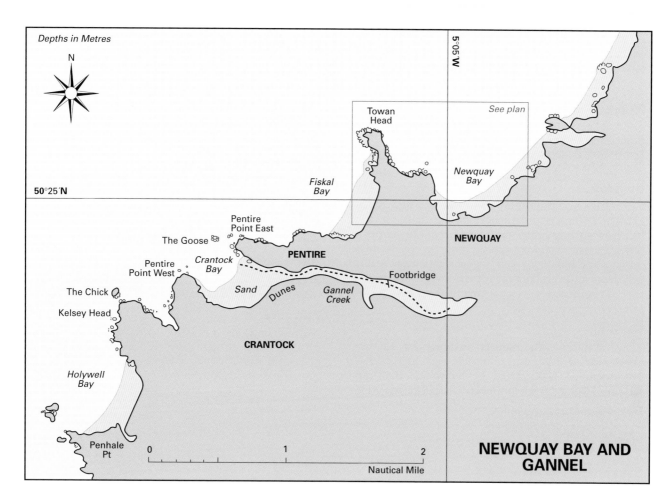

Newquay   *PRPA/Patrick Roach*

footbridge over the main channel ¾ mile from the entrance to the creek, which is exposed at LW and only passable by shallow-draught boats at HW.

Newquay

⊕ 50°25'·8N 5°05'·2W ½M NE of Towan Head
Population 15,280 (1981)
Local High Water is Dover –0604
Charts Admiralty *1168, 1149*; Imray *C7*

General

Cornwall's biggest holiday resort boasts a number of expansive, exposed beaches which make it the foremost surfing centre in the country. The harbour is a sufficient distance from the town centre to miss most of the holidaymakers' noisier activities, whilst still being close enough for provisioning. The drying harbour is shared between a small fishing fleet and a number of pleasure craft.

Warning

There is water in the harbour entrance for 3 hours either side of HW, and alongside the quay within 2½ hours of HW. Swell in Newquay Bay can produce strong surges in the harbour; otherwise it is reasonably well protected. The swell decreases at the harbour entrance closer to HW.

Approach

By day Newquay Bay is entered between Towan Head and Trevelgue Head, 1¼ miles to the east. There are two conspicuous hotels between Towan Head and Newquay. Old Dane Rock (dries 6·2m) lies 3 cables offshore ½ mile southeast of Towan Head. Listrey Rock, with a depth of 0·5m, lies 1 cable east of Old Dane Rock.

By night Approach by night is not recommended because of the lack of major lights. The harbour is lit with 2F.G(vert)5m2M on the north pier and 2F.R(vert)4m2M on the south pier.

Anchorage in the approach

Anchor in 5m sand 2½ cables to the northeast of the harbour in settled conditions.

Entrance

Narrow entrance between north and south piers, turning south immediately on entering to pass east of central pier.

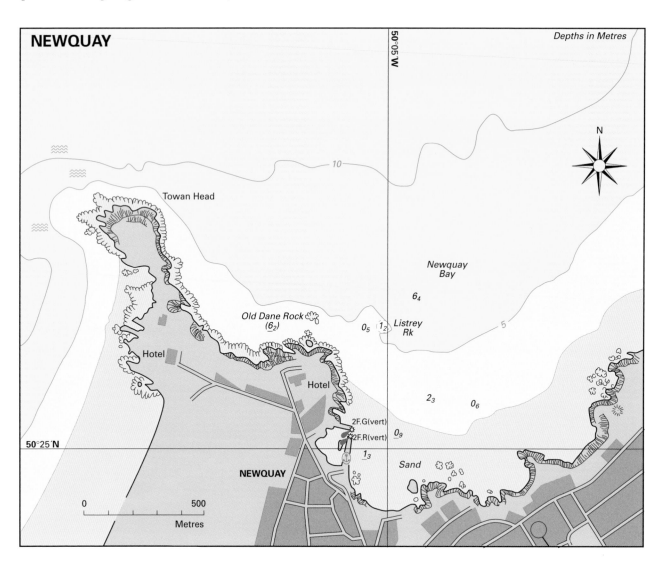

Berthing

Along west side of south pier. There are ladders, but these are in poor condition.

Harbourmaster

On south pier.

VHF radio telephone

Call *Newquay Harbour* on Ch 16, work Ch 12 or 14.

Charges

There are harbour charges.

Facilities

Fuel From tanker which visits frequently.
Water From tap on south pier; key for tap with harbourmaster.
Provisions Good range of shops in town.
Post office In town centre.
Refuse disposal Litter bins on quay.

Trevose Head

The headland has an elevation of 51m, although its hinterland is much lower. The white tower of the lighthouse (Fl.7·5s62m21M) stands on its northwest corner. The Bull is an above-water rock 3 cables to the southwest of Trevose Head. The Quies are a group of above-water rocks 5 to 8 cables west of The Bull. In settled conditions it is possible to pass between The Bull and The Quies.

Polventon Bay

Anchorage is available in 4m sand off the lifeboat slip, although the bay is exposed to the northwest through north to east.

River Camel estuary

The River Camel flows into Padstow Bay and tidal waters make their way many miles inland.

Approach

By day From the west Gulland Rock can be passed on either side. From the northeast it is possible to pass between Newland (with its off-lying rocks) and Roscarrock shoals in settled weather, but it is advisable in any other conditions to pass to seaward of Newland.

Padstow Bay is entered between Stepper Point (with its conspicuous 12-metre-high stone tower daymark) and Pentire Point.

By night The estuary can be reached using the following lights:

Trevose Head Fl.7·5s62m21M Horn(2)30s
Stepper Point LFl.10s12m4M

Anchorage in the approach

It is possible to find a sheltered anchorage in the lee of Stepper Point in all conditions (except with the wind between north and west) while waiting for water at the Doom Bar.

Entrance

There is always water over the Doom Bar at the entrance to the estuary; however, it is impassable at MLWS. The same applies at MLWN except in very

calm conditions. Extra care should be taken at half-ebb and below when any swell is running. The bar also becomes impassable in strong northwest winds.

The channel lies to the east of the estuary, the first red buoy (Fl(2)R.10s) marking the limit of the rocks off Trebetherick Point. Leave the green Bar buoy (Fl.G.5s) to starboard and head for the red Channel buoy (Fl.R.5s).

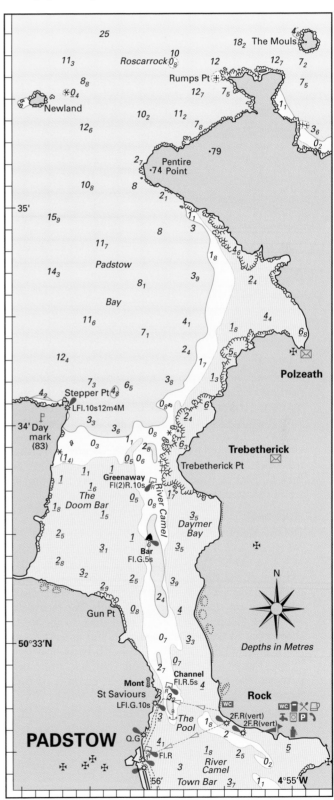

Padstow   *PRPA/Patrick Roach*

Padstow

⊕ 50°34'·6N 4°56'·7W ½M N of Stepper Point
Population 2,806 (1981)
Local High Water is Dover –0550
Charts Admiralty *1168, 1156*; Imray *C58*

General

An attractive fishing port and holiday resort, with a network of narrow streets leading down to the harbour. The trading nature of the harbour declined with the advent of larger vessels and the silting of the estuary. The outer harbour is now busy with fishing vessels; the inner harbour (in which, thanks to the new lock gates, vessels now lie afloat in 3.5m) is mostly used by pleasure craft. The inner harbour is well protected from all winds.

Approach

By day Keep well clear of Newland Island and its off-lying reef. There is a conspicuous white daymark (83m) 3 cables W of Stepper Point. There is only 0·5m over the bar at MLWS and approach should not be made LW±1½. In strong onshore winds seas can break on the bar and in the adjacent channel. From the Channel red buoy, keep close to the west shore after St Saviour's Point. Red and green buoys mark the channel between the north quay and the Town Bank, a large sand spit that has built up between the harbour and the main channel of the River Camel.

By night Be vigilant of the unlit islands on the approach to the estuary. The harbour can be reached using the following lights:

Stepper Point LFl.10s12m4M
Greenaway buoy Fl(2)R.10s
Bar buoy Fl.G.5s

Channel buoy Fl.R.5s
St Saviour's Point LFl.G.10s
North quay 2F.G(vert)6m2M
South quay 2F.R(vert)7m2M

Anchorage in the approach

In the pool to the south of the Channel buoy for vessels waiting to enter the inner harbour or wishing to stay afloat. The anchorage becomes uncomfortable with strong SE winds against the flood.

Entrance

Between the north and south quays, and through the lock gate, which is open for 2 hours either side of HW; then pass through into the inner harbour.

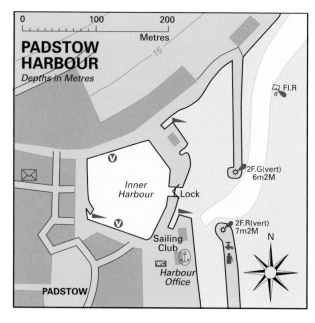

Berthing

Alongside in the inner harbour as directed by the harbourmaster.

Harbourmaster

Office by the harbour.

VHF radio telephone

Padstow Harbour Ch 16, 14 (0900–1700).

Charges

There are harbour charges.

Facilities

Fuel Diesel on south quay.
Water On south quay, and tap at harbour office.
Toilets, showers and laundry In new red brick building to N of lock gate.
Slip Three slips as indicated on harbour plan.
Provisions Good range of shops in town centre.
Camping gas Clues DIY, opposite post office.
Post office Duke Street.
Yacht club Padstow Sailing Club.
Chandlery Rig Marine, at south end of inner harbour.
Marine engineers G B Smith, Wadebridge and MF Engineering, Padstow.
Boat repairs At south end of inner harbour.
Refuse disposal Bins on quay.

Rock

There are moorings available off the small town of Rock on the opposite side of the Camel estuary to Padstow. The moorings dry onto firm sand. Rock Sailing Club operates from a converted warehouse on the foreshore and there is a chandlery nearby.

Wadebridge

The channel of the River Camel is constantly changing, but is navigable up to Wadebridge, which should ideally be reached just before the last of the flood. Quayside moorings are available, although the southwest quay has silted and is only suitable for fin-keelers to lie to. There are moorings in the main channel to the northwest of the town centre. There is a sailing club and a boat repair yard.

Port Isaac

⊕ 50°36'·3N 4°50'·1W ½M N of harbour entrance
Local High Water is Dover –0555
Charts Admiralty *1156*; Imray *C58*

General

A small fishing harbour within a cove made attractive by the small cottages and narrow streets that make up the town. There is limited space in the part of the harbour that dries to firm sand, due to the large outcrop of rock to the west of the harbour and the moorings of the resident fishing craft.

Warning

The harbour can only be entered for 2 hours either side of HW. Strong onshore winds make the

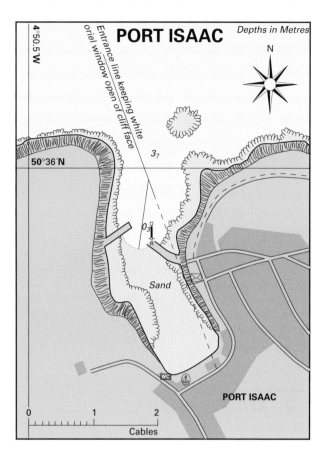

entrance impassable and produce a strong surge in the harbour itself.

Approach

By day St Endellion Church with its square tower is conspicuous 1¼ miles south of Port Isaac; approaching the church on a bearing of 171° will lead to Port Isaac.

By night A night approach and entrance should not be attempted.

Entrance

There are drying rocks to the east of the harbour entrance. A building with distinctive oriel windows fronting the shingle beach should be kept open of the east cliff face to avoid the rocks until Lobber Point is abeam. Make directly for and enter between the two stone breakwaters.

Entrance to Port Isaac. Keep white oriel window open of cliff face to avoid off-lying rocks to west of harbour entrance

Port Isaac and Port Gaverne

Moorings

Anchor fore and aft as close as possible to the fishing-boat moorings and check that you will be drying on sand by asking the harbourmaster or local fishermen. Alternatively, test physically with a long pole as the water shallows; on a calm day the sea bed is often visible.

Harbourmaster

Office by the shingle beach.

Charges

There are harbour charges.

Facilities

Provisions Adequate shops for everyday requirements.

Post office On the road to the east of the harbour.

Port Gaverne

A narrow creek ½ mile east of Port Isaac. The houses at the head of the creek are prominent as the entrance opens. There is no protection from onshore winds. The creek dries to a stone and pebble bottom.

Boscastle

⊕ 50°41'·45N 4°43'·0W ½M W of harbour entrance
Local High Water is Dover –0543
Charts Admiralty *1156*; Imray *C58*

General

An intricate entrance between the cliffs leads to the harbour, beyond which is a picturesque village restored and preserved by the National Trust. The small drying harbour is home to a small number of fishing boats and pleasure craft.

Warning

Entrance should only be made in settled weather; onshore winds or ground swell can make the harbour inaccessible and produce surges in the harbour itself. Enter up to 2 hours either side of HW. The harbour dries to a firm bottom of sand and small stones near the entrance, with rock outcrops along the north side and further up the harbour.

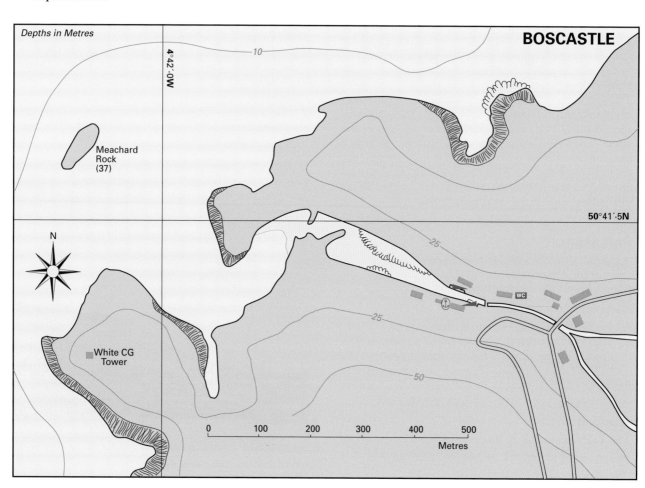

Approaching Boscastle looking east

Pencarrow Point, looking east

Approach

By day Tintagel Head with its prominent hotel is conspicuous to the south. Meachard Rock must be identified at the harbour entrance and can be passed on either side, although leaving it to the north would make for an easier first-time entrance.

The white former coastguard lookout tower on the headland to the south of the harbour is conspicuous, resembling a keep with its turreted corners.

By night A night approach and entrance should not be attempted.

Entrance

Make for the centre of the bay until the channel opens up to the north. Keep to the centre of the channel and head for the small stone breakwater. Leave the outer breakwater to port, and keep close to the end of the inner mole when turning into the harbour.

Berthing

Alongside the south quay.

Harbourmaster

Office on the south side of the quay.

Charges

There are nominal harbour charges.

Facilities

Slip Two slips at the head of the harbour.
Provisions Small range of shops in the village.
Post office Up the old road into the village.

Bude Haven

⊕ 50°50'·0N 4°34'·1W ½M W of harbour entrance
Population 2,789 (1981)
Local High Water is Dover −0540
Charts Admiralty *1156*; Imray *C58*

General

A holiday resort famous for its surfers' beaches. Bude Canal, which opened in 1823 to carry sea sand inland for use as an agricultural fertiliser, now provides sheltered accommodation for visiting yachtsmen, although facilities are limited.

Warning

Entrance to the harbour can only be made up to 2 hours either side of HW, and as close to HW as possible is advisable, as the breaking surf moves further up the beaches away from the harbour entrance. The entrance is impassable in strong onshore winds or with a large ground swell running.

Approach

By day The radio dish aerials 3½ miles to the north of the harbour are conspicuous. Approaching from the southwest, the harbour lies at the north end of a 2-mile-long line of low cliffs with a stone tower at the north end.

By night A night approach and entrance should not be attempted.

Entrance

Identify and align the leading marks on the hillside to the north of the harbour: a white post with a yellow diamond topmark and a white flagstaff above and beyond it. The leading marks give a course of 075·5° passing close to Barrel Rock, marked with a post topped with a barrel. Immediately on passing Barrel Rock turn to starboard, picking up the leading marks close to the lock gates (two white posts with yellow triangular topmarks) on a bearing of 131·5°. A sand spit has started to build up off Chapel Rock. This should be given a little more clearance than the leading marks indicate.

Moorings

It may be possible to find a vacant drying mooring in the outer harbour, but there is little room to anchor.

Approaching Bude

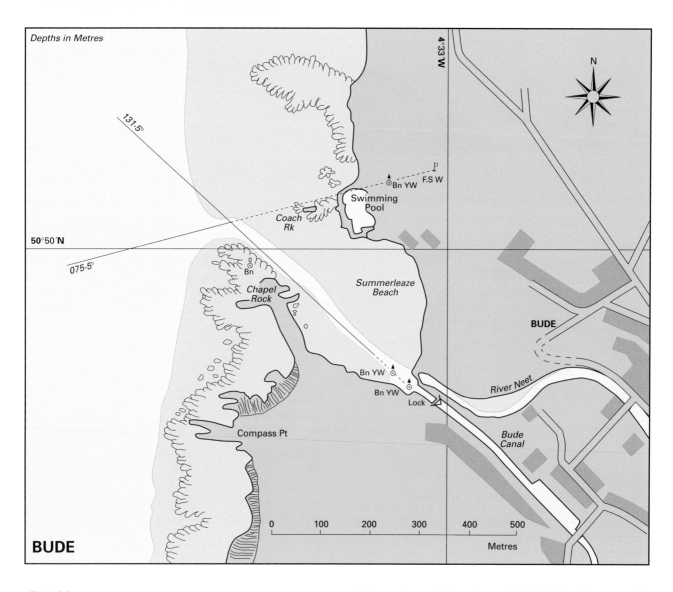

Depths in Metres

131.5°

075.5°

50°50′N

4°33′W

N

Bn YW F.S W

Coach
Rk

Swimming
Pool

Bn

Chapel
Rock

Summerleaze
Beach

BUDE

Bn YW

Bn YW

Lock

River Neet

Bude
Canal

Compass Pt

0   100   200   300   400   500

Metres

BUDE

Berthing

The lock requires a water level of approximately 5m over chart datum to operate. Yachts can then pass through into the shelter of the canal basin.

Harbourmaster

Office by canal basin.

VHF radio telephone

Call Bude Haven on Ch 16, work Ch 12.

Charges

There are harbour charges and lock fees.

Facilities

Provisions A good range of shops in the town.

Hartland Point

A 100-metre tableland slopes steeply to the sea at the headland, with adjoining perpendicular rocks. The white round tower and white buildings of the lighthouse (Fl(6)15s37m25M) are halfway down the cliff face. Tense Rocks are drying rocks extending 2 cables northwest from the foot of the cliffs. A tidal race extends 2 miles to the northwest

of the point, and is to be avoided during the strength of the tidal streams.

The tidal stream can reach 3 knots at springs; it begins in a northeast direction at HW Dover +0120 and in a southwest direction at HW Dover −0440.

Hartland Point at low water, looking NE, with the appropriately named Tense Rocks exposed

II. Hartland Point to Sand Point

Lundy Island

Position 51°10'·0N 4°40'·0W
Population 52 (1981)
Local High Water is Dover –0530
Charts Admiralty *1164;* Imray *C58*

General

A small island, 2½ miles long and ¾ mile wide, with steep granite cliffs rising to more than 120m in places. It is owned by the National Trust and is administered as a bird sanctuary by the Landmark Trust.

Warning

Lundy Island is surrounded by tidal races and overfalls, and should only be approached near slack water. The east-going stream begins at HW Dover –0030 and the west-going stream at HW Dover –0530. The streams run at 4 knots at springs, 2½ knots at neaps.

A race known as The White Horses forms over the Stanley Bank 3 miles northeast of the island, being particularly turbulent during the east-going stream.

Similar races extend 1 mile north of the island and 1½ miles east of Rat Island. During the west-going stream tidal races exist, although they are of less ferocity, with the race off the south of the island extending 1 mile southwest of Shutter Point.

Approach

The island lies 10 miles NNW of Hartland Point and 16 miles west of Morte Point. North West Point, the north extremity of the island, has a white round light tower (Fl.15s48m17M). A similar light tower (Fl.5s53m15M) is on a peninsula at the southeast end of the island.

The church tower 1½ cables northwest of the southeast lighthouse is conspicuous from the south or east. The stone tower of a disused lighthouse is conspicuous on the west side, ½ mile north of the south end of the island.

Anchorage

The only recognised anchorage is in the bay immediately to the north of the southeast lighthouse, in 6m shingle. Ample anchor scope is necessary, with a tidal range of up to 7m at springs and 3m at neaps. The anchorage is exposed to winds from the north through east to the southeast. Landing is made on the shingle beach of the cove.

In east winds shelter can be found in Jenny's Cove, on the west side of the island, although swell can make this uncomfortable.

Facilities

Provisions Limited provisions are available from the Marisco Tavern.

Clovelly

Position 50°59'·9N 4°23'·7W
Population 419 (1981)
Local High Water is Dover –0524
Charts Admiralty *1179;* Imray *C58*

General

Picture-postcard village with whitewashed cottages flanking the narrow cobbled main street that winds down the wooded hillside to the harbour. The small drying harbour provides limited shelter for a few small fishing and pleasure craft.

Warning

The harbour should only be entered close to HW. It should be avoided if there is any swell running, as this can cause surges in the harbour.

Approach

By day Easily visible as a built-up break in the wooded hillside when approached from the

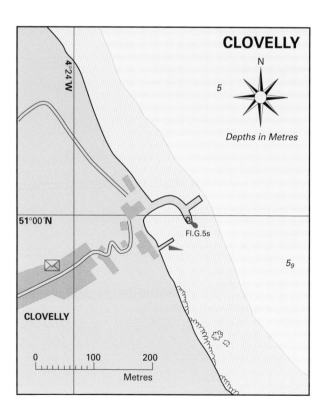

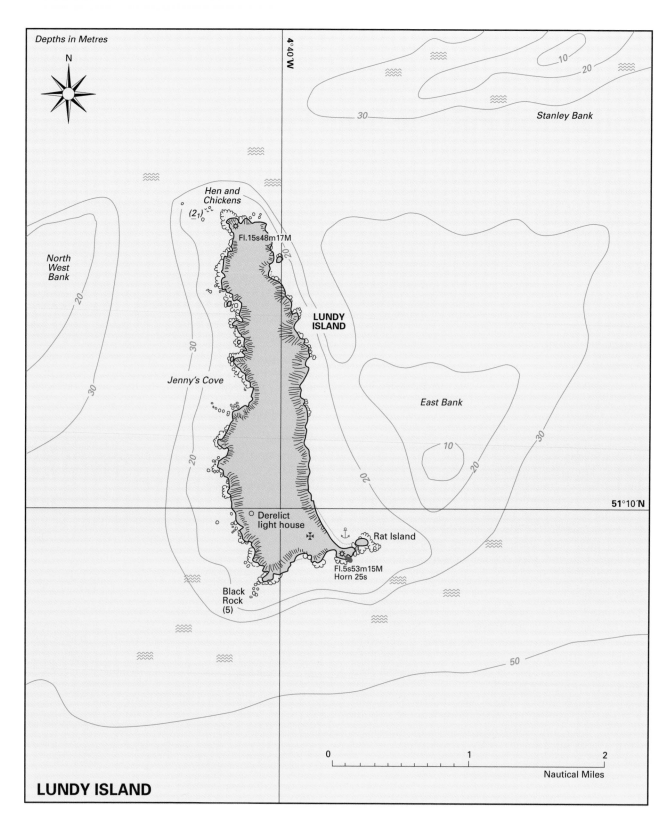

Depths in Metres

N

Stanley Bank

Hen and
Chickens

(2₁)

Fl.15s48m17M

North
West
Bank

LUNDY
ISLAND

Jenny's Cove

East Bank

51°10′N

Derelict
light house

Rat Island

Fl.5s53m15M
Horn 25s

Black
Rock
(5)

0   1   2

Nautical Miles

LUNDY ISLAND

northeast; less so from the west. There are no off-lying dangers.

By night The anchorage should only be approached with care; the light (Fl.G.5s5m5M) at the harbour entrance must be identified.

Anchorage in the approach

Anchor off the harbour in 5m mud. Shelter from offshore winds is good.

Entrance

The harbour is small. It should be entered keeping close to the end of the quay to avoid a shingle bank that has built up close by.

Approaching Clovelly

Berthing

There is limited space alongside the quay for use in settled weather. The harbour dries to a firm bottom of sand and small stones.

Harbourmaster

The harbourmaster lives close to the harbour, behind the lifeboat house.

Facilities

Water From the lifeboat house.
Provisions Limited provisions in the village.
Post office On the main street.

River Taw and River Torridge estuary

Local High Water at Appledore is Dover –0520
Charts Admiralty *1179, 1160;* Imray *C58*

General

The rivers flow into Barnstaple Bay and tidal waters extend several miles inland to a number of harbours and anchorages.

Warning

Entrance should not be attempted until 2½ hours before HW; strong onshore winds can produce a large, dangerous swell, any swell also making the buoys difficult to identify.

Approach

By day Barnstaple Bay is entered between Hartland Point and Baggy Point. The red and white Bideford Fairway buoy (LFl.10s) must be identified.

By night The estuary can be approached using the following lights:

Hartland Point Fl(6)15s37m25M Horn 60s
Bull Point Fl(3)10s54m20M+F.R.48m12M
Bideford Fairway buoy LFl.10s
Instow Ldg Lts 118° *Front* Oc.6s22m15M
  Rear 427m from front Oc.10s38m15M

Anchorage in the approach

Anchor in 5m sand only in the most settled conditions. Alternative anchorages in which to await the tide are Clovelly to the southwest and Morte Bay to the north, depending on the prevailing wind direction.

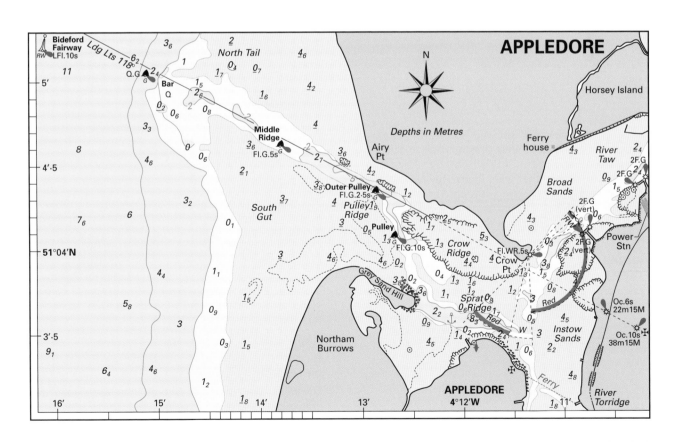

Entrance

Leading lights indicate the channel between the Bideford Fairway buoy and the drying Old Wall Rocks. In line the two white light towers bear 118°. This course is followed, passing three buoys to starboard: the Bar, Middle Ridge, and Outer Pulley light buoys. Passing the Outer Pulley, change course to 160° to leave the Pulley green conical buoy to starboard, heading close to the southeast tip of Greys Hill before turning to the pool to the north of Skern Point.

Appledore

A small shipbuilding and fishing town, said to have been granted 'free port' status by Elizabeth I in return for the part played by local ships and sailors in the defeat of the Spanish Armada. Yachts wishing to remain afloat can anchor in the pool to the north of Skern Point. It is possible to lie alongside the drying quay, but this gets busy in summer, and the mud and stone bottom can contain obstructions which could damage a yacht. There are virtually no ladders. Toilets and a post office are on the quay and there is a limited chandlery on Market Street.

Appledore

Bideford

The 2-mile channel up the River Torridge to Bideford is navigable after 2 hours before HW. An attractive town lies behind the long tree-lined quay. The quay along the west bank below Bideford Bridge is used by coasters, although it is possible for yachts to lie alongside and dry onto soft mud. There are no ladders. Toilets and the post office are on the quay.

Instow

The home of the North Devon Yacht Club, on the east bank of the River Torridge, with a large expanse of moorings drying onto firm sand. The moorings are exposed to northwest winds. Water has to be carried from the yacht club, where there are showers.

Fremington Quay

Passage up the River Taw should not be made until 2 hours before HW. Dangerous rocks on either side of the channel are marked with pole beacons. The river is navigable with care up to the former railway quay at Fremington. Now deserted, the drying quay is exposed to northwest winds; there are no facilities.

Barnstaple

The channel up the River Taw to Barnstaple is tortuous and liable to change. Navigation is possible with care for shallow-draught boats arriving in Barnstaple with the last of the flood. There is a quay along the north bank of the River Taw close to the town centre. Local boats lie alongside the quay of the River Yeo, where the shelving bank makes investigation prior to mooring necessary.

Baggy Point

Headland 3½ miles north of Bideford Fairway buoy. The Baggy Leap green conical buoy marks the end of the rock shoal 6 cables WNW of Baggy Point.

Morte Point

Low cliffed sloping headland 2½ miles north of Baggy Point. The Morte Stone green conical buoy marks the west extremity of the rock ledge extending from the headland. A dangerous race can be experienced off Morte Point during strong tides and contrary winds.

Bull Point

The white round tower of the lighthouse stands on the point 3½ miles west of Ilfracombe. At the strength of the tide, overfalls extend 2¾ miles north from Bull Point to Horseshoe Rocks. A north cardinal buoy marks the extremity of these rocks and overfalls. The tidal stream at springs can reach 3 knots. The east-going tide begins at HW Dover +0040, the west-going at HW Dover −0525.

Ilfracombe

⊕ 51°13'·15N 4°06'·6W ½M N of pierhead
Population 10,479 (1981)
Local High Water is Dover −0525
Charts Admiralty *1160, 1179, 1165*; Imray *C58, C59*

General

North Devon's largest holiday resort has terraces of elegant Victorian houses rising above a safe harbour. There are good facilities for yachts in this lively resort. The harbour is very busy during the summer, and the drying inner harbour can be full of resident boats. There is usually space available in the outer harbour, part of which dries to firm sand. There is water at the entrance to the harbour at all stages of the tide.

Approach

By day The approach is straightforward and there are no off-lying dangers.

By night The harbour can be reached using the following lights:

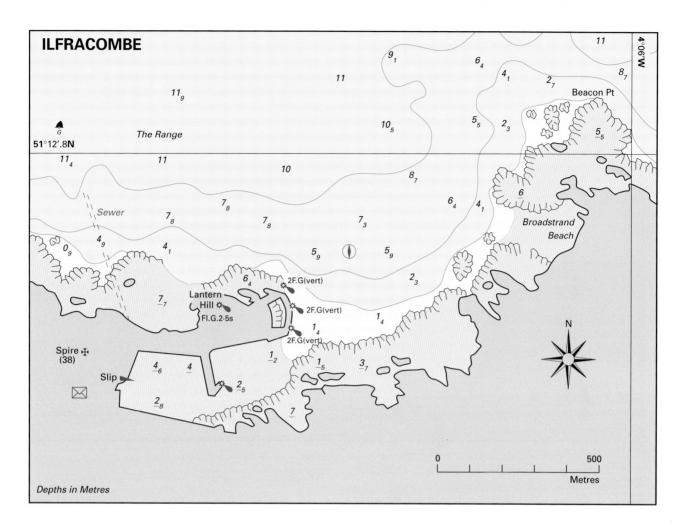

ILFRACOMBE

Depths in Metres

Bull Point Fl(3)10s54m20M+F.R.48m12M
Lantern Hill Fl.G.2·5s39m6M
Ilfracombe Pier 2F.G(vert)

Entrance

Entrance is made between Lantern Hill and Hillsborough, the headland to the east of the harbour, keeping close to the pier to avoid the rocks to the south of the harbour. The whole of the outer harbour is accessible at half-tide. The inner harbour is available for 2 hours either side of HW.

Moorings

Visitors' moorings are available in the outer harbour. Anchorage is also possible, keeping clear of the pier to allow passenger boats to manoeuvre.

Berthing

There is limited space available alongside the quays in the inner harbour.

Harbourmaster

Office on the quay to the northeast of the inner harbour.

Charges

There are harbour charges.

Facilities

Fuel Diesel from north wall of inner harbour, by

arrangement with harbourmaster. Petrol from filling stations on both main roads out of the town centre, each a 20-minute walk from the harbour.

Water By hose from quay (by arrangement with harbourmaster) or from tap by car park on main pier.

Slip At west end of inner harbour, although this must be kept clear for the lifeboat.

Provisions Occasional shop selling provisions amongst the plethora of gift shops, fast food outlets and restaurants.

Post office St James Place.

Yacht club Ilfracombe Yacht Club, in attractive premises over the harbourmaster's office on the quay. Bar, showers and washing facilities.

Calor Gas Harbour Chandlery and Marine.

Refuse disposal Bins on the quay.

Watermouth Cove

⊕ 51°13'·4N 4°04'·5W ½M N of harbour entrance
Local High Water is Dover –0525
Charts Admiralty *1164, 1165, 1179*; Imray *C58, C59*

General

A narrow haven, drying to sand and fine shingle, 4 cables east of Rillage Point. There is a small holiday camp at the head of the cove, close to Watermouth Castle.

23

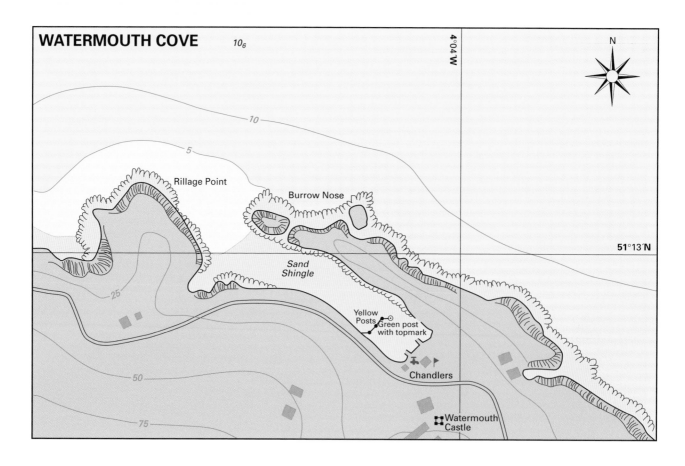

WATERMOUTH COVE 10₆

Rillage Point

Burrow Nose

Sand
Shingle

Yellow
Posts — Green post
with topmark

Chandlers

Watermouth
Castle

4°04´W

51°13´N

N

Warning

There is always water at the entrance to the cove, but the moorings within the cove are only available for 2½ hours either side of HW. The harbour is sheltered to all but the strongest northwest winds. The tide runs strongly across the entrance to the harbour, and conditions with contrary winds can produce rough water.

Approach

By day There are conspicuous cottages on Rillage Point (4 cables west of the harbour) and an observation post on Widmouth Head, immediately to the west of the entrance. The circular stone pill box on Burrow Nose, immediately to the east of the entrance, is conspicuous when approaching from the east.

By night A night approach and entrance should not be attempted.

Anchorage in the approach

Anchorage is possible within the harbour entrance at all states of the tide.

Entrance

Entrance to the harbour is made between Widmouth Head to the west and the lower Burrow Nose to the east.

Moorings

Visitors' moorings within the harbour are indicated by the red buoys with yellow handles.

Harbourmaster

The harbourmaster can be contacted at the chandlery at the head of the cove, and should be reported to on arrival.

Charges

There are harbour charges.

Facilities

Water Tap on wall of chandlery.
Slip There are two slips at the head of the cove.
Yacht club Watermouth Yacht Club, at the head of the cove.
Chandlery Watermouth Marine Services, adjacent to the yacht club.

Approaching Watermouth Cove

Combe Martin Bay

Temporary anchorage is available in 6m off the village of Combe Martin.

Lynmouth

⊕ 51°14'·6N 3°49'·6W ½M N of harbour entrance
Population 2,075 (1981)
Local High Water is Dover –0515
Charts Admiralty *1165, 1179*; Imray *C59*

General

One of Devon's most picturesque resorts, Lynmouth has a small drying harbour which should only be visited in the most settled conditions.

Warning

Entrance should only be made within one hour of HW. The east quay formed by the river training wall is covered at HW springs. The harbour is only available to shallow-draught craft at neaps and becomes uncomfortable if there is any north in the wind. Strong winds create a surge, making the harbour untenable.

Approach

By day From the green conical Sand Ridge buoy, 1½ miles west of Foreland Point, head directly for the poles marking the entrance to the harbour.

By night A night approach and entrance should not be attempted.

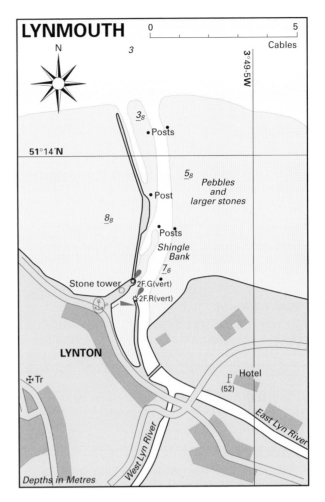

Lynmouth   *PRPA/Patrick Roach*

Anchorage in the approach

Anchorage may be had in 6m in Lynmouth Bay only in settled conditions.

Entrance

The line of the river is marked by timber posts as far as the harbour entrance.

Berthing

Visitors should tie alongside the east quay, although this is covered at HW springs.

Harbourmaster

Office on the quay above the slip.

Charges

There are harbour charges.

Facilities

Slip In northwest corner of harbour.

Foreland Point

The most prominent headland on this stretch of coastline has a lighthouse with a white round tower (Fl(4)15s67m18M). Foreland Ledge lies parallel to the coast ¾ mile north of Foreland Point. In strong tidal conditions with contrary winds there are dangerous overfalls extending over a mile to the northwest and northeast of the point.

Porlock Weir

⊕ 51°13'·6N 3°37'·6W ½M N of harbour entrance
Local High Water is Dover –0455
Charts Admiralty *1160, 1165, 1179*; Imray *C59*

General

A small, well sheltered drying harbour, surrounded by an attractive grouping of buildings, lying 1½ miles from the village of Porlock.

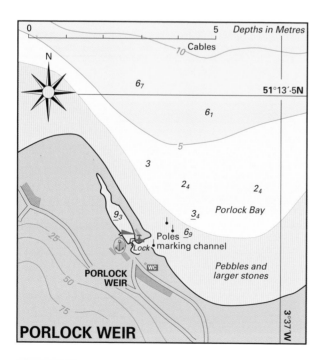

Entrance to Porlock Weir at low water, showing channel marker poles

Warning

The harbour can only be entered for 2 hours either side of HW.

Approach

By day Porlock Bay can be approached from any direction. There are no off-lying dangers.

By night A night approach and entrance should not be attempted.

Anchorage in the approach

Anchorage may be had in 5m shingle in Porlock Bay in settled conditions.

Entrance

The harbour entrance and channel are marked with poles, painted red and white, and green and white. They have been painted and positioned in such a way that the red and white posts must be left to port and the green and white posts to starboard both when entering and when leaving the harbour. There is a steep pebble bank to either side of the narrow entrance.

Moorings

There is limited mooring space in the outer pool.

Berthing

Keel boats may lie alongside the southwest quay in the inner harbour, although the space available is again limited.

Harbourmaster

Office at southwest corner of inner harbour.

Charges

There are harbour charges.

Facilities

Water From tap by lock gates to inner harbour.
Slip On west side of inner harbour.
Provisions Limited provisions in Porlock Weir. Full range of shops in Porlock, 1½ miles away. Restaurant and bar snacks are available at the hotel overlooking the harbour.
Post office In Porlock.

Minehead

⊕ 51°13'·1N 3°28'·1W 3 cables NNE of pierhead
Population 11,211 (1981)
Local High Water is Dover −0450
Charts Admiralty *1160, 1165, 1179*; Imray *C59*

General

A popular holiday resort, dominated by a large holiday camp at its eastern end. The drying harbour is set apart from the bustle of the town and provides good shelter in all except east winds, although seas have been known to break over the pier at MHWS during inshore gales. The harbour is busy in the summer months.

Warning

The harbour can only be entered for 2 hours either side of HW.

Approach

By day The harbour is best approached from the north or northwest to avoid the drying shingle bank ½ mile ENE of the pier. The holiday camp to the east of the harbour is conspicuous.

By night Approach at night can be made with care. The lights of the holiday camp are conspicuous; the Fl(2)G.5s4M light at the end of the pier must be identified.

Anchorage in the approach

Anchorage may be had (in 4m, north of the pier) only in settled conditions.

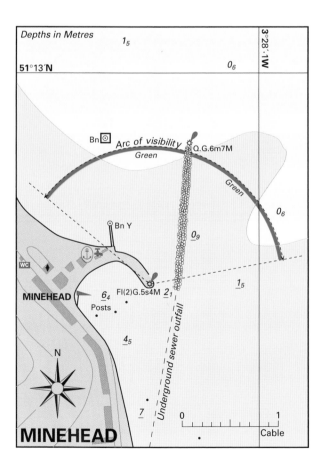

Entrance

Leave the green-topped beacon marking the end of the sewer outfall to starboard, and keep 200 feet away from the pierhead until able to turn into the harbour.

Moorings

There are 8 red buoyed visitors' moorings to seaward of the three wooden posts.

Berthing

Visitors can lie alongside the pier wall. There are good ladders; the harbour dries to a firm bottom of sand, mud and small stones. Visitors planning an extended stop and capable of taking the bottom will be moved up closer to the slip to dry out onto firm sand.

Harbourmaster

Office on north side of harbour.

Charges

There are harbour charges.

Facilities

Fuel Only from filling station about 1 mile from harbour.
Water From tap by harbourmaster's office.
Slip On west side of harbour.
Provisions Full range of shops in town centre, ½ mile from harbour.
Post office The Avenue, in the town centre.
Refuse disposal Litter bins on quay.

Watchet

⊕ 51°11'·5N 3°19'·7W ½M N of harbour entrance
Population 3,357 (1981)
Local High Water is Dover −0450
Charts Admiralty *1160, 1152, 1179*; Imray *C59*

General

An old-established commercial port with a well sheltered drying harbour which can take vessels of up to 2,500 tons. Work started in autumn 2000 on a 240-berth marina in the SE half of the harbour and the initial 100 berths were available in summer 2001. The fully serviced marina includes showers, toilets and laundry facilities ashore. There are chemical toilets, waste oil disposal points and storage facilities for boats ashore.

Warning

Entrance to the harbour can be made up to 2½ hours either side of HW. The marina can be entered between 2 and 2½ hours either side of HW, the tidal gates being opened at 6·9m above chart datum allowing a minimum 2·5 draught. There are least depths of between 1·5 and 3m within the marina. The tidal gates can accommodate vessels of up to 7·5m beam.

Approach

By day The two radio masts to the southwest are very conspicuous. When approaching from the north, Culver Sand must be avoided.

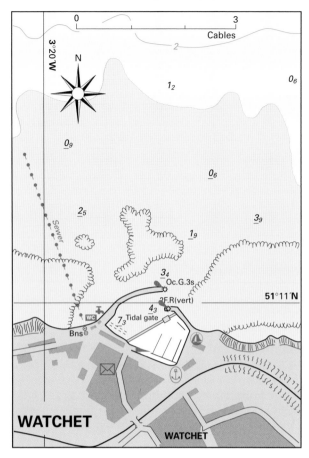

To clear the off-lying rocks it is advisable to keep ½ mile offshore until the entrance between the piers is well open. The harbour should then be approached directly.

By night The harbour can be approached using the following lights:

Lynmouth Foreland Fl(4)15s67m18M
West pierhead Oc.G.3s9m9M
East pierhead 2F.R(vert)3M

Entrance

The harbour is entered between the two stone piers. The Oc.G.3s light at the end of the west pier is displayed from a red tower. Allowance should be made for the strong currents that can be experienced close to the west pier, especially on the ebb.

Anchorage in the approach

Anchorage is available in Blue Anchor Roads (1 mile to the west of the harbour) in settled conditions.

Berthing

Berthing within the new marina as directed.

Harbourmaster

Office on the quay in the southeast corner of the harbour.

Watchet. The marina in the eastern half of the harbour was built since the photograph was taken   *RPA/Patrick Roach*

Charges

There are harbour charges.

Facilities

Fuel Diesel from marina fuelling quay. Petrol by arrangement with marina office.

Water and electricity From marina pontoons.

Slip On south side of harbour.

Provisions There is a good range of shops in the town.

Post office In town centre.

Yacht club Watchet Boat Owners' Association, at south end of west quay.

Chandlery Limited chandlery available from Swantel's, at the south end of the west quay.

Calor Gas and Camping Gaz Available from Swantel's.

VHF radio Call *Watchet Marina* Ch 80 ☎ 01984 631264.

Burnham-on-Sea

Position 51°15'·0N 3°00'·0W
Population 17,341 (1981)
Local High Water is Dover –0430
Charts Admiralty *1152, 1179*; Imray *C59*

General

A holiday resort offering sheltered moorings as a reward for negotiating the shoals of Bridgwater Bay.

Warning

Approach should only be made within 3 hours of HW. Entry should not be attempted in strong onshore winds.

Approach

By day Bridgwater Bay is entered between Stoke Bluff and Brean Down, a bold promontory 10 miles to the northeast. It is necessary to locate the Gore bell buoy. Hinkley Point power station to the south is very conspicuous.

By night Entry is possible at night, as the buoys and leading marks are lit; however, it is not advisable without local knowledge.

The following lights will assist a night time entry

Burnham-on-Sea entrance Fl.7·5s7m12M
Dir Lt 076° DirF.WRG.4m12-10M
Ldg Lts 112° 2F.R.12/6m3M
Brue Beacon Fl.R.3s5m2M
East Dunball Point Fl.R.3s5m2M

Anchorage in the approach

Yachts can lie afloat in 3m approximately 3 cables east of No.2 buoy.

Entrance

From the Gore bell buoy, a course of 80° is made towards Brent Knoll (133m; 2 miles ENE of Burnham) along the buoyed channel before picking up the leading marks: the old light tower with the

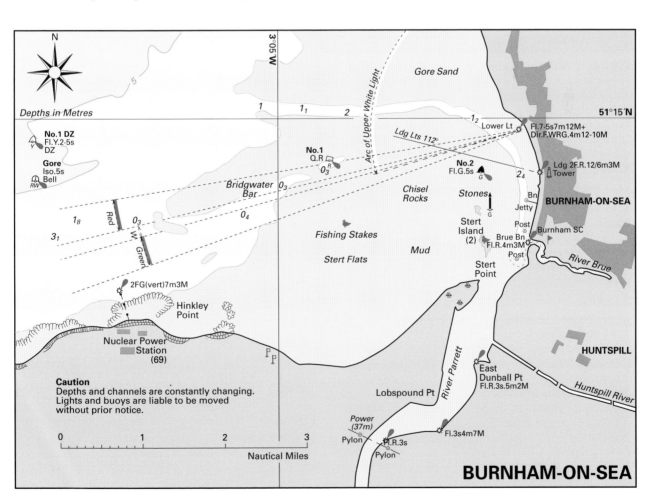

BURNHAM-ON-SEA

Burnham-on-Sea/Bridgwater Bay   *PRPA/Patrick Roach*

main lighthouse beyond. The lighthouse should be kept just open to the south of the old tower until the church tower (5 cables south of the lighthouse) and the white mark on the sea wall are in line on a bearing of 112°.

Moorings

The anchorage off the town is protected by Stert Island, but the best shelter is to be found in the River Brue. The river is best entered 2½ hours before HW, and dries to soft mud. There are moorings near the yacht club slipway for deep-keel boats.

Facilities

Water There are water taps in the public toilets by the yacht club.
Slip In the River Brue, by the yacht club.
Provisions There is a good range of shops in the town.
Post office In the town centre.
Yacht club Burnham-on-Sea Yacht Club, at the entrance to the River Brue.

Weston-super-Mare

Position 51°20'·8N 2°59'·3W
Population 62,261 (1981)
Local High Water is Dover –0435
Charts Admiralty *1152, 1176, 1179*; Imray *C59*

General

A popular holiday resort that expanded rapidly in Victorian times. Knightstone Harbour, at the north end of Weston Bay, dries to a bottom of small stones and firm mud, and is sheltered from all directions except south.

Warning

The harbour should only be entered up to 2 hours either side of HW.

Approach

By day Weston Bay is entered between Brean Down and Anchor Head. The whole of the bay dries to mud in a line from the centre of Brean Down to the west extremity of Birnbeck Island.

By night The harbour can be reached using the following lights:

Grand Pier 2F.G(vert)

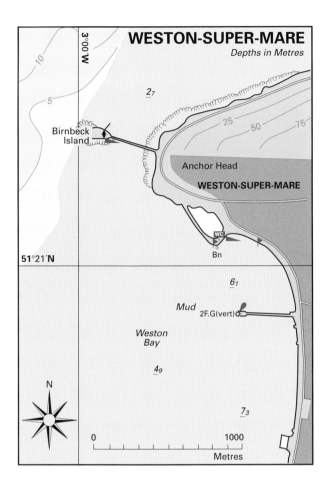

Entrance

Direct entrance, leaving the Grand Pier to starboard, and the causeway at the entrance to the harbour (marked with a beacon) to port.

Moorings

The yacht club should be contacted to ascertain which of the vacant moorings in the harbour are available. Sheltered moorings can be found in the River Axe, at the south end of Weston Bay. Entrance to the river, which dries to soft mud, is possible for 2 hours either side of HW, leaving Black Rock to port.

Berthing

Raft alongside the yacht club dolphin, leaving room alongside the slip for local boatmen.

Facilities

Slip In north corner of harbour.
Provisions Full range of shops in town.
Post office In town centre.
Yacht club Weston Bay Yacht Club.

III. Upper reaches of the Bristol Channel and the River Severn

Clevedon Pill

Position 51°25'·8N 2°52'·8W
Population 18,099 (1981)
Local High Water is Dover –0420
Charts Admiralty *1176, 1179*; Imray *C59*

General

Clevedon Pill lies ¾ mile southwest of the holiday resort of Clevedon, and offers a limited number of drying moorings on the banks of the pill by arrangement with the Clevedon Sailing Club.

Warning

The pill should only be entered between 2½ hours either side of HW. The moorings at the entrance to the pill are exposed to the west, although the moorings further up the pill offer good shelter. The damaged pier 1 mile northeast of Clevedon Pill must be given a wide berth. The tide runs at 3½ knots at springs.

Approach

By day From Sand Point to Clevedon, shoals with drying patches extend up to 3 miles offshore. There is a conspicuous radio mast 6½ cables southeast of Wain's Hill.

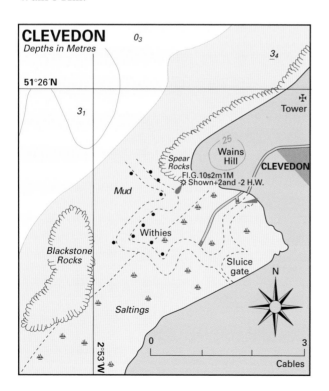

By night

By night A night approach and entrance should not be attempted.

Entrance

Entrance is made between Wain's Hill and Blackstone Rocks, the channel being marked with withies.

Moorings

Moorings are available on the banks of the pill by arrangement with Clevedon Sailing Club. The banks are steep and dry to soft mud.

Facilities

Slip The slip at the head of the pill can be used at HW springs.
Provisions From town centre, ¾ mile from the pill.
Yacht club Clevedon Sailing Club, on the promenade in Clevedon Bay.

Black Nore Point

Black Nore Point lies 1·2 miles WSW of Portishead Point, with a light (Fl(2)10s15M) shown from a white tower on a framework base.

Portishead

Position 51°29'·7N 2°45'·1W
Population 13,867 (1981)
Local High Water is Dover –0405
Charts Admiralty *1176, 1179*; Imray *C59*

General

Except in an emergency, yachts are not allowed to enter Avonmouth or Royal Portbury Docks. Shelter from southwest winds can be had temporarily off Portishead Dock, at the direction of the dockmaster. Work has now commenced (summer 2000) on a new marina in Portishead Dock. An initial 150 berths were available in 2001 of a projected total of 400/450 berths. The marina is fully serviced with toilets, showers, laundry facilities and a berth-holders lounge ashore. There is a 35-ton travel-hoist and storage yard.

Warning

The outer sill to the marina is at 3m above chart datum allowing access 3¾ hours either side of MHWS and 4½ either side of MHWN. Entrance is controlled by IALA light signals, 3F.R(vert) – do not enter; F.GWG(vert) – proceed on instruction.

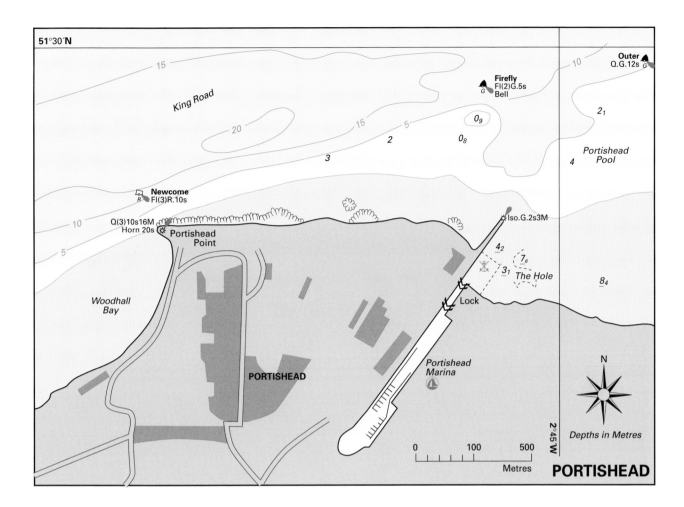

Approach

By day The Firefly Rocks, with a least depth of 0·9m, lie 2 cables NNW of Portishead Pier head. A green conical bell buoy marks their north extremity and should be rounded before approaching the pier.

By night The dock may be approached at night using the following lights:

Portishead Point Q(3)10s9m16M Horn 20s
Firefly buoy Fl(2)G.5s Bell
Portishead Pier Iso.G.2s5m3M

Anchorage

Anchor at the direction of the dockmaster to the east of the outer pier. Do not moor close to the permanent yacht moorings in the 'Hole', where there are some drastic changes in level. The approach is exposed to north to northeast winds, which will create choppy conditions and make taking the ground inadvisable.

VHF radio telephone

Call *Avonmouth Radio* on Ch 16, work Ch 12 or 14.
Call *Portishead Dock* on Ch 16, work Ch 12 or 14 (HW−2½ to HW+1½).
Call *Portishead Quays Marina* Ch 80 ☎ 01275 817440.

Facilities

Fuel Diesel and petrol available from fuel quay in marina.

Water and electricity Provided to all pontoon berths.
Slip On SE side of marina basin.
Boatbuilders and repairs Bristol Deep Boatyard.
Yacht brokerage Walton Marine Brokerage.

Bristol

Position 51°27'·0N 2°37'·0W
Population 420,234 (1981)
Local High Water (Avonmouth) is Dover −0405
Charts Admiralty *1859, 1176*; Imray *C59*

General

Bristol City Docks provide floating moorings alongside the quay in the heart of Bristol, after navigating the River Avon for 5½ miles from Avonmouth Docks.

Approach

On approaching Avonmouth Docks, contact Avonmouth Radio for instructions to enter the River Avon, calling *Avonmouth Radio* on Ch 12.

The tidal stream off the entrance to the River Avon runs at up to 5 knots at springs (being stronger on the flood) and 3 knots at neaps.

Do not enter the river until 2 hours before HW. Enter the river leaving the commercial dock to port, keeping close to the south pier until the leading marks (white posts) are in line on 127°. These should be kept in line until approaching the next

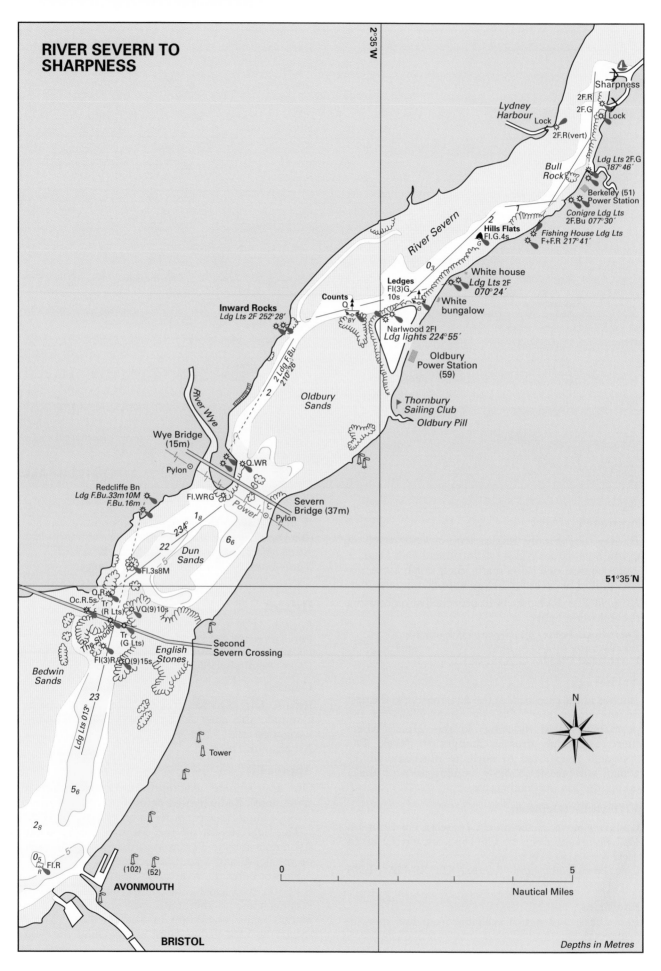

RIVER SEVERN TO SHARPNESS

2°35´W

Sharpness

2F.R
2F.G

Lydney Harbour
Lock
Lock

2F.R(vert)

Ldg Lts 2F.G
187° 46´

Bull Rock

Berkeley (51) Power Station

Conigre Ldg Lts 2F.Bu 077°30´

Hills Flats
Fl.G.4s

River Severn

Fishing House Ldg Lts F+F.R 217° 41´

White house
Ldg Lts 2F 070´ 24´

Ledges
Fl(3)G.
10s

Counts
Q

White bungalow

Inward Rocks
Ldg Lts 2F 252° 28´

Narlwood 2Fl
Ldg lights 224° 55´

BY

Oldbury Power Station (59)

2 Ldg F.Bu
210´26´

Oldbury Sands

Thornbury Sailing Club
Oldbury Pill

River Wye

Wye Bridge (15m)

Q.WR

Pylon

Redcliffe Bn
Ldg F.Bu.33m10M F.Bu.16m

Fl.WRG

Power

Severn Bridge (37m)

Pylon

234°

1_8

6_6

22

Dun Sands

Fl.3s8M

Q.R

Oc.R.5s
Tr
(R Lts)

VQ(9)10s

Tr
(G Lts)

Fl(3)R
Q(9)15s

English Stones

Second Severn Crossing

Bedwin Sands

23

Ldg Lts 013°

5_6

2_8

0_5
Fl.R
R

(102) (52)

AVONMOUTH

51°35´N

N

0   5

Nautical Miles

BRISTOL

Depths in Metres

34

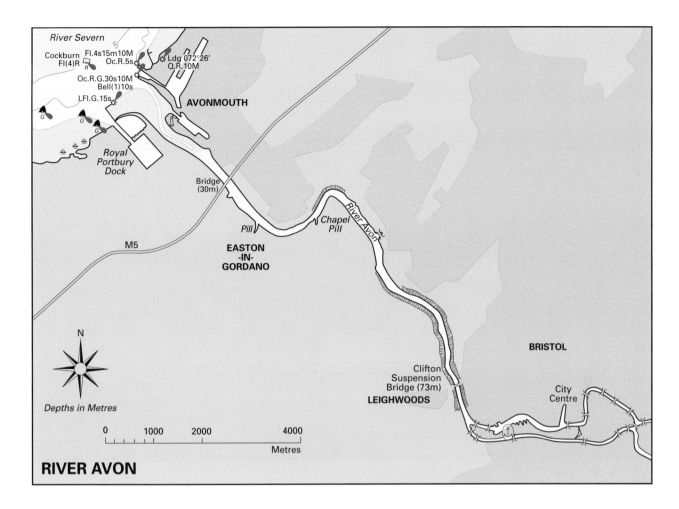

RIVER AVON

bend, from where yachts should keep to the centre of the channel.

There is limited mooring space available at Pill, the creek drying to soft mud, but mooring is only advisable with prior local knowledge.

Traffic signals are exhibited at two positions on the east bank of the river, 1½ and 2½ cables above Clifton Suspension Bridge. A fixed green light signifies 'come ahead with caution'; a fixed red light signifies 'stop and await orders'. Yachts should arrive at the Cumberland Basin entrance to the City Dock by HW. There are usually 3 lockings either way as from HW −2 hours 50 minutes. Yachts can lie alongside the pontoons before the docking signal at the Cumberland Basin entrance.

When proceeding inwards there will be less turbulence at the seaward end of the lock.

Moorings

Quayside moorings, as instructed by the dockmaster.

Dockmaster and office

Duty dockmaster's office is on south quay of entrance lock to Cumberland Basin. Dock office at Underfall Yard, on south side of City Docks by Junction Lock.

Charges

There are harbour charges.

VHF radio telephone

Call *Avonmouth Radio* on Ch 16, work Ch 12 or 14.
Call *City Docks Radio* on Ch 16, work Ch 12 or 14 (HW−3 to HW+1).

Facilities

Fuel Bristol Marina, on south side of City Docks.
Water At various points around City Docks.
Electricity At various points around City Docks.
Provisions Full range of shops, restaurants etc. in town centre.
Showers At the dock office and at Bristol Marina.
Chandlery Bristol Boating Centre and Bristol Yacht Centre.
Boat repairs, engineers Bristol Marine Engineering Centre; David Abel's, boatbuilders; Albion Marine Services.
Refuse disposal At various points around City Docks.

River Severn above Avonmouth

The Shoots

A narrow passage, only 1½ cables wide at its narrowest part, 4 miles north of Avonmouth Dock. An extensive area of rock, the English Stones, lies to the east of The Shoots; it is marked at is southwest

Bristol Docks   *PRPA/Patrick Roach*

Avonmouth   *PRPA/Patrick Roach*

Leading marks north of the shoots in the river Severn, above Avonmouth

and northwest ends by west cardinal marks. Leading marks for The Shoots are the white stone beacon on Charston Rock and the Redcliffe beacon, a white lantern on a black metal framework tower, 9 cables NNE of Charston Rock. Port and starboard lights are also attached to the tower supports of the new bridge.

Oldbury Pill

A pill drying to soft mud ½ mile south of the conspicuous Oldbury Power Station. Thornbury Sailing Club occupies conspicuous premises on the north bank of the pill. Entrance should only be made between 2 hours either side of HW. Visiting yachts requiring moorings should contact the club in advance.

Sharpness

Yachts can pass through the locked entrance to the commercial docks and into the marina at the entrance to the Gloucester and Berkeley Canal. The lock normally operates HW−2½ to HW+½. Yachts should arrive off Sharpness at about HW−1.

Tidal streams run at up to 6 knots at springs off Sharpness, with the flood beginning 2 hours before HW at Avonmouth and the ebb beginning 1 hour after HW at Avonmouth.

For VHF radio telephone, call Sharpness Control on Ch 16, work Ch 14.

Diesel fuel, water, *Calor Gas* and chandlery are available from Sharpness Marine, at the marina.

Lydney

Lock gates opening for 1 hour before HW give entrance to about one mile of canal offering secure moorings. The future of the lock is uncertain, and it should not be approached prior to checking locally as to its availability. Anchoring off the lock entrance is not possible, due to the strength of the tidal stream.

Newport

⊕ 51°31'·3N 2°58'·4W start of entrance channel
Local High Water is Dover −0420
Charts Admiralty *1176, 1152, 1179*; Imray *C59*

General

A commercial port on the banks of the River Usk,

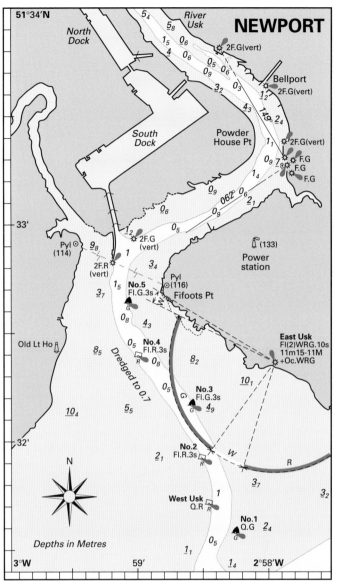

offering yachts sheltered moorings drying to soft mud.

Warning

The tidal stream in the river runs at 4 to 5 knots at springs at half-tide. Moorings off the yacht club dry to soft mud 3½ hours after HW.

Approach

By day The power station chimneys are very conspicuous. The West Usk buoy should be approached directly.

By night The moorings can be approached at night using the following lights:

East Usk LtHo
Fl(2)WRG.10s11m15/11M+Oc.WRG.10s10m11/9M
West Usk buoy Q.R
English & Welsh Grounds pillar light buoy
LFl.10s Whis Racon(T)
No.1 buoy Q.G
No.2 and **No.4** buoys Fl.R.3s
No.3 and **No.5** buoys Fl.G.3s
Alexandra Dock South Lock

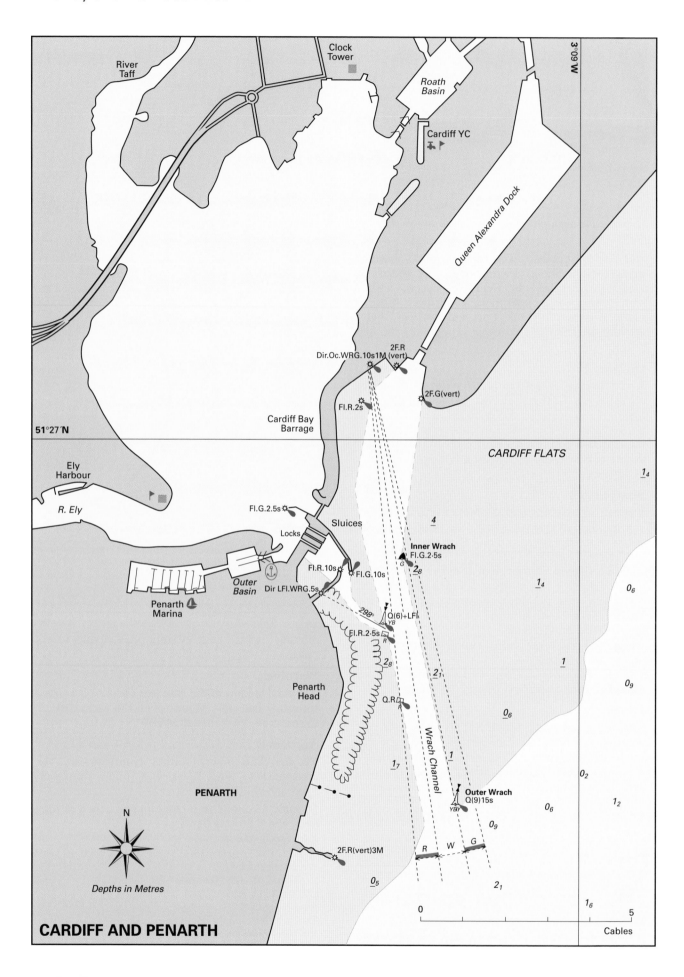

River
Taff

Clock
Tower

Roath
Basin

Cardiff YC

Queen Alexandra Dock

2F.R
(vert)

Dir.Oc.WRG.10s1M

2F.G(vert)

Fl.R.2s

Cardiff Bay
Barrage

51°27′N

CARDIFF FLATS

1_4

Ely
Harbour

R. Ely

4

Fl.G.2.5s

Sluices

Inner Wrach
Fl.G.2·5s

2_8

1_4

0_6

Locks

Fl.R.10s

Fl.G.10s

G

Outer
Basin

Dir LFl.WRG.5s

Penarth
Marina

$298°$

Q(6)+LFl
YB

1

Fl.R.2·5s

R

Penarth
Head

2_8

0_6

Q.R
R

1_7

2_1

Wrach Channel

1

PENARTH

Outer Wrach
Q(9)15s
YBY

0_6

0_9

0_2

1_2

N

2F.R(vert)3M

R   W   G

0_9

Depths in Metres

0_5

2_1

1_6

0   5

Cables

CARDIFF AND PENARTH

3°09′W

West pierhead 2F.R(vert)9m6M Horn 60s
East pierhead 2F.G(vert)9m6M
Julian's Pill Ldg Lts 062° F.G.4M

Entrance

Follow the buoyed channel to the South Lock entrance, then follow the river to the northeast. The moorings lie on the south side of the river, beyond the power station pier.

Moorings

Visitors' moorings, drying to soft mud 3½ hours after HW, are available on the sloping river bank. Keel boats can lie in the soft mud of Julian's Pill. Only temporary mooring for watering etc. is permitted alongside the pontoon.

Anchorage

It is possible to anchor immediately outside the moorings. An anchor light is essential at night.

Facilities

Water From the end of the sailing club pontoon.
Slip The slip by the sailing club is accessible at most states of the tide.
Yacht club Newport and Uskmouth Sailing Club.

Cardiff

⊕ 51°26'·0N 3°08'·7W start of entrance channel
Population 273,537 (1981)
Local High Water is Dover –0425
Charts Admiralty *1182, 1152, 1179*; Imray *C59*

General

The capital city of Wales is a commercial port where yachts may find good shelter. Cardiff was formerly one of the largest ports in the world; its early prosperity was based on coal. The docks are approximately 2 miles from the town centre. The Cardiff Bay Barrage has dramatically changed the area creating a 500-acre freshwater lake. An extensive dredging programme is planned which, it is hoped, will result in a depth of at least 2·5m throughout the bay.

Warning

The Outer Harbour to the Barrage locks is dredged to 0·7m below chart datum which should allow 24-hour access into the bay, dependent on draught, on all but the lowest spring tides. Call *Barrage Control* on Ch 18 to arrange lock-in. There is a waiting berth in the inner harbour. It is intended that the marina lock gates will now remain permanently open.

Approach

By day The Ranie buoy marks the extremity of the rocks and sand spit off Lavernock Point. The South Cardiff cardinal buoy marks the south extremity of the Cardiff Grounds. From a position between the two buoys make directly for the Outer Wrach west cardinal buoy.

By night The harbour can be reached making use of the following lights:
Monkstone LtHo Fl.5s13m12M

Ranie buoy Fl(2)R.5s
Cardiff Docks DirOc.WRG.10s1M
South Cardiff buoy Q(6)+LFl.15s
Mid Cardiff buoy Fl(3)G.10s
Penarth Pier 2F.R(vert)8m3M
Outer Wrach buoy Q(9)15s
Penarth Head buoy Q.R
Inner Wrach buoy Fl.G.2·5s
Queen's Dock
South pierhead 2F.G(vert) Dia 60s
North pierhead 2F.R(vert)

Moorings

Moorings belonging to Cardiff Yacht Club members are currently located in the northeast corner of the bay.

Berthing

There is a limited amount of space at the end of the pontoon for temporary berthing.

Facilities

Fuel Diesel fuel may be obtained from Castletown Oils, Collingwood Road. First right out of dock gates, approximately ½ mile from yacht club pontoon.
Water Tap at side of yacht club.
Electricity At the head of the slip.
Slip By yacht club.
Provisions Some shops near dock entrance. Town centre approximately 2 miles from docks.
Yacht club Cardiff Yacht Club.
Boat engineers The docks have numerous mechanical and electrical engineers.

Penarth

There are numerous moorings in the River Ely, and visitors may tie to the floating pontoon by the Penarth Motor Boat and Sailing Club.

Penarth Marina

A well sheltered marina, offering 420 fully serviced berths, within the former Penarth Dock.

Approach

The marina is approached as for Cardiff through the new Barrage locks, then turning to port to pass through the lock gates of the marina. These lock gates will only be in operation if the level of water in the bay has fallen.

Berthing

As directed by the berthing master. There are always visitors' berths available.

Charges

There are marina charges.

VHF radio telephone

Call *Penarth Marina* on Ch 80.

Facilities

Fuel Fuelling pontoons in inner basin.
Water On all pontoons.
Toilets and showers In Marina Services Building for

Cardiff. Penarth Marina   *PRPA/Patrick Roach*

Outer Basin and Inner Basin Services Building.
Provisions Full provisions available in Penarth, about
    10 minutes' walk from the marina.
Brokerage Penarth Boat Sales, by Marina Services
    Building.
Boat repairs and engineers Wigmore Wright Marine
    Services, The Boatyard, Marina Inner Basin.
    Cambrian Marine Services, River Ely.
Marine electronics RGB Electronics, Penarth.

IV. Lavernock Point to Worms Head

Barry

⊕ 51°23'·0N 3°15'·5W ½M S of harbour entrance
Population 46,520 (1981)
Local High Water is Dover –0430
Charts Admiralty *1182, 1152, 1179*; Imray *C59*

General

A holiday resort, with a large holiday camp close to the commercial docks. The outer harbour to the commercial docks is popular with yachtsmen, and there is sufficient water to enter at all states of the tide.

Warning

The outer harbour provides good shelter except in strong east or southeast winds, when yachts are advised to enter the docks (by prior arrangement). Although it is possible to enter the harbour at all times, the bays to the east and west of the outer harbour dry to soft mud at LW.

Approach

By day Sully Island and Bendrick Rock, to the east of the harbour, must both be passed to seaward; otherwise the approach is straightforward. The white round tower of the lighthouse is conspicuous at the head of the west breakwater.

By night The harbour can be approached and entered using the following lights:
West breakwater Fl.2·5s12m10M
East breakwater Q.G.7m8M

Entrance

Straightforward entrance between the two breakwaters. Keep clear of commercial traffic at all times. The dock can only be entered for 3 hours either side of HW.

Moorings

There are no moorings for visitors, but many owners will allow visiting yachts alongside, although they may not be left there unattended or overnight. Yachts wishing to stay for any length of time should contact the yacht club.

Berthing

Anchorage is possible in the east bay of the outer harbour, which dries to soft mud.

Charges

There are no harbour charges in the outer harbour.

VHF radio telephone

Call *Barry Radio* on Ch 16, work Ch 10, 11 or 22 (HW−4 to HW+4).

Facilities

Fuel Diesel fuel from Ray Harris Marine.
Water Tap by slip with hose extension out to side of lifeboat slipway.
Slip On west side of outer harbour.
Provisions Good range of local shops.
Yacht club Barry Yacht Club, with lounges, bar, toilets and showers.
Chandlery and repairs Ray Harris Marine, by the slipway.
Sailmakers and riggers Breaksea, No.1 Dock, Barry.

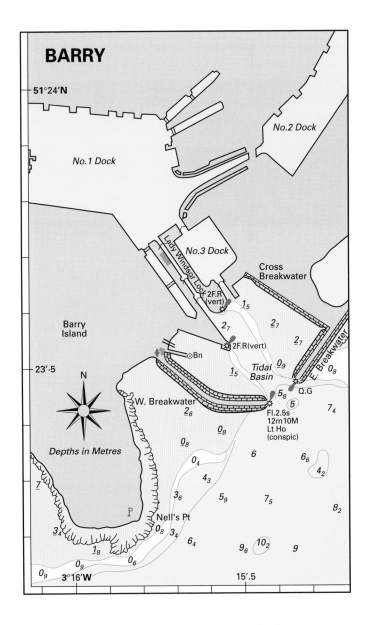

Barry Old Harbour

The old harbour lies 1 mile west of the main harbour and is rapidly silting. It is exposed to south winds and dries to firm sand.

Breaksea Point

A low headland 5½ miles west of Barry main harbour, with three very conspicuous power station chimneys. A low concrete tower with a domed top stands ½ mile SSW of the point, with a red buoy to its south side.

Nash Point

A prominent headland 5½ miles WNW of Breaksea Point. The white round tower of Nash lighthouse (Fl(2)WR.15s56m21/16M) stands 4 cables ESE of the point, with the white round tower of a disused lighthouse standing on the cliffs of the headland.

Nash Passage

A narrow passage (1 cable wide) running between the east end of Nash Sand and the rocky ledge at the foot of Nash Point. There is a least depth of 6m in the fairway. The east-going stream causes heavy overfalls off Nash Point. The east-going stream begins at HW Dover +0130 and the west-going stream begins at HW Dover −0445. The tidal stream runs at up to 5 knots at springs.

Porthcawl

⊕ 51°28'·0N 3°41'·9W 3 cables S of harbour entrance
Population 15,625 (1981)
Local High Water is Dover −0500
Charts Admiralty *1169, 1165, 1179*; Imray *C59*

General

A former commercial port; now a holiday resort. The commercial trade was ruined by the expansion of Barry harbour. The old dock was filled in to be used as a car park, although the outer harbour remains, with limited space for the use of pleasure craft.

Warning

The harbour should only be entered between 2 hours either side of HW; it dries to soft mud at half-tide.

Approach

By day From the east the approach is through the Nash Passage, between Nash Sand and the rock

Porthcawl   *PRPA/Patrick Roach*

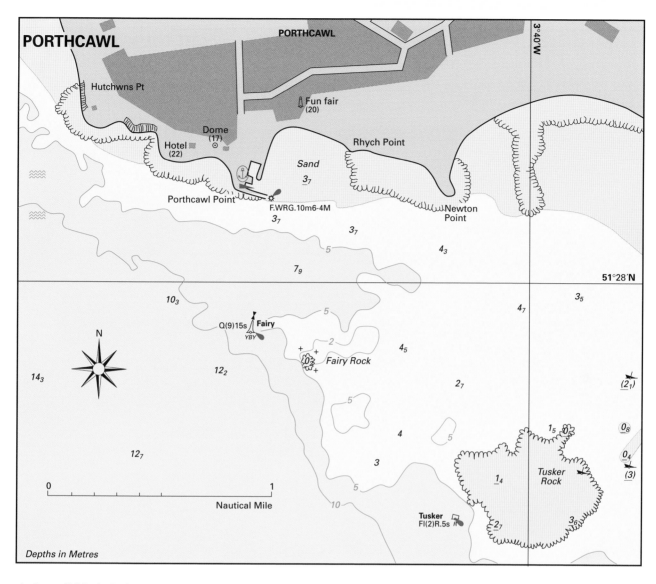

PORTHCAWL

PORTHCAWL

Hutchwns Pt

Fun fair
(20)

Dome
(17)

Hotel
(22)

Rhych Point

Sand
3₇

Porthcawl Point

F.WRG.10m6-4M

3₇

Newton
Point

3₇

4₃

3₇

7₉

51°28'N

10₃

3₅

Q(9)15s Fairy
YBY

4₇

5

2

Fairy Rock

4₅

14₃

12₂

0₃

+

2₇

(2₁)

12₇

5

4

5

1₅ 0₃

0₈

0₄

(3)

Tusker
Rock

1₄

Tusker
Fl(2)R.5s

2₇

3₆

0   Nautical Mile   1

10

Depths in Metres

ledge off Nash Point. Leave the red buoy marking the Tusker Rock (dries to 4·2m) to starboard and (heading no more than 312° to avoid Fairy Rock) make for a position 5 cables due south of the lighthouse and then directly for the harbour. Porthcawl lighthouse, at the end of the breakwater, has a white hexagonal tower with a black base.

From the west the ideal approach leaves Scarweather Sands to the north, passing south of the West Scar and South Scar cardinal light buoys. There is a passage to the north between the sands and the Hugo Bank, but this should only be used in settled weather. In such conditions passage may also be made between the Kenfig east cardinal buoy and Sker Point.

In conditions with strong tidal streams and contrary winds, overfalls can build up to the west of Porthcawl Point. Again the approach is to a position 5 cables south, erring west of south, of the lighthouse, and then directly to the harbour.

By night Numerous lights make approach and entrance possible, but the number of offshore hazards, coupled with strong tidal streams, makes this inadvisable without prior local knowledge.

Anchorage in the approach

This is possible off the harbour entrance only in the most settled conditions.

Entrance

Keep close to the end of the breakwater and then

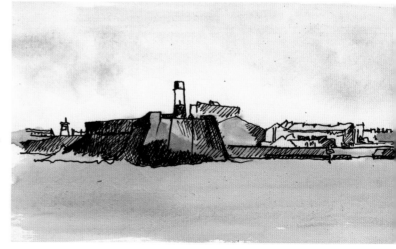

Entrance to Porthcawl

43

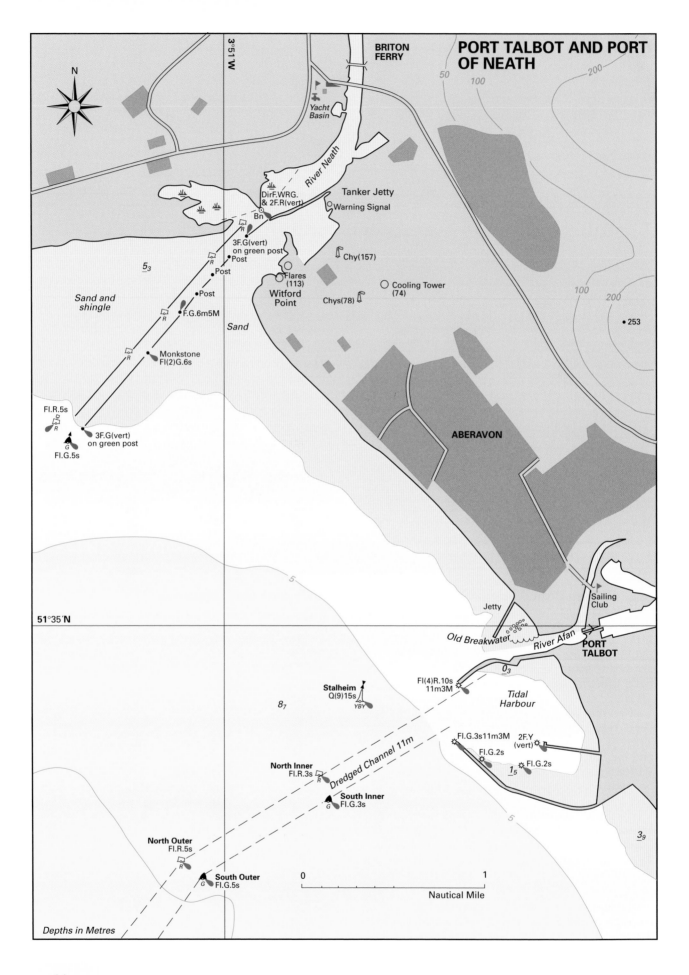

PORT TALBOT AND PORT OF NEATH

N

3°51'W

BRITON FERRY

50 100 200 200

Yacht Basin

River Neath

DirF.WRG. & 2F.R(vert)

Bn

Tanker Jetty

Warning Signal

3F.G(vert) on green post

Post

Post

Post

F.G.6m5M

Chy(157)

Flares (113)

Witford Point

Chys(78)

Cooling Tower (74)

5₃

Sand and shingle

Sand

R

R

R

Monkstone Fl(2)G.6s

100 200

•253

Fl.R.5s

R

3F.G(vert) on green post

G
Fl.G.5s

ABERAVON

51°35'N

5

Sailing Club

Jetty

Old Breakwater

River Afan

PORT TALBOT

Fl(4)R.10s 11m3M

0₃

Tidal Harbour

Stalheim
Q(9)15s
YBV

8₇

Dredged Channel 11m

Fl.G.3s11m3M

2F.Y (vert)

Fl.G.2s

Fl.G.2s

1₅

North Inner
Fl.R.3s
R

South Inner
G
Fl.G.3s

North Outer
Fl.R.5s
R

South Outer
G
Fl.G.5s

3₉

5

0   1

Nautical Mile

Depths in Metres

44

close to its north side until near to the slip, before turning north to avoid an old collapsed breakwater, marked with a pole (with a 'keep left' sign) at its south end.

Berthing

There is limited space for visitors to tie alongside the east quay of the harbour.

Harbourmaster

On south side of inner harbour.

Charges

There are harbour charges.

Facilities

Slip Alongside the breakwater at its west end.
Provisions Good range of shops in the town centre.
Post office On the main street in the town centre.
Calor Gas and Camping Gaz Protheroe's DIY, in town centre.

Port Talbot

A large commercial port, used principally for the importation of iron ore. The port is prohibited to pleasure craft. There are a number of industrial outfalls in the bay, marked with yellow buoys. The River Afan flows into Swansea Bay on the north side of the north breakwater. The ruins of an old breakwater project from the shore along the north side of the river channel. The Port Talbot Small Boat Club has premises on the east bank of the river ½ mile from the entrance; there are moorings alongside the clubhouse.

Briton Ferry

Position 51°36'·0N 3°52'·0W
Local High Water is Dover –0500
Charts Admiralty *1161, 1179*; Imray *C59*

General

A declining commercial port that offers sheltered accommodation for yachtsmen. The local sailing club have excavated a basin and laid out pontoons for yachts to complement their river moorings, although there is limited space for visitors.

Warning

The River Neath dries out at LW, and entry should only be made between 2½ hours either side of HW. Entrance should not be attempted in strong onshore winds.

Approach

By day Approach is direct across Swansea Bay, and the green post carrying the 2F.G(vert) lights at the head of the training wall must be identified. There is a group of chimneys, cooling towers and flares to the east of the harbour; these are conspicuous.

By night The harbour can be approached and entered by night, using the lights along the training wall. However, this is not recommended without prior local knowledge.

Entrance

A training wall extends 1·8 miles southwest from the harbour, marked with green posts. It should be left close to starboard. The northwest side of the entrance channel is formed by a training bank marked by red buoys. There is a warning signal exhibited from high above the tanker jetty which flashes red when a large vessel is manoeuvring; entrance is prohibited until the signal turns green. The sailing club is on the west bank of the river, with the new mooring basin to the south of the clubhouse.

Moorings

There are drying moorings on either side of the slip in front of the clubhouse.

Berthing

There are approximately 70 berths in the new basin, but these are allocated to club members.

Facilities

Water From tap by the clubhouse.
Slip Slip into the river in front of the clubhouse; another at the entrance to the new basin.
Yacht club Monkstone Cruising and Sailing Club.

Swansea

⊕ 51°35'·5N 3°56'·06W starboard-hand buoy 9 cables SSW of East Breakwater head
Population 186,907 (1981)
Local High Water is Dover –0515
Charts Admiralty *1161, 1179*; Imray *C59*

General

A large commercial port which houses the Swansea Yacht Haven, offering excellent facilities and marina berthing in former commercial docks. The completion of the Tawe Barrage has improved access to the marina and increased the number of berths to 360, with space available for visitors.

Approach

By day There is a conspicuous radio mast (245m) 1·5 miles to the north of the harbour. The dredged entrance channel should be approached directly once in Swansea Bay and clear of Mumbles Head. The tidal stream runs anticlockwise around Swansea Bay for 9½ hours from HW Swansea −0330 to +0600. During this time a race may form off Mumbles Head. At the start of the flood tide the flow reverses, running N round Mumbles Head and setting towards Swansea from HW Swansea −0620 to −0325.

By night The harbour can be approached and entered using the following lights (note that the marina is only open between 0700 and 2200):
Fairway buoy Q(6)+LFl.15s
Inner fairway buoy Fl(2)G.5s
East Breakwater head 2F.G(vert)10m6M Siren 30s
Jetty Ldg Lts 020° *Front* Oc.G.4s5m2M
    Rear F.G.6M
West Pier head Fl(2)R.10s11m9M

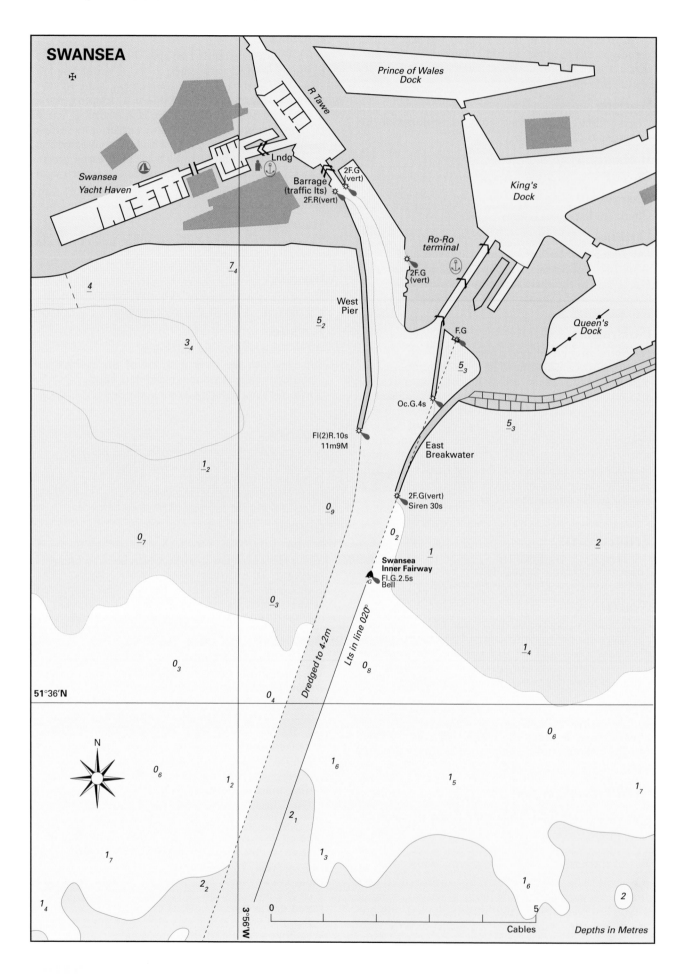

SWANSEA

Prince of Wales
Dock

R Tawe

Swansea
Yacht Haven

Lndg

Barrage
(traffic lts)
2F.R(vert)

2F.G
(vert)

King's
Dock

Ro-Ro
terminal

2F.G
(vert)

West
Pier

F.G

Queen's
Dock

Oc.G.4s

East
Breakwater

Fl(2)R.10s
11m9M

2F.G(vert)
Siren 30s

Swansea
Inner Fairway
Fl.G.2.5s
Bell

Lts in line 020°

Dredged to 4·2m

51°36'N

N

3°56'W

0   5

Cables

Depths in Metres

Swansea Marina   *PRPA/Patrick Roach*

Entrance

Entrance to the docks and marina is controlled by traffic signals, displayed at the west side of the entrance to Kings Dock. There are three rows of red and green lights in three columns. The middle row light of the left-hand column controls the movement of yachts. When a red light is shown yachts are prohibited from entering the port or the approach channel. When a green light is shown yachts may proceed to the Barrage Sea Lock. Entrance should be made close to the West Pier. Two holding buoys are situated downstream of the barrage lock, although these should not be used at LWS because of the danger of drying out. Access to the Yacht Haven is via the Barrage Sea Lock, usually on demand. The lock can hold some 25 yachts, and is controlled by traffic signals. It will close when the tide reaches 1·0m above chart datum – usually only during LW spring tides. The lock operates from 0700–1900 (0700–2200 at weekends) during the winter months, and from 0700–2200 during the summer. The last lock out is 30 minutes before the close of the business day. The marina lock operates the same hours as the barrage lock, the water level in the marina being one metre higher than the impounded level above the barrage.

Berthing

Marina berths in Swansea Yacht Haven.

Harbourmaster

Yachts are controlled by the marina master at the yacht haven.

Charges

There are marina fees, harbour dues and Tawe Barrage dues.

VHF radio telephone

Call *Swansea Yacht Haven* on Ch 80 and *Tawe Barrage* on Ch 18.

Facilities

Fuel Diesel from the marina between 0800–1800 (winter months) and 0800–2100 (summer months).

Water On all pontoons in the marina.

Slip In entrance basin to the marina.

Provisions Full range of shops in the town centre.

Showers Toilets and showers available 24 hours at the marina.

Laundry At Marine Reception.

Boatyard 18-ton marine travel-hoist. Boat storage and repair facilities.

Chandlery Cambrian Small Boat and Yacht Chandlery.

Swansea Yacht Haven   *PRPA/Patrick Roach*

Engineers Swansea Marine – inboard and outboard engine repairs. Cambrian Yacht Repairs – hull and rigging repairs.
Electronics Marconi Marine.
Refuse disposal Refuse skips at bridgeheads.

Mumbles

A large area of yacht moorings drying to sand, shingle and firm mud. There is water at the two

slipways in front of the Mumbles Yacht Club for 3 hours either side of HW. Visitors' moorings are provided by the yacht club. The easternmost moorings can be exposed to swell.

Mumbles Head

The outermost of two rocky islets, with a white octagonal tower lighthouse (Fl(4)20s35m15M). The Cherrystones are rocks creating broken water 2

The Mumbles and lighthouse   *PRPA/Patrick Roach*

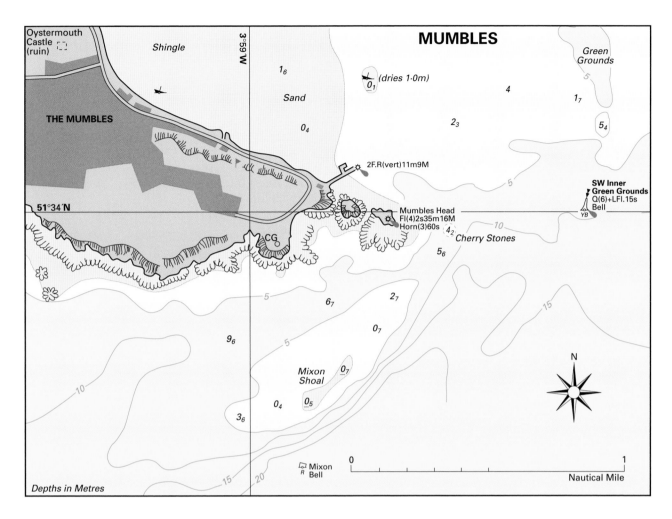

cables east of Mumbles Head; they should be rounded to seaward. The Mixon Shoal is a drying sandbank SSW of Mumbles Head, with its south extremity marked by a red bell buoy. The channel to the north of the bank can be used in settled conditions, keeping 1 cable offshore.

Oxwich Bay

Lies between Oxwich Point and Pwll-du Head, a bold bluff 3½ miles west of Mumbles Head. There is good shelter from the north and west for yachts, anchoring in 6m sand. The northwest portion of the bay dries to firm sand.

Port Eynon Bay

Lies between Port Eynon Point and Oxwich Point. Anchor in 7m in the centre of the bay, sheltered from the north and west. In strong tidal conditions with contrary winds there are overfalls off Oxwich Point.

Helwick Sands

The sands, extending 7 miles west from a position 3 cables south of Port Eynon Point, are marked at either end by cardinal buoys. Tidal streams run (at up to 3 knots at springs) northeast and southwest across the bank. There is a narrow passage between the sands and Port Eynon Point which can be used in settled weather.

V. Worms Head to St David's Head

Burry Port

⊕ 51°40'·0N 4°15'·0W ½M S of harbour entrance
Population 7,805 (1981)
Local High Water is Dover –0500
Charts Admiralty *1167, 1076, 1179;* Imray *C60*

General

A former commercial port, the harbour now provides good shelter for yachtsmen 3½ miles inland from Carmarthen Bay.

Warning

Burry Inlet should not be entered in strong onshore winds. The channel is not buoyed and is liable to change. The best time to enter the inlet is during the 2 hours before HW. The outer harbour at Burry Port dries to firm mud and should only be entered between 2 hours either side of HW.

Approach

By day Burry Inlet is entered between The Nose and Burry Holms.

By night A night approach and entrance should not be attempted.

Anchorage in the approach

A good anchorage, with shelter from the south and east, may be had in 5·5m mud in Rhossili Bay, 5 cables northeast of Worms Head.

Entrance

The channels through Burry Inlet are liable to change and are best negotiated on a rising tide. Even in moderate west or southwest winds the bar can become quite turbulent on the ebb. A post with a Fl.R.3s5M light lies 1 cable south of the harbour entrance. The west breakwater has a white

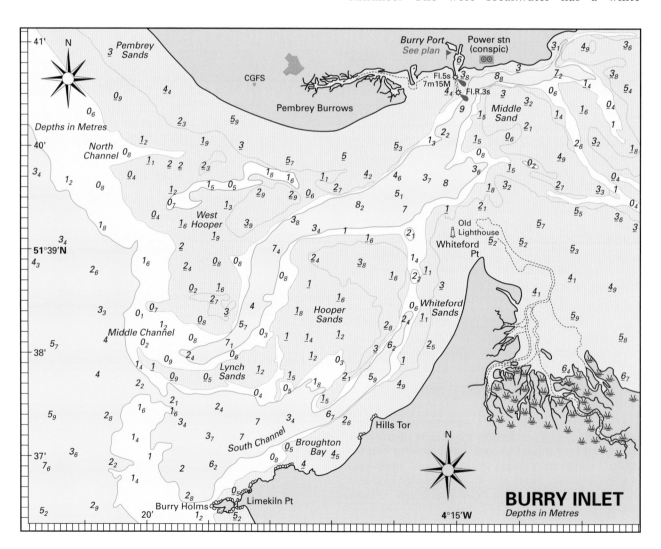

50

Entrance to Burry Port

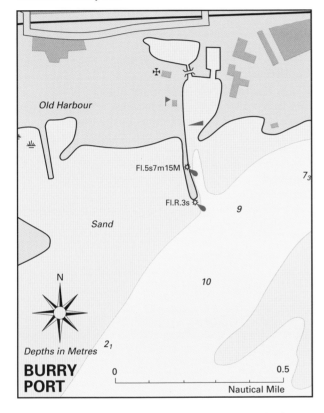

BURRY PORT

Depths in Metres

N

0   0.5

Nautical Mile

lighthouse tower with a red cupola, displaying a Fl.5s7m15M light.

Moorings

The outer harbour is entirely filled with moorings.

Berthing

It would be possible for visitors to lie alongside in thick mud in parts of the inner harbour.

Facilities

Fuel Diesel fuel from Burry Port Yacht Services.
Slip On east side, by harbour entrance.
Provisions Adequate range of shops nearby.
Yacht club Burry Port Yacht Club.
Chandlery Burry Port Yacht Services, overlooking west dock.

Llanelli

A former commercial harbour, 3 miles east of Burry Port up the River Loughor. The entrance channels and the docks dry to soft mud. There are no facilities for yachtsmen.

Ferryside

A small town on the east bank of the River Tywi, 5 miles beyond the Carmarthen Bar. The channels of the estuary are liable to change and should be entered on a rising tide within 2 hours of HW. Strong onshore winds can make the bar impassable. The River Towy Yacht Club has its premises at Ferryside, and visitors' moorings can be provided by prior arrangement with the club. The moorings dry to soft mud. There is room to anchor close by the moorings, but this should be done with care, as the river bottom shelves rapidly a little distance from the shore.

There is a firing range in Carmarthen Bay, the limits of which are marked by DZ buoys. Red flags (and lights by night) are displayed on Pendine Burrows and Laugharne Burrows when practices are taking place.

Saundersfoot

⊕ 51°42'·7N 4°40'·9W ½M E of harbour entrance
Population 2,373 (1981)
Local High Water is Dover −0510
Charts Admiralty *1482, 1076, 1179*; Imray *C60*

General

A popular holiday resort, its drying harbour providing good shelter for yachtsmen.

Warning

The harbour can only be entered for 2 hours either side of HW. Shelter is good, although a swell can enter the harbour in strong south winds.

Approach

By day Saundersfoot can be approached directly from seaward. Monkstone Rock is the outermost point of a rocky ledge extending from Monkstone Point; it must be avoided.

By night The harbour can be approached at night using the following lights, although local knowledge is necessary prior to entering:

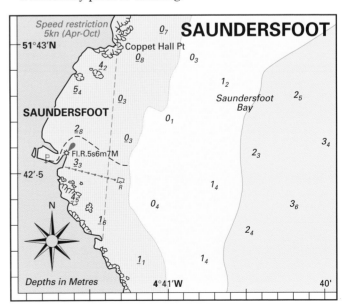

Saundersfoot   *PRPA/Patrick Roach*

Caldey Island Fl(3)WR.20s65m13/9M
Tenby Pier head F.R.7m7M
Saundersfoot Pier head Fl.R.5s6m7M

Anchorage in the approach

Anchorage may be had in 4m sand to the east of the harbour in settled conditions.

Entrance

The harbour is entered directly between the two breakwaters.

Moorings

There are only a limited number of moorings in the centre of the harbour, although a space may be allocated by the harbourmaster. The moorings dry to firm sand.

Berthing

There is limited space alongside the breakwaters, and berthing must be with the permission of the harbourmaster. There are good ladders. The stream flowing through the harbour has cut steep banks which must be avoided.

Harbourmaster

Office on quay in northwest corner of harbour.

Charges

There are harbour charges.

Facilities

Water Tap at midpoint of south quay.
Slip In northwest corner of harbour.
Provisions Good range of shops in the town.
Post office On the main street, behind the sailing club.
Calor Gas and Camping Gaz Frost's Hardware, High Street.
Chandlery On the south quay.
Boat repairs Jones and Teague, Harbour Boatyard, on south quay.

Tenby   *PRPA/Patrick Roach*

Tenby

⊕ 51°40'·65N 4°41'·0W ½M NE of Castle Hill
Population 5,657 (1981)
Local High Water is Dover –0510
Charts Admiralty *1482, 1076, 1179*; Imray *C60*

General

This popular holiday resort has terraces of Georgian and Regency buildings overlooking the harbour. Space within the harbour (which dries to firm sand) is limited, although shelter is good.

Warning

The harbour dries to firm sand, and can only be entered for 2½ hours either side of HW.

Approach

By day Woolhouse Rocks lie 1·5 miles southeast of the harbour, and are marked at their south extremity by an unlit cardinal buoy. St Catherine's Island, to the south of the harbour entrance, should be given a wide berth to avoid Sker Rock (dries to 1m), ½ cable southeast of the island, and its associated rocky ledges.

By night The harbour can be approached at night using the following lights, although local knowledge is necessary prior to entering:

Caldey Island Fl(3)WR.20s65m13/9M
Tenby Pier head F.R.7m7M+F.1M

Anchorage in the approach

There is a good anchorage (in 5m sand) northeast of Castle Hill, giving shelter from all directions except the east and southeast. An alternative anchorage is to the north of Caldey Island.

Entrance

The harbour is entered by rounding the pier.

Moorings

There are a number of moorings in the centre of the harbour, although space is limited. Private moorings lie to the northeast of the harbour, and beyond them is good holding ground for yachts to lie at anchor.

Berthing

There is limited space to lie alongside the pier (only with the permission of the harbourmaster). There are good ladders.

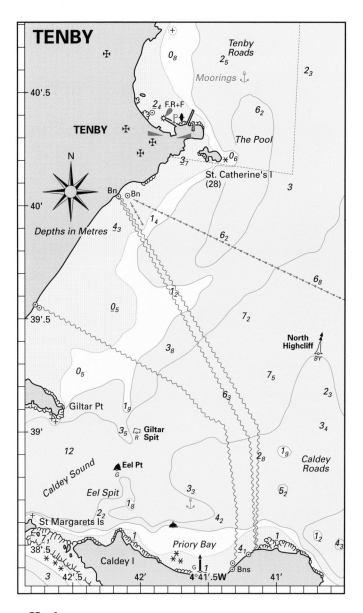

Approaching Tenby

Harbourmaster

On the road leading up from the pier to the southeast of the harbour.

Charges

There are harbour charges.

Facilities

Water Tap by the sailing club.
Slip On the west side of the harbour.
Provisions A good range of shops in the town.
Post office Warren Street.
Yacht club Tenby Sailing Club, with premises on the harbour.
Chandlery Limited chandlery from Morris Bros, St Julian's Street.
Calor Gas and Camping Gaz Morris Bros.

Caldey Island

The island lies 2 miles south of Tenby, and is home to a thriving monastery of Cistercian monks. The round white tower of the lighthouse (Fl(3)WR.20s 13/9M) is conspicuous.

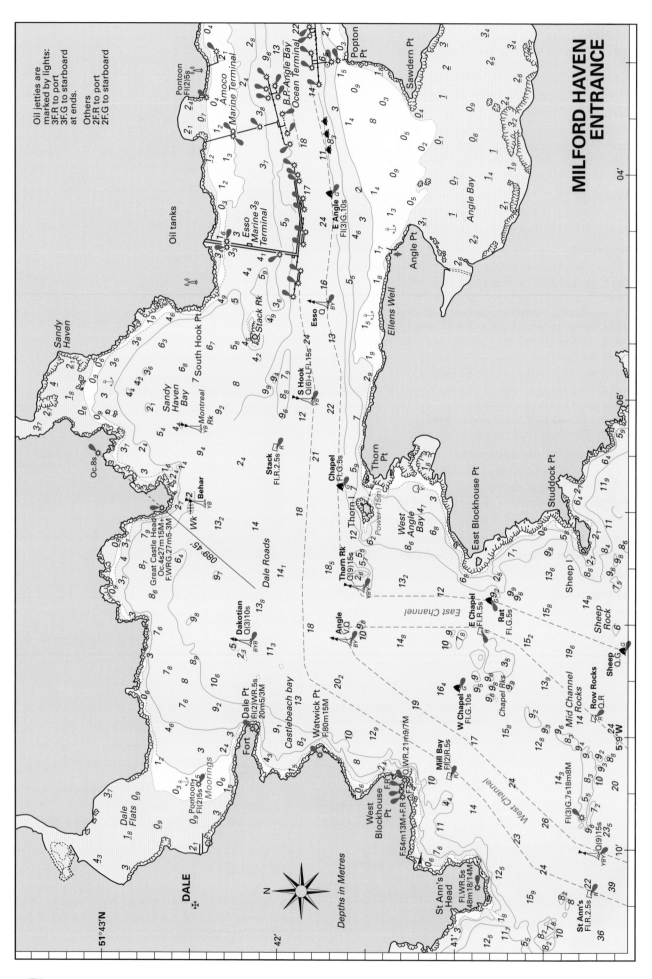

MILFORD HAVEN ENTRANCE

St Margaret's Island lies 2 cables west of Caldey Island, to which it is connected by a drying rocky reef.

There is a good anchorage (in 4m) 3 cables east of Eel Point, in Priory Bay, off the landing jetty. Landing requires the permission of the abbot at the monastery.

St Govan's Head

This is a prominent perpendicular cliff, 37m high, 10 miles southeast of the entrance to Milford Haven. In strong tidal streams with contrary winds overfalls build up off the headland. St Gowan Shoals lie 3·5 miles southwest of St Govan's Head, creating overfalls and breaking seas in heavy weather. St Gowan light vessel lies to the SSW of the shoals, 6 miles SSW of St Govan's Head.

Castlemartin Firing Range

There is live ammunition firing from the Castlemartin Range on most weekdays from April to November. The range extends from St Govan's Head in the east to Linney Head in the west. The range seaward is usually 3 to 4 miles, but can extend to 10M. Prior information regarding firing times can be obtained by telephoning 01646 661321 ext 4241. During firing, range safety vessels patrol the area. Both Castlemartin Range Control and the patrolling vessels operate on VHF radio.

Milford Haven

The magnificent natural harbour of Milford Haven consists of 25 miles of navigable waterway, offering shelter in all conditions. There is a major anchorage at Dale, the excellent marinas at Milford Haven and Neyland, moorings in picturesque surroundings at Lawrenny Yacht Station, and many other moorings and anchorages.

There is a constant movement of commercial traffic in the lower reaches, and it is imperative that yachts keep well clear of all commercial vessels. Yachts must keep a minimum of 90m away from oil terminals, ships alongside terminals, and ships under way and at anchor. This is a safety precaution that must be strictly adhered to.

The tankers operating in the lower reaches tend to manoeuvre relatively slowly. However, the B & I Ferry, operating from Pembroke Dock, can be moving quickly by the time it has reached the oil terminals.

Charts Admiralty *3274, 3275, 1478, 2878*; Imray *C60*

VHF radio telephone Milford Haven harbour is controlled by the Milford Haven Conservancy Board, operating from the port signal station at Hubberston Point. Yachts are not obliged to report their arrival and destination to the signal station (Milford Haven Radio), but doing this would help the harbourmaster to follow traffic movements.

The signal station is prepared to advise yachts regarding anchorages or traffic movements. A listening watch should be kept on VHF Ch 12 once inside the haven.

Weather forecasts for the haven and the neighbouring coastline are given by Milford Haven Radio on VHF Ch 12 and 14 at 0300, 0900, 1500 and 2100 UT. Gale warnings are broadcast on receipt.

Entrance

Entrance is possible in all weathers, although onshore winds against the ebb meeting the cross-tidal stream can cause turbulence, especially around Middle Channel Rocks. St Ann's Head should be given a wide berth in unsettled conditions, in which the projecting rock ledge can give rise to confused seas.

St Ann's Head is a bold promontory, 37m high, with a light (Fl.WR.5s48m18/14M) shown from a white octagonal tower near the cliff edge.

Middle Channel lighthouse exhibits its light (Fl(3)G.7s18m8M) from a black round metal tower at the west end of Middle Channel Rocks, 6½ cables SSE of St Ann's Head.

Leading lights are exhibited from tall concrete towers on West Blockhouse Point and Watwick Point, and the harbour is sufficiently well lit to make night access straightforward as far as Neyland Marina.

Watwick Bay and Castlebeach Bay

Good anchorages for yachts at the entrance to the harbour, sheltered from all except east winds.

Dale

Position 51°42'·4N 5°09'·2W
Population 384 (1981)

General

Excellent anchorage, sheltered from all except northeast or east winds, with facilities for yachtsmen provided in the village.

Warning

Dale Roads, extending onto Dale Shelf and into Sandy Haven Bay, is a reserved anchorage for commercial shipping. Dale Flats is designated as an area of natural scientific interest. Yachts are prohibited from anchoring in either area.

Entrance

Dale harbour is entered by rounding Dale Point, with a light shown from a metal column (Fl(2)WR. 5s20m5/3M).

Moorings

There are numerous moorings in Dale. Visitors' moorings, for which there are charges, are allocated by Dale Sailing Co. There is also a mooring pontoon provided for visiting yachts.

Anchorage

Anchorage is possible beyond the moorings, subject to the above-mentioned limitations.

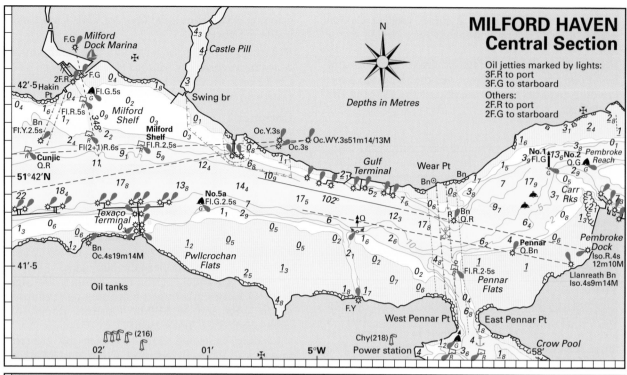

MILFORD HAVEN
Central Section

Oil jetties marked by lights:
3F.R to port
3F.G to starboard

Others:
2F.R to port
2F.G to starboard

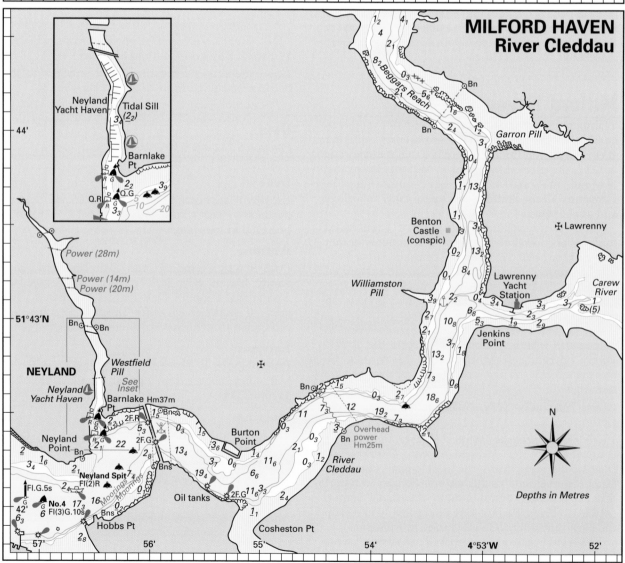

MILFORD HAVEN
River Cleddau

Facilities

Fuel Diesel from Dale Sailing Co. Petrol from filling station at the head of the slip.

Water Dale Sailing Co.

Slip At west end of bay.

Provisions Limited provisions are available in the village.

Post office In the village.

Yacht club Dale Yacht Club. Open in the summer months, with showers, bar and restaurant.

Chandlery Dale Sailing Co.

Calor Gas Dale Sailing Co.

Sandy Haven

A beautiful, secluded anchorage on the north side of the haven, drying (except for a shallow stream) to firm sand. Entrance should be within 1½ hours of HW. The modern houses with slate roofs and timber-clad upper storeys should be kept open to avoid Bull Rock; then keep close to the moorings on the west side of the haven. Anchorage can be found above the landing beach at the small village. There are no facilities.

West Angle Bay

A good anchorage in settled conditions, it is subject to a southwest swell. The shoreline is rocky and care must be taken when anchoring. A reverse eddy tends to keep yachts pointing northeast on the flood and the ebb. Shelter is fair in strong east winds, but not as good as that off Popton Point, at the entrance to Angle Bay.

Chapel Bay

Good anchorage (close to the shore) in strong south winds.

Angle Bay

There is a floating anchorage to the northeast of Angle Point, with landing by the lifeboat slip. Angle Bay itself dries to soft mud. There is a good anchorage to use in east winds between Popton Point and Sawdern Point, although the water is shallow.

Gelliswick Bay

Home to the Pembrokeshire Yacht Club, the bay provides a good anchorage, but is exposed to southeast winds.

Milford Haven Conservancy Board

The Board's jetty is only to be used for alongside berths in an emergency, with permission from the signal station. The Board also have some moorings, which may be used by yachtsmen in similar extreme circumstances.

Milford Shelf

There is an area of shallow moorings close to Milford Docks that is exposed to the southwest. Yachts must keep clear of the dredged area that is used to allow vessels to swing.

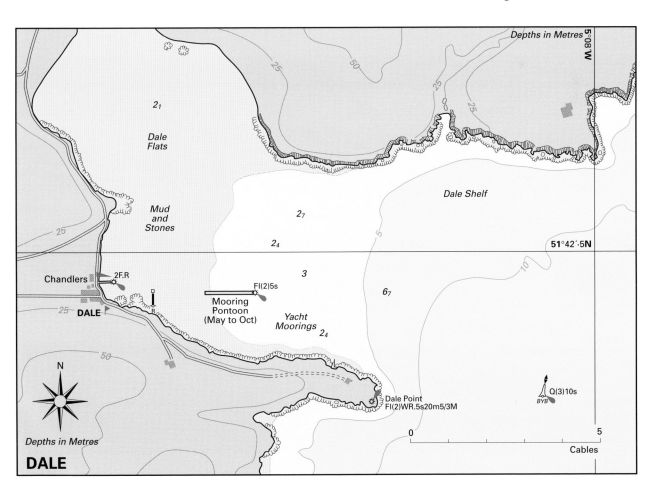

Milford Marina

A new 150-berth yacht marina in the E part of Milford Docks. Access is via the lock gates, which are open for the 4 hours before and 3½ after HW. There is a waiting pontoon immediately to the east of the lock entrance or shelter can be found in the lock itself if required.

All berths are provided with water and electricity. The marina office houses toilets, showers, a lounge and bar, and a chandlery. Cleddau Boatyard, on the W side of the dock, carries out boat and engine repairs, and has boat storage facilities ashore.

VHF radio telephone: call *Pierhead* on Ch 12, and they will contact the marina.

Pwllcrochan Flats

Yachts must keep clear of these flats, as there are uncharted obstructions.

Pennar Gut

There is limited anchoring space beyond the few laid moorings. A channel has been dredged to allow ships access to the power station, and although rarely used it should be left clear. The power station immediately to the west of Pennar Gut has a very conspicuous chimney (218m) with red lights.

Neyland Yacht Haven

The excellent marina at Neyland, some 10 miles from the entrance to the haven, offers access at all states of the tide, and berths in an attractive setting for 450 boats.

Entrance

The dolphins at the entrance are to be left to port; the channel is buoyed.

Berthing

Berths in the lower marina basin are accessible at all states of the tide. The upper basin is entered over a sill which gives access to yachts drawing 1·5m for 3 hours either side of HW. Berths can be arranged in advance by telephoning 01646 601601.

VHF radio telephone

Neyland Yacht Haven operates on Ch M.

Facilities

Fuel Diesel and petrol available from fuelling pontoon.

Water Water to all pontoons in lower basin, and to most in upper basin.

Electricity Electricity to all pontoons in the lower basin, and to most in the upper basin.

Provisions Good range of shops in Neyland, a short walk from the marina.

Toilets, showers and launderette At the marina centre.

Chandlery At the marina centre.

Boat repairs and engineers Dale Sailing Co., adjacent to the marina centre.

Sailmakers Brunel Quay Sails, at the rear of Dale Sailing Co.

Hobb's Point

There is a large area of moorings north of the point. Apply to Kelpie Boats for a visitor's mooring. Kelpie Boats operate a chandlery and a boat repair and

Milford Marina   *PRPA/Patrick Roach*

Neyland Yacht Haven   *PRPA/Patrick Roach*

engineering service from beside the slip. Yachts should not anchor close to Pembroke Dock, which is busy with commercial traffic.

From the Cleddau Bridge for 1·2 miles upstream to the overhead power cables is the only area in the haven allocated for use by water-skiers. Yachtsmen should recognise this right and not anchor between these points.

Williamston Pill

One of the best, and best sheltered, anchorages in the haven, although it is pretty full with resident moorings. There is limited space to anchor beyond the moorings without lying in the main stream.

Lawrenny Yacht Station

Moorings for 100 yachts at the entrance to the Carew River in a picturesque setting. Moorings can be arranged in advance by telephoning 01646 651212.

The stream can run quickly through the anchorage, and it is the yachtsman's responsibility to ensure that the mooring he has taken is suitable for his yacht. Payment is made at the chandlery for the use of a mooring.

The yacht station has a floating pontoon, with a water tap, where yachts may tie alongside (stay limited to 10 minutes). Dinghies should tie to the inside of the pontoon. There is a fuel quay with diesel, petrol and water.

The station operates a chandlery (with *Calor Gas* available), a boatyard, boat repairs and a slip. There is a small café nearby, and the hotel offers a restaurant and bar meals. There are no other provisions available locally. The village of Lawrenny is ½ mile from the yacht station and has a sub-post office. There is little space to anchor beyond the moorings without drying out.

Castle Reach

To the north of Benton Castle and the off-lying Castle Rocks is a delightful anchorage, although it is not a simple matter to find a position that will not dry yet is out of the main stream. Garron Pill should be avoided, as there are obstructions and oyster beds.

Llangwm

Llangwm Pill dries to soft mud. There are moorings laid along the west bank of the River Cleddau above the pill, and a safe anchorage off the east bank, in a position just out of the main stream but not drying. Provisions and a post office can be found in Llangwm. There is a landing slip just to the north of Black Tar Point.

Above the moorings off Llangwm navigation becomes more difficult. The water off Fowborough Point is very shallow, and it is necessary to head over towards the Landshipping Quay, on the east bank of the river, before turning north to Picton Point and the confluence of the East and West Cleddau.

East Cleddau

There is an area of moorings beyond the quay to the north of Landshipping. Anchorage may be found beyond these moorings. This is the limit of practical navigation, as the channel then becomes narrow and winding.

West Cleddau

The moorings off Hook and the possible adjacent anchorage mark the limit of practical navigation, although vessels have historically made their way up the river to Haverfordwest.

Skomer Island

The island is a nature reserve owned by the Nature Conservancy Council and run by the West Wales Naturalists' Trust. A fee is payable to the warden on landing. Anchorage is in the North or the South Haven, depending on wind direction. When entering either bay, keep close to the west shore to avoid rocks on the east side of the bay.

The Wildgoose Race forms west of Skomer and Skokholm Islands during the strength of the streams in both directions. It is particularly dangerous near springs with a contrary or cross wind blowing, and must be given the widest possible berth.

Lawrenny Yacht Station   *PRPA/Patrick Roach*

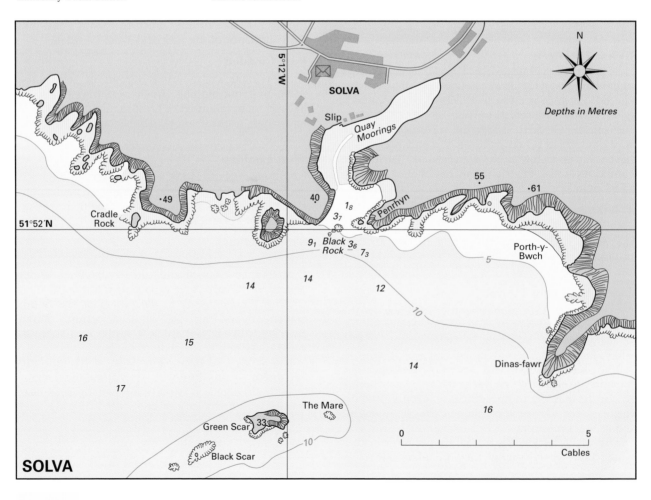

Jack Sound

A narrow channel (about 1 cable wide) lying between Midland Island and Wooltack Point, with a stream that can reach 7 knots at springs.

Passage through the sound should be made in daylight at slack water, or by using the stream in settled conditions. At the strength of the stream a contrary wind will create turbulent water at the end of the sound from which the wind is blowing.

The south-going stream begins at Dover HW −0300 and the north-going stream at Dover HW +0300.

Approaching from the southeast, head directly for Blackstones (above-water rocks 2 cables south of Midland Island). Approximately 50m from Blackstones, turn NNE, heading for Tusker Rock (dries 2m, ¾ cable west of Wooltack Point). The passage is between the Crabstones (drying rocks 3·7m extending east from Midland Island) and Cable Rock (drying rock 1 cable northwest of The Anvil).

With contrary winds, the worst of the turbulence can be avoided by keeping close to the north shore of Midland Island when heading north, and by heading close over to the Blackstones as soon as clear of the Crabstones when heading south.

Grassholme Island

This is a rugged island 6 miles west of Skomer Island. Overfalls surround the island and extend up to 2 miles SSE at the strength of the tidal stream. There is a clear passage 5 miles wide to the east, between these overfalls and the Wildgoose Race off Skomer and Skokholm Islands.

The Smalls

A group of low rocks 13 miles west of Skomer Island. A light (Fl(3)15s36m25M) is shown from a white round tower with red bands. The light has a red sector (F.R.33m13M) overlooking Hats and Barrels, patches of shallow rock extending over 4 miles east from The Smalls. Hats and Barrels are generally alive with tide rips and overfalls.

At the strength of the tidal stream with a contrary wind turbulence can extend some distance west from The Smalls, and when passing in these conditions the islands must be left at least 2 miles to the east.

St Brides Bay

In south or east winds, anchorage may be had between Little Haven and Borough Head in the southeast corner of the bay. Porth-clais is a drying inlet 3 miles west of Solva, giving shelter to small craft.

Solva

⊕ 51°51'·8N 5°11'·7W 2 cables S of harbour entrance
Local High Water is Dover −0450
Charts Admiralty *1478, 1973*; Imray *C60*

General

An attractive winding inlet providing good shelter for drying moorings in the inner harbour.

Warning

The inner harbour dries to a bottom of firm sand, and can only be entered for 2½ hours either side of HW. Strong south winds can make the entrance difficult.

Approach

By day Green Scar, Black Scar and The Mare are islets lying ½ mile south of the harbour entrance.

By night A night approach and entrance to the harbour should not be attempted.

Entrance

Black Rock, an islet with drying rocks that extend ¼ cable west, lies in the entrance to the harbour. The rock can be passed on either side, and anchorage may be had in 3m in the pool behind the rock, although this is not tenable in strong SW winds. The deep water river channel into the harbour runs to the west and north of the laid moorings.

JACK SOUND

Entrance to Solva harbour

Moorings

The inner harbour around the dogleg of the inlet is well sheltered and crowded with moorings. Red buoys along the southeast side of the inlet indicate visitors' moorings.

Berthing

There is a small quay, with good ladders, for temporary alongside berthing.

Facilities

Water Tap in gents' toilets.
Slip At west end of quay.
Provisions Limited provisions may be found in the upper village.
Post office In the upper village.
Yacht club Solva Boat Owners' Association.

Ramsey Sound

A navigable channel lying between Ramsey Island and the mainland, with tidal streams running at up to 6 knots at springs.

Passage must be in daylight, and should ideally be made at slack water. At the strength of the tidal stream strong eddies can take a yacht off its heading; however, if it is correctly aligned away from the areas of danger this will not be a problem. At the strength of the tidal stream strong contrary winds will create some turbulence at that end of the sound from which the wind is blowing.

The south-going stream begins at Dover HW −0200 and the north-going stream at Dover HW +0400.

The Bitches are a ledge of rocks extending 2 cables east from the midpoint of the east side of Ramsey Island. There is a least width in the sound of 2 cables at this point, and passage should be made through the centre of this channel. Horse Rock (dries 0·9m, 5 cables to northeast of The Bitches) must be avoided.

There is a sheltered anchorage and landing place on Ramsey Island, close to the north of The Bitches.

Whitesand Bay, with St David's Head at its north end, provides an anchorage sheltered from the south and east in 6m sand.

The Bishops and Clerks

A group of islets and rocks lying within 2½ miles west and northwest of Ramsey Island. A light (Fl.5s44m16M) is shown from a white round tower on the summit of South Bishop, the southwesternmost islet of the group. North Bishop is the northernmost islet of the group, lying 3·2 miles NNE of South Bishop. Within the group are a number of dangerous rocks and islets which produce heavy overfalls and tidal rips. If not taking the passage through Ramsey Sound, the Bishops and Clerks should all be passed on the seaward side.

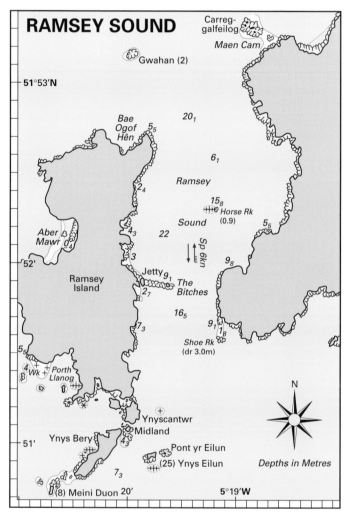

VI. St David's Head to Bardsey Island

Cardigan Bay lies between St David's Head to the S and Bardsey Island to the N. The majority of its harbours lie on a lee shore and are protected by bars, making for limited times of access and for dangerous conditions in strong onshore winds. To counter this the harbours are invariably attractive, in scenic surroundings.

The major ports of refuge are Fishguard, which can be entered at any state of the tide and in any conditions, and Pwllheli harbour, with access at most states of the tide and in most conditions. Limited shelter with access at all states of the tide can be found at New Quay and St Tudwal's Roads.

Sarn Badrig or St Patrick's Causeway, Sarn-y-Bwch and Cynfelyn Patches are three dangerous shoals extending to seaward in the north half of the bay.

Tidal streams for the most part follow the line of the coast. They are strong at St David's Head and Bardsey Island, but become progressively weaker into the bay.

Firing exercises controlled from Aberporth take place in the southern half of the bay. Unlit targets and mooring buoys are frequently moved to accommodate these exercises.

St David's Head

A 30m-high headland extending NE from the entrance to Ramsey Sound. The coast to Strumble Head consists of perpendicular cliffs interspersed with sandy bays. Keep ¾M offshore between St David's Head and Porthgain to avoid outlying rocks.

Strumble Head

A conspicuous headland at the NW end of Pen Caer promontory. The lighthouse (Fl(4)15s45m26M) has a white circular tower. When heading S, an inshore tidal eddy, beginning some 3 hours before the general tidal stream, can be used to assist passage through Ramsey Sound before the stream builds to full strength. There are overfalls on Strumble Bank, about one mile offshore, in contrary wind and tide conditions.

Fishguard

⊕ 52°01'·0N 4°57'·9W 3 cables NNE of head of N breakwater
Local High Water is –0350 Dover
Charts Admiralty *1484, 1973*; Imray *C60, C61*

General

The main harbour was developed by the Great Western Railway as a terminal for transatlantic liners, but its trade was later taken by Southampton. Fishguard Harbour, now belonging to Sealink, subsequently became a main ferry port for trade with Ireland. Lower Fishguard is an attractive old fishing village that was used as the setting for the film version of Dylan Thomas's *Under Milk Wood*.

Warning

The main harbour and the outer harbour at Lower Fishguard can be entered at any state of the tide and in any conditions. Strong winds from the N or NE can cause a heavy swell in both harbours, although some shelter can be obtained in the outer harbour behind Castle Point. The inner harbour at Lower Fishguard dries to firm mud and clay, and can only be entered for 1½ hours either side of HW.

Approach

By day Strumble Head, with its lighthouse, is conspicuous to the W of Fishguard, with the wedge-shaped Dinas Head to the E. There are drying rocks to the N of the root of the N breakwater, but no other dangers to the approach.

By night The harbour can be reached making use of the following lights:
Strumble Head Fl(4)15s45m26M
N breakwater Fl.G.4·5s18m13M Bell(1)8s
E breakwater Fl.R.3s10m5M

Entrance

The main harbour is entered between the two breakwaters. Lower Fishguard is entered between Saddle Point and Castle Point.

Moorings

There are private moorings laid to the SW of a line between the ro-ro terminal and the head of the E breakwater in the main harbour. There are private moorings laid in the outer harbour and inner harbour at Lower Fishguard.

Anchorage

Anchorage is prohibited NE of the line between the ro-ro terminal and the head of the E breakwater in the main harbour. If draft permits, anchorage may be obtained beyond the moorings laid to the SW of this line, or close to the moorings in the outer harbour at Lower Fishguard. The ends of the sewer outfalls at Lower Fishguard are marked with green triangular topmarks on poles. There are deeper anchorages off Saddle Point and between Saddle Point and the E breakwater.

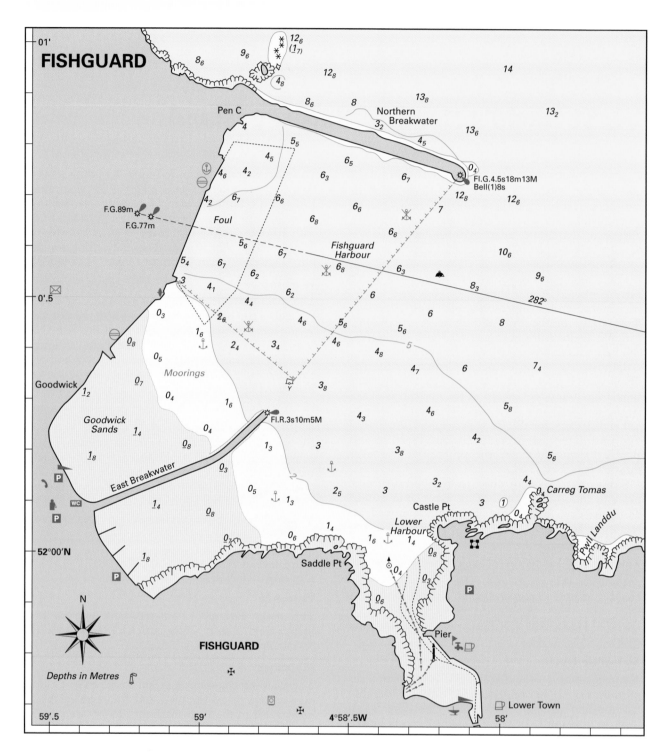

Berthing

There are drying berths alongside the pier in the inner harbour at Lower Fishguard; however, priority is given to fishing vessels, and these berths should only be used with the consent of the harbourmaster.

Harbourmaster

Lower Fishguard ☎ 01348 404453.

VHF radio telephone

None.

Facilities

Fuel Marine diesel from Goodwick Marine, behind PFS near slip at head of main harbour.

Water By toilets at head of main harbour, and from tap on wall of YC in Lower Fishguard.

Slip There are numerous slips in both harbours.

Provisions Provisions are obtainable in Goodwick for yachts in the main harbour, and in Fishguard (which is a short walk, but up a steep hill) from Lower Fishguard. EC Wednesday.

Post office There are post offices in Goodwick and Fishguard.

Fishguard *PRPA/Patrick Roach*

Yacht club Fishguard Bay Yacht Club, Lower Fishguard. Bar and showers.

Calor Gas From PFS at head of main harbour.

Chandlery Fishguard Yacht and Boat Co. Ltd, High Street, Fishguard, and Goodwick Marine.

Refuse disposal Bins on the quay.

Newport Bay

Shelter may be obtained from winds from S through SE to E by anchoring in 5m off the mouth of the Afon Nyfer, or by drying on the firm sand of the estuary in settled conditions only.

Cardigan

⊕ 52°08'·0N 4°43'·0W 8 cables W of Cardigan Island

Local High Water is −0350 Dover

Charts Admiralty *1484, 1973*; Imray *C61*

General

Formerly an important port; silting of the estuary has restricted its use to principally pleasure craft. Good shelter from all wind directions can be found on the drying moorings to the S of Pen yr Ergyd, and in the deep-water pool where the Afon Teifi narrows a mile further upstream.

Warning

The entrance is dangerous in strong W through NW to N winds. The bar dries, but there is over 2·5m at MHWS and 1·5m at MHWN. The channel between Pen yr Ergyd and Bryn-du is subject to continual change and is not buoyed. Entrance should be made on the flood when making for the deep-water moorings upstream.

Approach

By day Cemaes Head is a prominent headland, rising steeply to an elevation of over 180m. Approach is straightforward, with no off-lying dangers. Cardigan Sound, between Cardigan Island and the mainland, should not be attempted without local knowledge.

By night There are lights: 2F.R(vert) to the S of the conspicuous hotel on the E side of the bay and Fl(2)5s on the steel beacon in the approach. There are no further lights at the river entrance, and approach without local knowledge is not recommended.

Anchorage in the approach

Shelter may be found from SW winds below

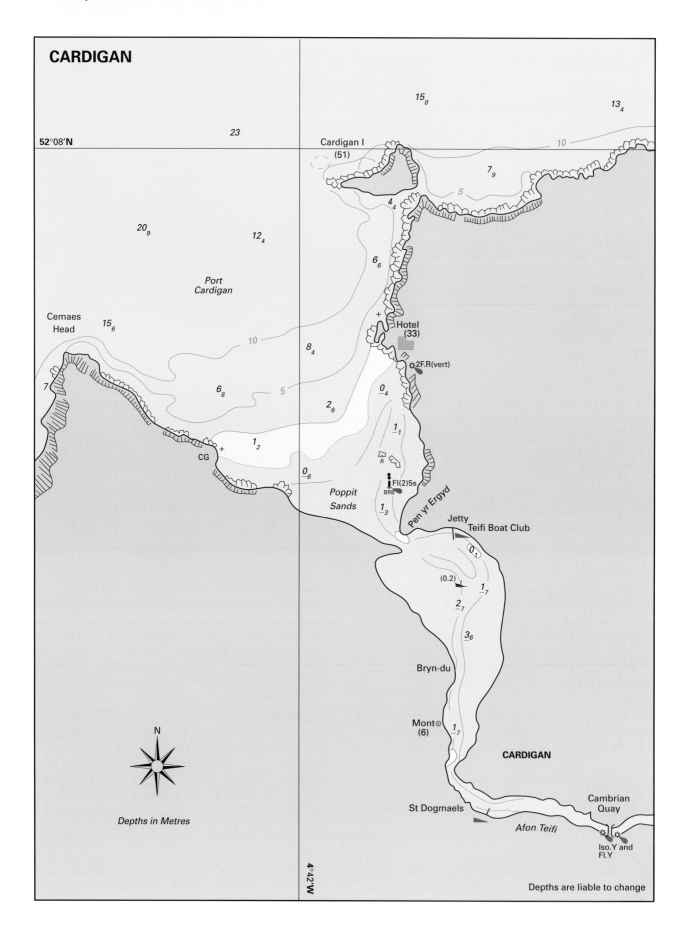

CARDIGAN

52°08'N

Cardigan I
(51)

Port
Cardigan

Cemaes
Head

CG

Hotel
(33)

2F.R(vert)

Fl(2)5s
BRB

Poppit
Sands

Pen yr Ergyd

Jetty
Teifi Boat Club

Bryn-du

Mont⊙
(6)

CARDIGAN

N

Depths in Metres

St Dogmaels

Cambrian
Quay

Afon Teifi

Iso.Y and
Fl.Y

4°42'W

Depths are liable to change

Moorings off Teifi Boating Club, Cardigan

Cemaes Head, and from E winds below the hotel on the E side of the bay.

Entrance
Approach on a SE course to leave the red can buoy to port and the steel beacon close to starboard before passing between the points, leaving Pen yr Ergyd to port.

Moorings
There are visitors' moorings (which mostly dry), belonging to the Teifi Boat Club, to the south of Pen yr Ergyd.

Berthing
Yachts that can take the ground can anchor close to the moorings S of Pen yr Ergyd. Deep-water anchorages can be found where the river narrows one mile to the S of the entrance, and in pools between St Dogmaels and Cardigan.

Facilities
Water From tap on wall of Teifi Boat Club.
Yacht club Teifi Boat Club.
Provisions Full provisions, post office, chandlery and petrol filling station can be found in Cardigan. EC Wednesday.

Aberporth
Aberporth is a small fishing village to the east of Pencribach, the head providing some protection from SW or W winds. A Government missile test centre, airfield and research establishment are sited close to the village. A number of targets, moorings and buoys marking scientific instruments can be found within 20 miles of Pencribach, some marked with flashing lights. Their positions are frequently changed; the latest information may be obtained from the Marine Officer, RAE, Aberporth ☎ 01239 810205 ext 462.

New Quay
⊕ 52°13'·4N 4°21'·3W 4·5 cables N of outer breakwater
Local High Water is –0330 Dover
Charts Admiralty *1484, 1972*; Imray *C61*

General
A holiday resort and fishing village. The bay offers limited protection, although it can be entered at any state of the tide. There are floating moorings in New Quay Bay; to the S of the breakwater the harbour dries to firm sand. The pier was built in 1835, when there was a thriving shipbuilding trade.

Warning
The harbour is protected from winds E through S to W, although a swell can affect the moorings at any time. Strong winds from N or NW can produce a dangerous sea, making the moorings untenable, with conditions only slightly improved in the shelter of the breakwater. An inner breakwater gives some additional protection, but this drying area is crowded with local small fishing boats.

Approach
By day New Quay Head is the first conspicuous headland to the N of Cemaes Head. Carreg Ina are drying rocks extending 3 cables to the NW of Ina Point, on the E side of New Quay Bay. Their extremity is indicated by a N cardinal mark. Beacons ashore indicate alignment of a sewer outfall extending 7 cables NNW from Ina Point.

Approaching New Quay

New Quay harbour

67

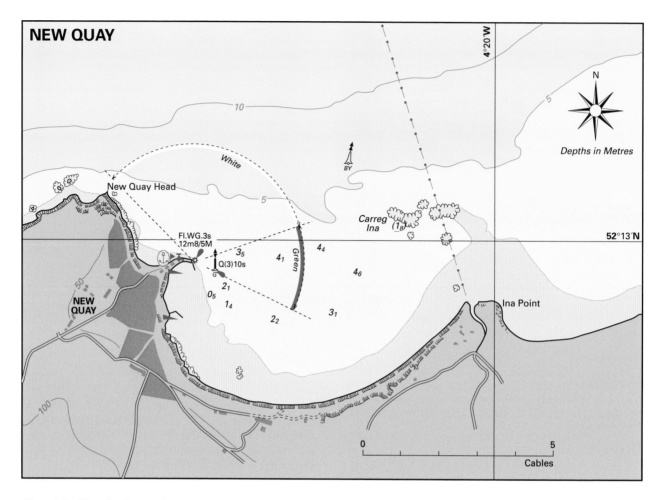

By night The harbour should be approached with care until the following lights are identified:

New Quay outer breakwater Fl.WG.3s12m8/5M
New Quay inner breakwater Q(3)10s

Entrance

New Quay Bay is entered between the end of the outer breakwater and the N cardinal mark off Carreg Ina. There is a further stone groyne running 50m SSE from the end of the outer breakwater. This affords some additional protection to vessels alongside the breakwater. Its extremity is marked by a green beacon, which must be left to starboard.

Moorings

There are private moorings in New Quay Bay, some of which dry to firm sand. Moorings for visitors, when available, may be allocated by the harbourmaster.

Berthing

Anchorage is possible close to the laid moorings in New Quay Bay and outside the breakwater in settled conditions. Berthing alongside the breakwater is only with the permission of the harbourmaster, and priority is given to fishing boats. The harbour inside the breakwater dries to firm sand.

Harbourmaster

Office at the head of the breakwater.

Facilities

Fuel Available from fishermen.
Water From tap on wall of yacht club.
Slip At head of outer breakwater.
Provisions Provisions are available in the town.
Post office On road looking down over the harbour.
Yacht club At head of outer breakwater.

Aberaeron

⊕ 52°15'·0N 4°16'·35W 5 cables NW of harbour entrance
Local High Water is –0325 Dover
Charts Admiralty *1484, 1972*; Imray *C61*

General

A picturesque harbour, flanked by Regency houses painted in contrasting pastel colours, at the mouth of the Afon Aeron. Its development owes much to the foresight of a local landowner, the Reverend Alban Gwynne, at the beginning of the last century. Formerly a busy coastal port and shipbuilding centre, it is now a holiday resort, its drying harbour providing limited shelter for pleasure craft and small fishing boats.

Warning

The harbour mostly dries to a bottom of firm mud and small stones, and should only be entered between 1½ hours either side of HW. Strong onshore winds make the entrance dangerous, and

Harbour entrance Aberaeron

Aberaeron harbour

the swell continues into the harbour, making it for the most part untenable.

Approach

By day The church tower 1·2M ENE of the harbour

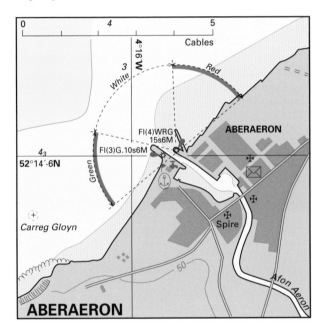

Harbour entrance Aberaeron

entrance is easily identified. There is foul ground with depths of 1·5m extending 3 cables offshore for ¾M to the SW of the harbour entrance. Carreg Gloyn, with a least depth of 0·3m, lies 3·5 cables to the SW of the harbour entrance. Sarn Cadwgan, with a least depth of 1·8m, extends ½M offshore from Cadwgan Point, ½M to the NE of the harbour entrance.

By night The harbour may be approached with care until the following lights are identified:

Aberaeron north pier Fl(4)WRG.15s10m6M
Aberaeron south pier Fl(3)G.10s11m6M

Anchorage in the approach

Anchorage is possible (in 5m off the harbour entrance) only in the most settled conditions.

Entrance

The harbour is entered between the two stone piers that extend WNW from the shore. The pierheads dry.

Moorings

The harbour is crowded with private drying moorings that may only be used with the permission of the harbourmaster.

Berthing

Limited space for visiting yachts against the NW wall of the harbour by the yacht club. Yachts may tie alongside the NE quay in settled conditions only.

Harbourmaster

Office by yacht club. No VHF radio telephone.

Facilities

Water From tap on wall of yacht club.
Slip In W corner of harbour.
Provisions Full provisions are available in the town.
Yacht club Aberaeron Yacht Club, on W side of the harbour.

Aberystwyth

⊕ 52°24'·8N 4°06'·0W 5 cables NW of harbour entrance
Local High Water is –0325 Dover
Charts Admiralty *1484, 1972*; Imray *C61*

General

The principal holiday resort of West Wales, Aberystwyth houses the National Library of Wales and one of the colleges that form the University of Wales. The ruins of Aberystwyth Castle stand on Castle Point, the headland in the centre of the town. The castle was begun in 1277 by Edward I and later captured and held by Owain Glyndwr. The harbour, at the mouth of the Afon Rheidol, mostly dries, but affords good shelter. The new Aberystwyth Marina and its associated dredging work has greatly improved the access and revitalised the facilities to be found in the harbour.

Warning

Entrance to the harbour should only be made between 3 hours before and 4 hours after HW. First time visitors are recommended to approach within 2 hours of HW. Entrance should not be attempted in strong onshore winds, and there can be a ground swell on the bar even on calm days. The harbour mostly dries to a bottom of stone and gravel overlaid with mud but dredging is maintaining a depth of 1·7m in the marina and a channel depth of 0·5m at MLWS. It is well sheltered, although some swell can enter the harbour at HW with strong onshore winds.

Approaching Aberystwyth harbour entrance

Approach

By day There is a conspicuous TV mast 3M to the S of the harbour entrance. The Wellington Monument (124m) on Pendinas, 5 cables to the SE of the harbour entrance, is also conspicuous. Rocky ledges extend 1½ cables offshore from Castle Point. The Wellington Monument in line with the head of the N breakwater on a course of 140° will keep a vessel clear of these rocks.

By night The harbour can be approached using the following lights:

Aberystwyth south pier Fl(2)WG.10s12m10M
Aberystwyth north pier Q.WR.9m4M
There are two F.R leading lights within the harbour entrance on a bearing of 133°.

Aberystwyth · PRPA/Patrick Roach

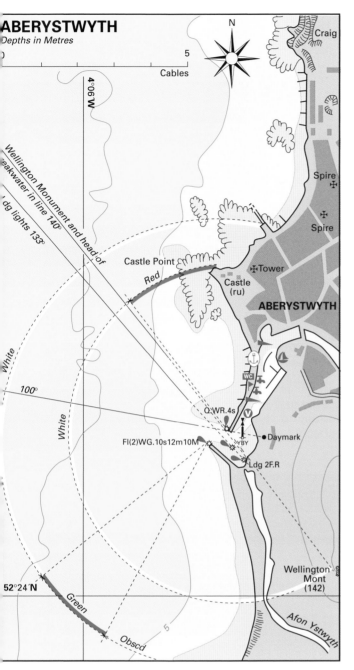

Aberystwyth Marina

Anchorage in the approach

Anchor off the harbour entrance only in the most settled conditions.

Entrance

The harbour is entered between the S stone pier and the N wooden pier. There are leading marks within the harbour entrance: a white pole in front of a white painted mark on the stone quay wall, in line at 138°. A patch of rocks extends some 20m N from the head of the S pier and a shingle bank extends W from the N pier. Once level with the end of the stone pier turn onto 100° using the transit of the W cardinal mark and the yellow daymark (on the lamppost on the street above the harbour). On passing the end of the N pier the channel turns sharply to the N, being marked initially by the W cardinal mark and then a port-hand marker. Head directly for the marina pontoons.

Moorings

All moorings within the harbour are taken by local boats.

Berthing

There are visitors' berths available in the 104-berth marina. This is a fully serviced, secured marina with water and electricity on the pontoons, toilets, showers and launderette ashore in the central reception building.

Approaching Aberystwyth

Harbourmaster

Office at head of Town Quay. ☎ 01970 611433.

Charges

There are marina charges. ☎ 01970 611422.

VHF radio telephone

The harbourmaster operates a hand-held VHF radio; call Ch 16, work Ch 14. Aberystwyth Marina, call Ch 16, work Ch 80.

Facilities

Fuel Diesel from marina fuel quay and petrol by cans from Moduron Anthony Motors filling station, on E side of harbour.

Water From marina pontoons and taps on wall on Town Quay.

Slip On Town Quay.

Provisions Full provisions are available in the town.

Post office Great Darkgate Street, in town centre.

Yacht club Aberystwyth Sea Angling and Yacht Club, on Town Quay.

Calor Gas and Camping Gaz From marina office.

Sarn Cynfelyn and Cynfelyn Patches

Sarn Cynfelyn and Cynfelyn Patches, with a least depth of 1·5m, are stone and shingle spits extending some 6·5M WSW offshore from a point 2·5M N of Aberystwyth harbour entrance. There is a ½M-wide channel with a least depth of 4·9m between Sarn Cynfelyn and Cynfelyn Patches. The channel is not buoyed. The W end of Cynfelyn Patches is rock, and is known as Outer Patch, with a least depth of 1·5m. The Patches buoy is a W cardinal mark in clear water ¾M W of Outer Patch. In unsettled weather conditions passage should be to the W of the Patches buoy.

Aberdovey

⊕ 52°31'·75N 4°06'·2W Aberdovey Outer buoy
Local High Water is –0320 Dover
Charts Admiralty *1484, 1972*; Imray *C61*

General

An attractive holiday resort at the mouth of the Afon Dyfi, Aberdovey provides reasonable shelter, with both floating and drying berths alongside the jetty and quay in the heart of the town.

Warning

Aberdovey Bar is constantly changing and the buoys are moved accordingly. The flood stream reaches 2–3 knots and the ebb 3–4 knots at springs. The ebb stream at the jetty has been recorded at 6 knots. Entrance should not be attempted before half-tide. It is possible to enter after HW, but because of the strength of the ebb any strong onshore wind will quickly make the entrance impassable. Entrance is possible in strong onshore winds just before HW, but only recommended with local knowledge.

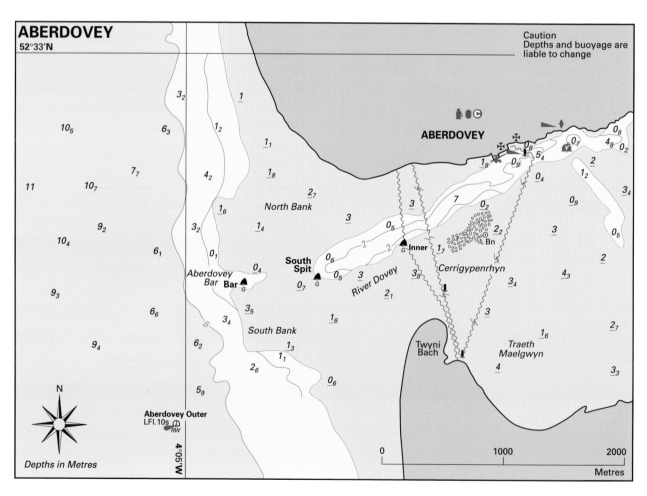

Aberdovey · *PRPA/Patrick Roach*

Approach

By day Aberdovey is the first major inlet S of Cader Idris. On the N side of the estuary the hills rise steeply to an elevation of 275m, with lower-lying land to the S.

By night There are no official lights; a night entrance should not be attempted.

Entrance

The spherical RW Aberdovey Outer buoy should be located. The Bar buoy, the first of 3 green conical buoys, lies one mile to the ENE of the Outer buoy. Follow the channel past the South Spit and Inner green buoys, then head directly towards the harbour jetty. A ruined iron refuge beacon stands to the south of the channel.

Moorings

There are a few moorings within the harbour, and one may be allocated by the harbourmaster if required.

Berthing

Anchorage is not permitted within the harbour, as there are submerged cables crossing the estuary. Sandbanks continually shift within the estuary, and all visiting boats should preferably berth alongside the jetty or quay. Yachts wishing to remain afloat should berth alongside the outer jetty; the inner quay dries to firm sand. All berthing is at the direction of the harbourmaster.

Harbourmaster

Office on quay.

Charges

There are harbour charges.

VHF radio telephone

Call *Aberdovey Harbour* Ch 16, work Ch 12.

Facilities

Fuel Diesel fuel will be delivered by local yard depending on quantity required; contact harbourmaster. There are petrol filling stations 300m along the road heading E and that heading W out of the town.

Water Tap on jetty, or by container from toilets.

Slip Adjacent to the quay.

Provisions Adequate provisions are available in the town.

Post office On road fronting estuary, to W of the quay.

Yacht club Dovey Yacht Club, on quay. Bar and showers.

Chandlery Dovey Marine, behind Dovey Inn.

Calor Gas and Camping Gaz Dovey Marine.
Refuse disposal Bins on quay.

Borth

A channel on the S side of the Afon Dyfi estuary is freshly marked each year with buoys and withies to give access to the Aber Leri Boatyard, Ynys-las, Borth. There is a steel can fendered waiting buoy at the channel entrance. Approach should only be made between 2 hours either side of HW. Limited visitors' mooring space is available (both drying moorings and alongside berths). A deep-water berth is only available by prior arrangement. Water is provided on the quay, and repairs can be carried out. Boat storage facilities are available.

Sarn-y-Bwch

Sarn-y-Bwch, consisting of large stones and rocky boulders, extends 4M WSW offshore from Pen Bwch Point. It dries in patches for about one mile offshore, and depths of less than 5m extend for a further 2M. The outer end is marked by the Bwch buoy, a W cardinal mark.

Barmouth

⊕ 52°42'·6N 4°04'·77W Barmouth Outer buoy
Local High Water is −0250 Dover
Charts Admiralty *1484, 1971*; Imray *C52, C61*

General

Barmouth is a holiday resort at the mouth of the beautiful Mawddach estuary. It is an excellent base for walking. Dinas Olan, which rises behind the town, became the first piece of land to be owned by the National Trust in 1895. It is the starting point for the Three Peaks International Yacht Race, held each June. Competitors race to Fort William, stopping en route to allow runners to reach the tops of Snowdon, Scafell Pike and Ben Nevis. The harbour offers good shelter, although strong onshore winds can make entrance impossible.

Warning

Entrance to the harbour should only be made between 2½ hours either side of HW. Tidal streams within the harbour can run at over 4 knots at springs, and a dangerous sea can build up with the ebb. With strong onshore winds, entrance becomes impossible. The bar is subject to change and the buoys are moved accordingly.

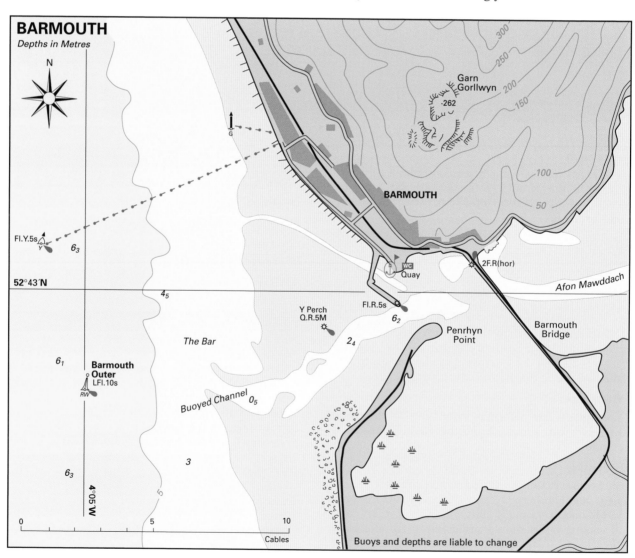

Barmouth

Barmouth   *PRPA/Patrick Roach*

Barmouth Harbour

Approach

By day Barmouth, viewed from seaward, lies on a well defined estuary, with land rising to the north and south of the harbour, and the peak of Cader Idris (890m) 5M to the ESE. Fegla Fawr, a small rounded hill, lies on the S side of the harbour.

By night The harbour can be approached using the following lights:

Barmouth Outer buoy LFl.10s
Y Perch Q.R.4m5M
SE end of Ynys y Brawd groyne Fl.R.5s5M
NW end of railway bridge 2F.R(hor)

Anchorage in the approach

Anchor off the harbour entrance only in the most settled conditions.

Entrance

The spherical RW Barmouth Outer buoy should be located. The channel is marked by red port-hand buoys which are moved as necessary. Y Perch marks the S end of a stony ledge extending 3·5 cables SW from Ynys y Brawd, and is left to port. There is an off-lying sandbank some 70m from the town quay, with its W end marked by a green buoy. On rounding the SE end of the Ynys y Brawd groyne, a sharp turn N towards the quay will avoid the sandbank, leaving the green buoy to starboard. Except at slack water, there will be a strong tidal stream running at the end of the groyne. The estuary is navigable for several miles beyond the railway bridge (5·5m clearance), although the channel is constantly changing and is not buoyed.

Moorings

There are both floating and drying moorings within the harbour; these may be used as directed by the harbourmaster.

Berthing

Anchorage is not permitted within the harbour because of the power cables laid across the estuary. Visitors may lie alongside the town quay as directed by the harbourmaster. The quay dries to firm sand and small stones.

Harbourmaster

Office on the quay.

Charges

There are harbour charges.

VHF radio telephone

Call *Barmouth Harbour* Ch 16, work Ch 12.

Facilities

Fuel Diesel may be delivered to the quay. Contact harbourmaster.
Water On wall of toilets on quay.
Slip E end of quay.
Provisions Full provisions are available in the town.
Yacht club Merioneth Yacht Club. Bar and showers.
Chandlery Seafarer Chandlery.

Sarn Badrig or St Patrick's Causeway

Sarn Badrig, or St Patrick's Causeway, extends 11M SW offshore from just S of Mochras Point, and dries in patches for most of its length. The inner portion is composed of small loose stones, whilst further to seaward there are extensive rock patches with large stones and rocks. The causeway is relatively steep-to on its S side and shoals to the N. The SW extremity is marked by the Causeway buoy, a W cardinal mark.

The East Passage is an inshore passage, about ½M offshore, between the NE end of the causeway and the mainland. This passage may be used between about 4 hours either side of HW, depending on draught and conditions. Moel-y-Gest, to the W of Porthmadog, in line with Mochras Point leads E of the NE end of the causeway; then keep some ¾M offshore as Mochras Point is approached in order to avoid Mochras Spit.

Mochras Lagoon

⊕ 52°49'·83N 4°08'·33W 5 cables NW of harbour
   entrance
Local High Water is −0245 Dover
Charts Admiralty *1512, 1971*; Imray *C52, C61*

General

Well sheltered, mostly drying lagoon at the mouth of Afon Artro, with limited facilities. The S half of the lagoon is protected by Shell Island, a peninsula that was formed by the diversion of the Afon Artro in 1819. A leisure complex has been developed on the peninsula, with vehicular access via a tidal causeway.

Warning

There is a depth of approximately 1·2m over the bar for 2 hours either side of HW, and approach must be made within this period. Swell can make the bar dangerous even in calm weather, and in strong onshore winds entrance becomes impossible.

Approach

By day The entrance is one mile to the NE of Mochras Point. The ruins of Harlech Castle lie a further 2M to the NNE. When viewed from the SW, the castle is seen in silhouette and is conspicuous; when viewed from the W or NW it is more difficult to identify.

By night The harbour entrance displays a Fl.WRG.4s sectored light, the white sector

Yacht moorings, Mochras Lagoon

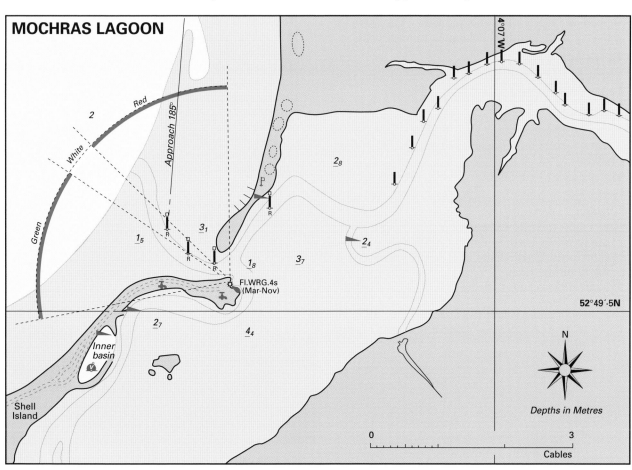

MOCHRAS LAGOON

Depths in Metres

indicating the line of correct approach; however, a night entrance should only be attempted with local knowledge.

Anchorage in the approach

Anchor off the harbour entrance only in the most settled conditions.

Entrance

The entrance, between the sandhills, is marked by three green buoys on the S side and by three posts with red topmarks to the N. The bar lies to seaward of the first green buoy, extending N in a gentle arc. At HW and in settled conditions approach can be made directly from the NW. To avoid the worst of the bar in alternative conditions, final approach should be made parallel to the N shore on a course of 185° towards the first red-topped post.

Once inside the lagoon, the channel to the N is initially marked with two red posts, then with red and green port and starboard can buoys, the course of the Afon Artro being marked as far as the railway station, where there are slips and water is available.

The channel to the S of the lagoon is marked by three red port-hand buoys leading into the lagoon. Good shelter may be found within the whole lagoon in all conditions.

Moorings

Private moorings are laid throughout the lagoon. There is a basin on Shell Island where shallow-draught boats may lie afloat. Leading marks indicate the line of entrance, in the shape of two poles ashore topped by black diamond markers. The basin is crowded with moorings belonging to local boats.

Berthing

Anchorage for boats that can take the ground may be had on firm sand throughout the lagoon.

Charges

Harbour charges are levied by the Shell Island Leisure Centre on those boats that make use of their facilities.

Facilities

Water There are a number of water taps on Shell Island.

Slip There is a slip to the yacht club boathouse to the N of the harbour entrance. There are further slips in the Shell Island deep-water basin and to the N of the basin.

Provisions Provisions may be obtained at the Leisure Centre shop.

Yacht club Llanbedr and Pensarn Yacht Club.

Calor Gas and Camping Gaz From the Leisure Centre shop.

Porthmadog

⊕ 52°52'·87N 4°11'·02W Porthmadog Fairway buoy
Local High Water is −0230 Dover
Charts Admiralty *1512, 1971*; Imray *C52, C61*

General

Porthmadog was created in the early 19th century, when the local MP, William Maddocks, built the mile-long embankment across the Glaslyn estuary to reclaim 7,000 acres of land. The town achieved prosperity as the sea outlet for the local slate trade; the narrow-gauge Ffestiniog railway was built to transport the slate from the mines, the station being situated in the NE corner of the inner harbour. Local ships transported slate from Porthmadog to destinations all over the world.

The town is now a thriving holiday centre, and the harbour offers good shelter to those prepared to negotiate the 3·5M-long estuary channel.

Warning

Entrance to the harbour should only be made between 2 hours either side of HW. The channel is subject to change and the buoys are moved accordingly. An up-to-date chart showing the position of the buoys is obtainable from the harbourmaster. Strong onshore winds can build up a dangerous sea, particularly against the ebb, making the harbour impossible to enter. The inner harbour is well protected in all conditions; the outer harbour is more exposed to strong winds from the S or SW.

Approach

By day Porthmadog lies on the N side of the estuary formed by the confluence of Afon Dwyryd and Afon Glaslyn. Moel-y-Gest is a conspicuous, isolated hill (260m) to the north of the entrance, and Criccieth Castle, sited on a bold, grassed promontory, is conspicuous 2·5M NW of the Fairway buoy. Harlech Castle, to the S, forms an excellent navigational mark when approaching from the SW, although it may be difficult to identify against its background when approaching from the NW or W.

Approaching Porthmadog harbour

Porthmadog

Porthmadog   *PRPA/Patrick Roach*

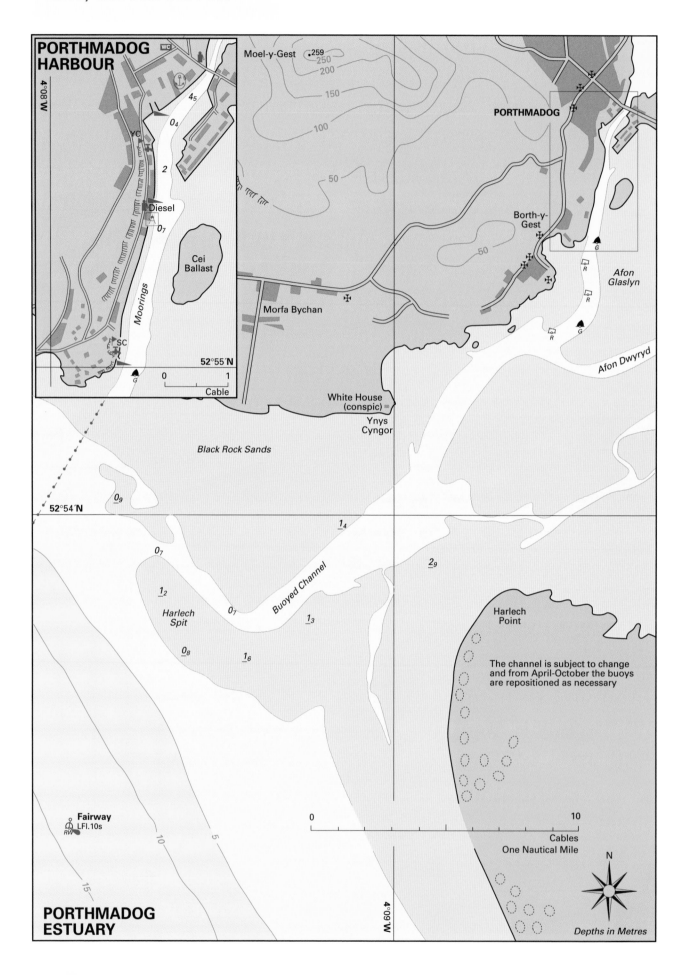

PORTHMADOG HARBOUR

4°08′W

WC

YC

Diesel

4_5

0_4

2

0_7

Cei Ballast

Moorings

SC

G

52°55′N

0   1

Cable

Moel-y-Gest   •259
250
200
150
100
50

PORTHMADOG

50

Borth-y-Gest

Afon Glaslyn

R

R

G

R

G

Afon Dwyryd

Morfa Bychan

White House (conspic)

Ynys Cyngor

Black Rock Sands

52°54′N

0_9

1_4

0_7

2_9

1_2

0_7

Buoyed Channel

Harlech Spit

0_7

1_3

Harlech Point

0_8

1_6

The channel is subject to change and from April-October the buoys are repositioned as necessary

Fairway
LFl.10s
RW

10

5

0   10

Cables

One Nautical Mile

15

PORTHMADOG ESTUARY

4°09′W

N

Depths in Metres

By night The Fairway buoy is lit (LFl.10s) and the buoys have reflective topmarks, but a night entrance should not be attempted without local knowledge.

Anchorage in the approach

Anchor off the harbour entrance only in the most settled conditions.

Entrance

The striped RW Fairway buoy must be located. The channel is marked for its full length with red and green lateral buoys, which are relocated as necessary.

Berthing

Drying berths for visitors are available alongside the yacht club quay. Yachts wishing to stay afloat should take a river mooring just before entering the inner harbour, at the direction of the harbourmaster.

Harbourmaster

Office on NW quay ☎ 01766 512927.

Charges

There are harbour charges.

VHF radio telephone

Call *Porthmadog Harbour* Ch 16, work Ch 12 or 14. Call *Madoc Yacht Club* Ch 80.

Facilities

Fuel Robert Owen Marine, on quay (adjacent to the chandlery).
Water Tap on yacht club wall; key required (from steward or a club member).
Slip On NW side of inner harbour.
Provisions Full provisions are available in the town. EC Wednesday.
Post office High Street, Porthmadog.
Yacht club Madoc Yacht Club. Bar and showers. Porthmadog and Transfynydd Sailing Club.
Calor Gas and Camping Gaz Gwynedd Caravans, Madoc Street.
Chandlery Glaslyn Marine, Oakley Wharf.
Marine engineer Robert Owen Marine, Oakley Wharf.

Pwllheli Harbour

⊕ 52°52'·75N 4°23'·3W 5 cables SSE of harbour entrance
Local High Water is −0300 Dover
Charts Admiralty *1512, 1971*; Imray *C52, C61*

General

The biggest town on the Lleyn peninsula, Pwllheli has been an important market town and harbour since it was given its charter as a borough by the Black Prince in 1355. A street market is still held every Wednesday in the Maes. Substantial improvements have recently been made to the harbour, to improve access and to form Hafan Pwllheli, a well sheltered marina with 420 alongside berths (summer 1999) and excellent onshore facilities. It is one of only a few publicly owned marinas in the country, having been developed by Dwyfor District Council with financial assistance from the EC, and is managed by Yacht Havens Management Limited.

Depths in the channel are continually being monitored, and at present access is available at all states of the tide to yachts of moderate draft in virtually all conditions (one metre at MLWS).

Approach

By day Pwllheli harbour lies 3·5M NE of Llanbedrog Head, and can be identified by Carreg yr Imbill or Gimblet Rock, a 40m-high conspicuous mass of granite, to the S of the harbour entrance.

By night The harbour may be approached at night using the following lights:
St Tudwal's Island Fl.WR.15s46m14/10M
Pwllheli harbour entrance Q.G.3m3M and
    Q.R.3m3M
It should be noted that the harbour entrance lights are obscured by the land to the W, and cannot be seen until a yacht is virtually due S. Sufficient offing should be maintained until these lights are identified. The training wall and the channel through to the marina are lit.

Anchorage in the approach

Anchorage may be found in 3m sand off the harbour entrance, giving shelter from winds from W through NW to N.

Entrance

Entrance is made between the new training wall to the N and Pwllheli Point. There is a groyne running NW from Pwllheli Point and an outfall running N; both are marked with beacons with red topmarks. The training wall is submerged after half-tide, and its position is marked with poles with green topmarks, all of which must be left to starboard. There are piled trot moorings to the S side of the channel.

Berthing

All yachts must report to the marina office, where they will be allocated a berth. ☎ 01758 701219.

Harbourmaster

Office on S side of harbour.

VHF radio telephone

Call *Hafan Pwllheli* Ch 80.

Facilities

Hafan Pwllheli is a fully serviced marina, with water and electricity provided on the pontoons, and toilets, showers and a launderette ashore. There is a separate fuelling pontoon to the S of the pontoons, a slip and a 40-ton travel-hoist.
Slip There is a further slip to the S side of the harbour.
Provisions Full provisions are available in the town, although the centre is ¾M from the marina offices.

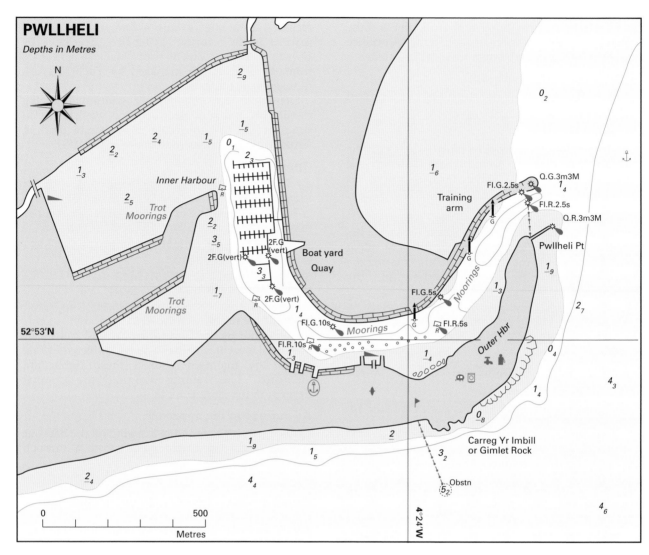

PWLLHELI

Depths in Metres

N

Inner Harbour

Trot Moorings

Trot Moorings

2F.G (vert)
2F.G(vert)
2F.G(vert)

Boat yard Quay

52°53'N

Moorings

Fl.G.10s
Fl.R.10s

Training arm

Q.G.3m3M
Fl.G.2.5s
Fl.R.2.5s
Q.R.3m3M
Pwllheli Pt

Moorings

Fl.G.5s
Fl.R.5s

Outer Hbr

Carreg Yr Imbill or Gimlet Rock

Obstn

0   500
Metres

4°24'W

Yacht club Pwllheli Sailing Club. Bar and showers.
Boat repairs and engineers Partington Boatyard and Firmhelm Boatyard, both on S side of harbour.
Chandlery Firmhelm Boatyard, on S side of harbour.
Calor Gas and Camping Gaz Partington Boatyard.
Marine electronics Rowlands Marine Electronics, on S side of harbour.
Sailmakers JKA Sails ☎ 613266 and Tudor Sails ☎ 613141.

Trwyn Llanbedrog or Llanbedrog Head

A steep-sided, bold promontory, rising to an elevation of 131m. There are a small number of local boat moorings. Anchorage may be had to the N of the headland, close to and to seaward of the perch marking the end of the sewer outfall, in stones and sand, giving shelter from SW and W. Limited provisions may be obtained from the village ashore.

Abersoch

⊕ 52°49'·46N 4°28'·05W one mile E of yacht club jetty, and 52°47'·26N 4°28'·7W
7 cables SSW of St Tudwal's Island lighthouse, at the S entrance to St Tudwal's Sound
Local High Water is –0315 Dover
Charts Admiralty *1512, 1971*; Imray *C52, C61*

General

A popular holiday and boating centre, Abersoch offers limited shelter to yachts in St Tudwal's Roads. There is a small drying inner harbour, formed by the channel of the Afon Soch, that can be accessed at HW, but has no space for visiting yachts. St Tudwal's Islands are privately owned, and landing is not allowed.

St Tudwal's Island West

Pwllheli Marina   *PRPA/Patrick Roach*

Warning

St Tudwal's Roads are sheltered from S through W to N. The anchorage is exposed to the E, and heavy seas can build in strong winds from this sector.

Approach

By day Overfalls can build ½M offshore off Trwyn Cilan in contrary wind and tide conditions. St Tudwal's Sound, between the West Island and the mainland, is clear of dangers. West Island has a white tower lighthouse (Fl.WR.15s46m14/10M) and white buildings. The islands themselves are steep-to except at their N ends, where shoals extend from both islands; these N ends should be given a clearance of at least 200m. Passage between the islands should be on a N-S course midway between the two. Careg-y-Trai is a dangerous patch of drying rock, often used by seals, 3 cables ESE of East Island. It is marked at its seaward end by a red bell buoy.

There is a sewer outfall pipe running 1·5 cables ENE from Penbennar, close to the yacht club, its end being marked by a perch. This also serves to mark the low-water line of spring tides.

By night St Tudwal's Roads may be approached using the following lights:

Bardsey Island Fl(5)15s39m26M Horn Mo(N)45s
St Tudwal's West Island Fl.WR.15s46m14/10M

Moorings

There are a large number of moorings laid to the SE and E of Penbennar. Contact the yacht club to arrange the use of a visitors' or vacant mooring.

Anchorage may be found in sand and small stones clear of the moorings. There is a launch service arranged by the yacht club running to the yacht club jetty. There is an anchorage midway along the NE side of St Tudwal's East Island, although the tidal stream can run through strongly at springs.

VHF radio telephone

Call *South Caernarfon Yacht Club* on Ch 37.

Facilities

Fuel Petrol and diesel from Abersoch Land and Sea Services.
Water By container from yacht club.
Provisions Full provisions are available in the town.
Yacht club South Caernarfon Yacht Club. Bar and showers.

Entrance to Inner harbour, Abersoch

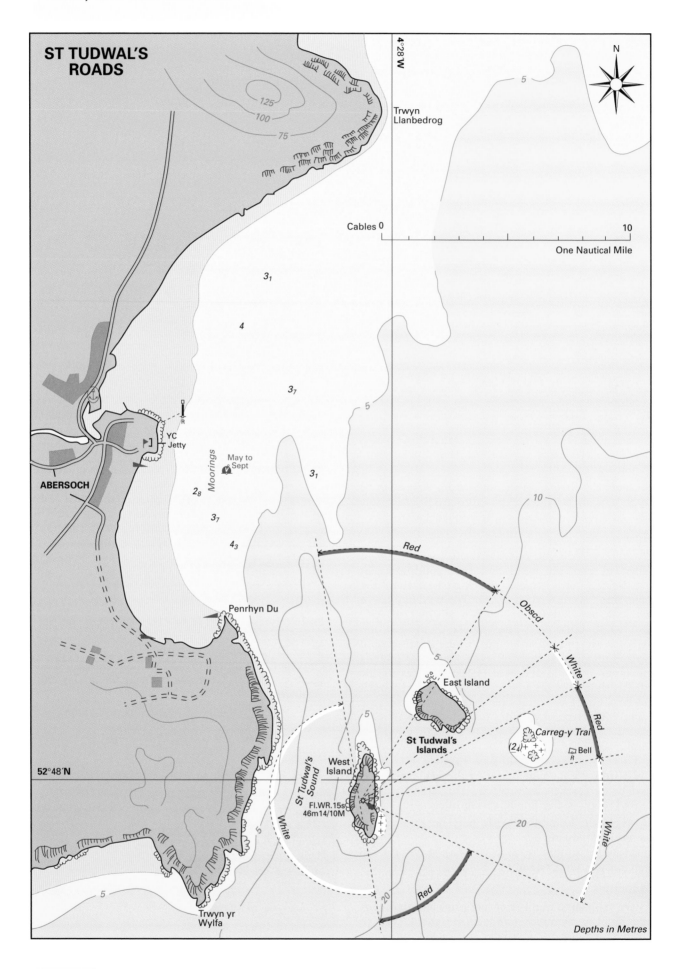

ST TUDWAL'S
ROADS

4°28′W

N

Trwyn
Llanbedrog

Cables 0

10

One Nautical Mile

3₁

4

3₇

5

YC
Jetty

R

Moorings

May to
Sept

5

ABERSOCH

2₈

3₁

3₇

10

4₃

Red

Obscd

Penrhyn Du

White

Red

5

East Island

St Tudwal's
Islands

Carreg-y Trai

(2₄)

Bell
R

West
Island

St Tudwal's Sound

Fl.WR.15s
46m14/10M

White

5

20

White

52°48′N

5

Red

20

5

Trwyn yr
Wylfa

Depths in Metres

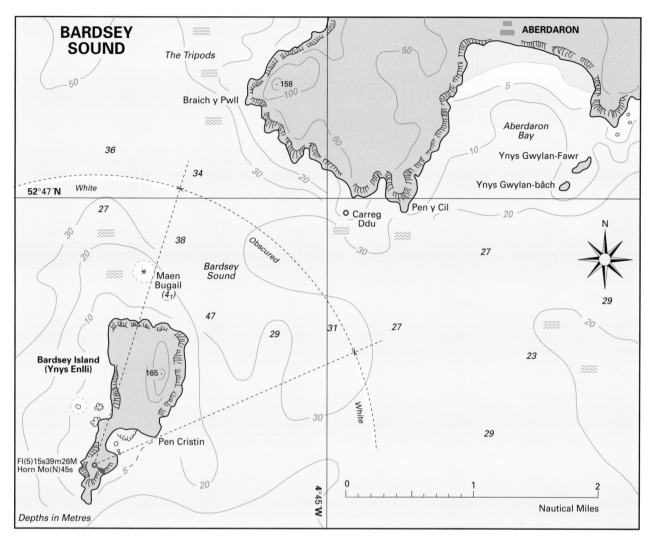

BARDSEY SOUND

The Tripods

ABERDARON

Braich y Pwll

· 158

100

50

36

34

52°47'N White

27

Aberdaron Bay

Ynys Gwylan-Fawr

Ynys Gwylan-bâch

Pen y Cil

Carreg Ddu

38

Obscured

Bardsey Sound

Maen Bugail (4₁)

27

N

29

47

29

31

27

White

23

Bardsey Island (Ynys Enlli)

165 ·

29

Pen Cristin

Fl(5)15s39m26M
Horn Mo(N)45s

5

20

Depths in Metres

4°45'W

0   1   2

Nautical Miles

Chandlery Abersoch Land and Sea Services, and Abersoch Boatyard Ltd.

Marine engineers Hookes Marine ☎ 01758 712458.

Aberdaron

A small village, set in a fold in the rugged coastline. The bay offers limited protection as an anchorage, but is a convenient stopping place in settled weather when waiting for the tide in Bardsey Sound. The 12th-century church was originally built a respectable distance from the shore, but erosion by the sea has required the construction of a protective sea wall. The anchorage, off Aberdaron Church, is protected from W through N to NE winds, although a swell may find its way into the bay at any time. Anchor with care, as the holding ground is poor. Landing may be effected on the beach, and limited provisions and a post office can be found in the village.

Ynys Gwylan Fawr and Ynys Gwylan Fach are two islands lying at the SE entrance to Aberdaron Bay. There is a 3·5-cables-wide sound between Ynys Gwylan Fawr and the mainland, with a least depth of 5·8m through the centre of the sound. There is also a deep-water passage between the islands.

Bardsey Island

Bardsey Island, or Ynys Enlli, lies at the SW tip of the Lleyn peninsula. It is 1½M long and ¾M wide, and its S promontory is joined to the main part of the island by a narrow isthmus. The N coastline is about ½M long, and the cliffs are rugged and steep, rising to the heights of Mynydd Enlli (165m) in the E. Mynydd Enlli falls steeply into the sea on its E side. The remainder of the coastline is jagged but

Llanbedrog Head

Aberdaron

lower-lying. The lighthouse (Fl(5)15s39m26M) is a white square tower standing on the S promontory.

The island has long been a refuge for holy men; the earliest church is thought to have been begun in the 6th century. The ruins of the Abbey of St Mary of Bardsey, dating from the 13th century, still remain. The island is now managed as a farm and nature reserve, and visitors landing on the island are asked to respect the farming and wildlife interests.

There is an anchorage, for settled weather only, at the entrance to Henllwyn Cove, to the W of Pen Cristin, on the E side of the island. Smaller craft may anchor within the cove itself. Entrance to the cove must be made with great care, as there are isolated rocks and shoals extending from the shore. Anchor with care, as holding is poor. There is a slip on the N side of the cove.

Passage to the S of Bardsey Island should be to the S of both Bastram Shoal and the Devil's Ridge, as heavy overfalls are created by the tidal streams and exacerbated by any contrary wind.

Bardsey Sound

Lying between Bardsey Island and the SW tip of the Lleyn peninsula, the 1·5M-wide Bardsey Sound allows daylight passage in suitable conditions of tide and wind. The only obstructions within the sound are Carreg Ddu, a small island on the N side, and Maen Bugail, a rock (drying 4·1m) on the S side of the sound.

The sound should preferably be passed through at or near slack water. The main tidal streams through the sound run NW and SE. The NW stream begins at +0500 Dover and the SE stream at −0100 Dover. During the last of the ebb, an eddy stream runs from Trwyn Cilan inshore along Porth Neigwl, passing through the sound between Ynys Gwylan Fawr and the mainland, anticlockwise around Aberdaron Bay, around Pen y Cil, and inshore of Carreg Ddu to Braich y Pwll. This stream begins 2 hours before the main stream in Bardsey Sound turns to the NW. A similar stream sets in the opposite direction 2 hours before the main stream sets SE. Yachts can take advantage of these eddies in settled conditions.

There are races off Pen y Cil, Braich y Pwll and Maen Bugail at the strength of the tide, and strong winds can cause a confused and breaking sea in these localities. Strong winds contrary to the main tidal flow can cause heavy and confused seas, making the sound impassable.

Approaching the anchorage, Bardsey Island

VII. Braich y Pwll to Conwy

The coastline from Braich-y-Pwll to Caernarfon Bar is one of spectacular scenery, but with only Porth Dinllaen offering any realistic shelter, and that only from some of the prevailing winds, and with the often inhospitable Caernarfon Bar, it is a coast to be treated with respect. Tidal streams run N-S across the mouth of the bay, their strength lessening further into the bay as the stream follows the curve of the coast.

Anglesey offers an excellent cruising ground. Tidal streams are strong around the island and can be utilised to good effect.

Holyhead is an excellent port of refuge, with good shelter and access at all times and in all conditions. The variety of harbours and anchorages around the island between them offer shelter from all wind directions.

The Tripods

A shoal extending N for about 1½M and running about one mile offshore from a point ¾M N of Braich y Pwll. There is a least depth of 10m, but the bank produces overfalls at the strength of the tidal stream, and with a contrary wind builds up a considerable sea. Keeping Carreg Ddu open from the N side of Bardsey Sound leads S of the shoal.

Porth Dinllaen

⊕ 52°57'·3N 4°34'·1W 5 cables WNW of Careg y Chwislen beacon
Local High Water is –0240 Dover
Charts Admiralty *1512, 1971*; Imray *C52, C61*

General

A small cove at the W end of the north-facing Dinllaen Bay, protected by a narrow promontory extending N on its W side. It was nearly chosen instead of Holyhead as the road and rail terminal for the Irish ferries. The tiny hamlet comprises an inn and a row of cottages.

Warning

Dinllaen Bay can be entered at any state of the tide. Shelter is good in S to W winds, but N or NE winds can cause heavy seas and make the anchorage untenable.

Approach

By day When approaching from Braich y Pwll, an offing of ¾M will avoid the offshore rocks and islets. Carn Fadryn (369m), a cone-shaped mountain 3·5M S of Porth Dinllaen, is conspicuous; when approaching from the N, a bearing of 182° on Carn Fadryn will lead about one cable east of Careg y Chwislen. Approaching from the SW, Carreg-y-chad, a rock with a least depth of 1·6m, lying 7 cables SW of Trwyn Porth Dinllaen, must be left to starboard. Carreg Ddu are drying rocks extending one cable N of the headland. Careg y Chwislen, drying to 1·5m, lies 2 cables ENE of the headland. It is marked by an iron beacon with a globe top and should be left well to starboard, as there is a tendency for the stream to set on to Careg y Chwislen from inshore.

By night There are no official lights, apart from the F.R displayed occasionally from the top of the lifeboat slip; a night approach is not recommended.

Approaching Porth Dinllaen

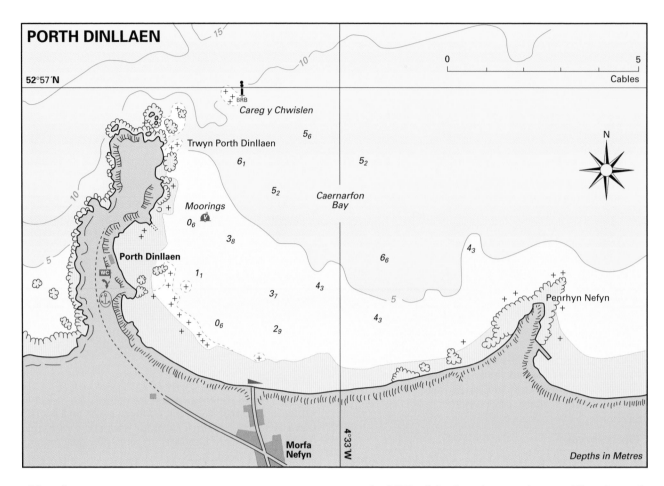

PORTH DINLLAEN

52°57′N

Careg y Chwislen

Trwyn Porth Dinllaen

Moorings

Porth Dinllaen

Caernarfon Bay

Penrhyn Nefyn

Morfa Nefyn

4°33′W

Depths in Metres

0 — 5 Cables

Moorings

There are a number of private moorings laid within the cove.

Berthing

Anchor in sand clear of the laid moorings, avoiding Carreg Oysters (rocks which dry 4·3m) on the S side of the cove.

Facilities

There are no facilities ashore for yachtsmen, apart from the inn, and provisions have to be carried from Morfa Bychan, up a steep road from the beach on the S side of the anchorage.

Trevor

A small cove 5 cables E of Trwyn-y-Tal, drying to sand with stone patches. The small harbour is protected from S through W winds, and a stone pier extending 100m E provides shelter from the NW. There is 2·5m alongside the pier at MLWN. There is a slip on the W side of the harbour, but there are no further facilities ashore. Provisions are available from the village, some 15 minutes' walk from the harbour.

Caernarfon Bar

⊕ 53°07′·18N 4°24′·37W C1 buoy

Drying sandbanks extend for 3M W of the coast. The channel over the bar leads into the Menai Strait through the narrow entrance at Abermenai. The white tower of the lighthouse on Llanddwyn Island,

to the NW of the bar, is conspicuous. The channel should only be used for 3 hours either side of HW.

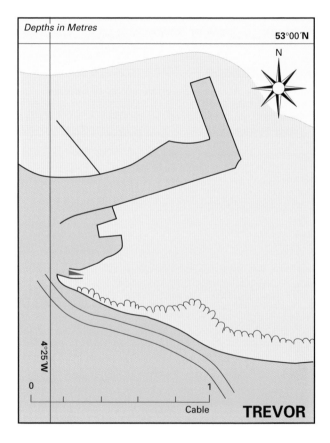

Depths in Metres

53°00′N

4°25′W

0 — 1 Cable

TREVOR

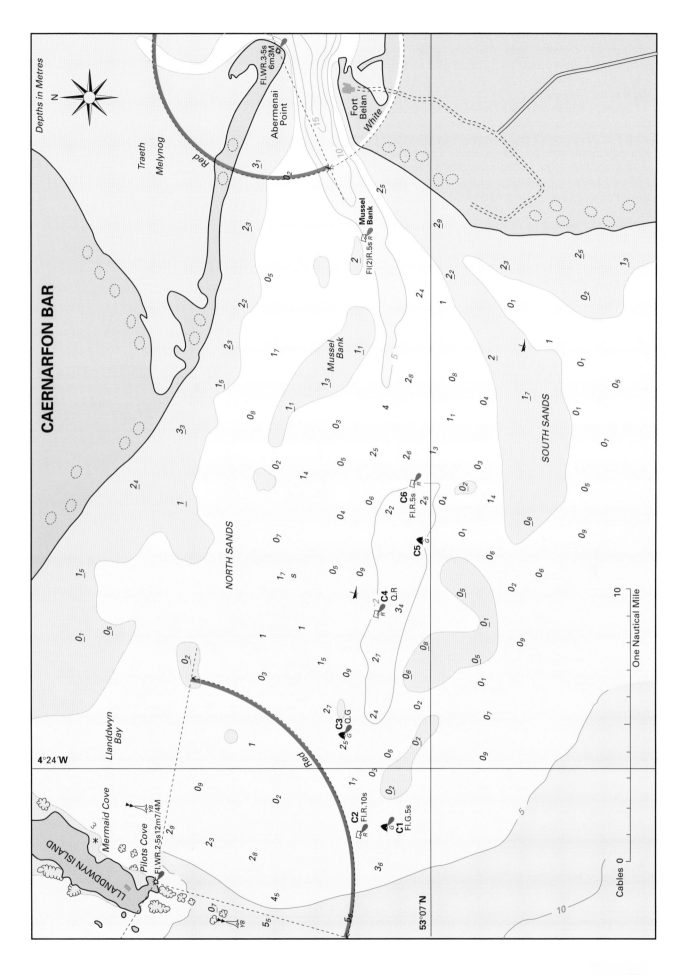

CAERNARFON BAR

Depths in Metres

N

Traeth Melynog

Abermenai Point

Fl.WR.3.5s 6m3M

Red

3₁

Fort Belan

White

Mussel Bank

Fl(2)R.5s R

2

2₃

2₅

2₉

2₅

1₃

0₂

2₂

2₃

2₄

0₅

2₂

Mussel Bank

1₁

0₁

2₅

3₃

2₃

1₇

1₃

1₁

5

2₈

0₂

2₄

0₈

1₁

4

0₈

0₂

0₁

0₁

0₅

0₁

1₇

SOUTH SANDS

1₅

3₃

0₃

0₅

2₅

2₆

0₄

0₃

0₄

0₇

0₆

1

2₄

0₂

1₄

0₅

0₂

C6

Fl.R.5s R

2₅

0₄

0₂

0₆

0₉

0₁

NORTH SANDS

0₇

0₆

0₄

0₉

C5 G

0₅

0₆

0₉

0₅

0₇

1₇ s

0₅

0₉

C4 Q.R R

3₄

0₆

0₁

0₅

1

1₅

2₇

0₈

0₉

0₂

0₅

1

0₃

0₉

2₇

2₄

0₆

0₇

C3 Q.G G

2₅ G

0₅

0₂

0₉

Llanddwyn Bay

4°24′W

1

Red

0₃

0₂

Mermaid Cove

YB

0₉

1₇

2₉

C2 Fl.R.10s R

0₂

2₃

Pilots Cove

Fl.WR.2.5s12m7/4M

2₈

G

C1 Fl.G.5s

53°07′N

LLANDDWYN ISLAND

0₇

YB

0

3₆

5₅

4₅

5₅

5

10

Cables 0

One Nautical Mile

10

89

The depths and position of the sandbanks are subject to change, and the buoys are moved accordingly. At springs, the tidal stream can exceed 5 knots at Abermenai Point, and use of a fair tide or slack water is necessary.

Contrary winds and tide can build severe seas on the bar, particularly when a swell has built up in the Irish Sea. Even moderately strong winds against the ebb can make the bar impassable. The buoys are mostly lit, but night entrance is not recommended without prior knowledge, and settled conditions would in any case be necessary.

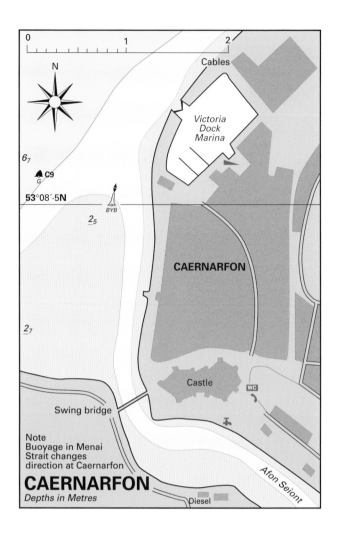

Caernarfon

⊕ 53°08'·53N 4°16'·82W C9 buoy
Local High Water is –0130 Dover
Charts Admiralty *1464, 1970*; Imray *C52, C61*

General

A totally sheltered, mostly drying harbour within the estuary of the Afon Seiont, 2M NE of the SW entrance of the Menai Strait. The harbour is dominated by the magnificent 13th-century castle, the town having been a fortified centre since pre-Roman times. Victoria Dock has recently been redeveloped with lock gates to form a secure marina.

Warning

Entrance to the inner harbour should be made within 3 hours either side of HW. Access to Victoria Dock Marina is via lock gates which are controlled by lights and open 2 hours either side of HW. The tidal stream sets strongly across the entrances to the harbours, except at slack water, and strong winds

Victoria Dock Marina, Caernarfon   *PRPA/Patrick Roach*

Entering Victoria Dock Marina, Caernarfon tidal dock

contrary to the tide can create rough conditions. The inner harbour dries except for the bed of the river.

Approach

By day The castle and town walls are conspicuous when approaching Caernarfon from either direction. It should be noted that the direction of buoyage changes in the Menai Strait, at the S cardinal mark to the NW of Caernarfon.

By night The only official lights are the 2F.G(vert) lights at the entrance to and to the N of the tidal basin; however, the proximity of the entrance channel to the lights of the town makes a night entrance feasible. The River Seiont footbridge is left permanently open between the hours of 2300 and 0700.

Anchorage in the approach

Anchorage may be had in 5m off the town, but the tide can exceed 3·5 knots at springs and the holding ground is uncertain. Yachts that can take the ground can anchor out of the tidal stream to the W of the entrance channel.

Entrance

Victoria Dock Marina is entered via lock gates between the stone quays to the N of the town walls. The inner harbour entrance is marked with an E cardinal buoy, which must be left to starboard. Three green beacons mark the starboard side of the channel, and a red pole beacon marks the extremity of a stone pier to port. There is a pedestrian swing bridge across the channel which is manned when there is enough water to enter the harbour. It may be necessary to give a sound signal B (−···) using foghorn in order to have the bridge opened.

Moorings

Private moorings are laid along the channel of the Afon Seiont.

Berthing

There are secure pontoon moorings in 2m in Victoria Dock Marina. Drying wall berths along the north bank of the River Seiont may be available, as directed by the harbourmaster.

Harbourmaster

Office on quay. Caernarfon Marina ☎ 01492 593000.

Charges

There are harbour charges.

VHF radio telephone

Call *Caernarfon Harbour* Ch 16, work Ch 12 or 14 (office hours only). *Victoria Dock Marina* Ch 80.

Facilities

Fuel Diesel from Caernarfon Marine, on S side of Afon Seiont.
Water Hydrants on quay and in Victoria Dock Marina.
Slip Slip in tidal basin to Arfon Oceaneering.
Provisions Full provisions are avilable in the town. EC Thursday.
Post office Castle Square.
Yacht clubs Royal Welsh Yacht Club (bar). Caernarfon Sailing Club (bar).
Chandlery Caernarfon Marine and Owen Tudor, on quay.
Calor Gas and Camping Gaz Owen Tudor and Calor Gas Centre, Pool Street.
Marine engineers Arfon Oceaneering.

Abermenai

Temporary anchorage may be had at the SW entrance to the Menai Strait, within the shelter of Abermenai Point. The anchorage is protected from SW to NW but exposed to winds from the E sector. There are no facilities. A similar anchorage may be found on the S side of the entrance to the E of the fort at Belan.

Llanddwyn Island

Temporary anchorage may be found in suitable weather conditions off Pilot's Cove or Mermaid Cove, to the E of Llanddwyn Island. The attractive anchorages offer shelter from W through N to NE winds; in strong SW winds a swell runs round the headland into the cove. Small S cardinal buoys indicate the positions of rocks to the S and E of the headland. Approach to the anchorages should be made with care, as there are a number of drying rocks that are not buoyed, particularly to the S of the islet off Mermaid Cove. There are no facilities, but Pilot's Cove can provide an ideal anchorage in which to wait for the right conditions for entering the Menai Strait.

Rhosneigr

Shelter may be found from winds from N through E to SE off the village of Rhosneigr. Reefs extend in tongues offshore in a SW direction on either side of Crigyll Bay. Approach should be from a SW direction, in order to identify and avoid the reefs. Approach and anchor with care, as there are further isolated rocks within the bay. The bay is exposed to the SW. Provisions are available in the village.

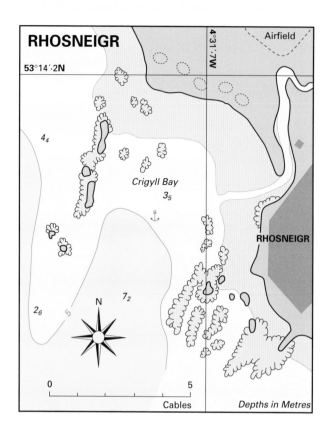

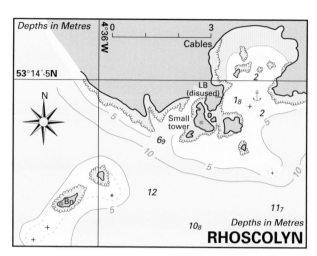

Trearddur Bay

Anchorage may be found on the S side of Trearddur Bay, giving shelter from winds from NW through N to SE. The bay is exposed to the SW. Maen Piscar (dries 1·8m) must be avoided when approaching from the S. There are conspicuous buildings on the N headland to help identify the bay. There are extensive patches of drying rocks in the N of the bay. Trearddur Bay is a popular holiday resort, and anchored yachts will have to contend with the wash from powerboats during the day in fine weather. Provisions are available in the village. Porth Diana, to the S of Trearddur Bay, is a small bay protected by off-lying rocks. It is crowded with private moorings, and there is no space for a yacht to anchor.

Rhosneigr

Rhoscolyn

Rhoscolyn Bay offers shelter to yachts except in strong winds from the S or SE. A rock with a least depth of 1·8m at MLWS is situated at the midpoint of the narrow entrance to the bay. There is a limited amount of space in which to anchor close to the moorings laid within the bay. There is a small castellated tower on the islet to the S of the disused lifeboat station. Approach to the bay should be from the SE. Tidal streams set strongly across the entrance. Rhoscolyn Beacon marks the Beacon Rocks, lying 2 cables SW of Rhoscolyn Point and extending for ½M in a SW direction. Provisions are available in Rhoscolyn.

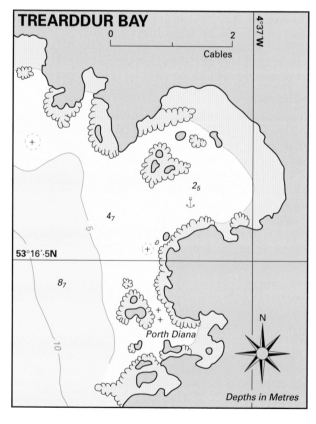

Conspicuous buildings to north of harbour entrance, Trearddur

South Stack

A small island off the NW of Holy Island, to which it is joined by a pedestrian suspension bridge at the foot of a steep flight of cliff steps. The island is topped with the white round tower and associated buildings of South Stack lighthouse (Fl.10s60m20M). A fog signal station is situated on North Stack, one mile NE of the lighthouse. At springs, tidal streams can run at over 5 knots off South Stack. The N-going stream begins at +0530 Dover and the S-going stream at −0030 Dover. During the N-going stream, races extend 1½M NW of South Stack and ½M W from North Stack. During the S-going stream a race extends ½M W of South Stack. In the most settled conditions, advantage may be taken of the narrow passage inside the races, close under the cliffs. In normal conditions the Stacks should be given an offing of 2M, if passage is not being made at slack water. Strong winds can extend the race for up to 7M offshore. Strong contrary winds can build a heavy and dangerous sea off the headlands.

Holyhead

⊕ 53°20'·1N 4°37'·1W 3 cables N of end of
   breakwater
Local High Water is −0040 Dover
Charts Admiralty *2011, 1413, 1970*; Imray *C52, C61*

General

An excellent port of refuge, Holyhead can be entered in any conditions and is well sheltered from all directions, although strong NE winds can raise an uncomfortable sea in the harbour. The 1½M-long breakwater which protects the New Harbour was completed in 1873. The breakwater lighthouse is a white stone tower with a black painted band. Holyhead is a busy commercial port, from which the Sealink ferry runs regularly to Dun Laoghaire. Work started in summer 2000 on a 500-berth marina off Soldier's Point in the outer harbour and it is intended to provide an initial 100 berths by spring 2001. The plan includes comprehensive haul-out, chandlery and boatyard facilities.

Approach

By day The races off North and South Stack have been described above; the passages around Carmel Head will be described later. There are no off-lying dangers when approaching the harbour from the west. The 127m-high chimney 2M to the SSE of the harbour entrance is conspicuous. When making passage from Holyhead, departure should be timed so as to reach Carmel Head or South Stack at slack water.

By night The harbour may be approached at night using the following lights:

South Stack LtHo Fl.10s60m24M Horn 30s
The Skerries LtHo Fl(2)10s36m22M+F.R.26m16M
   Horn(2)20s
Clipera Rocks can Lt buoy Fl(4)R.15s
Breakwater head LtHo Fl(3)G.10s21m14M Siren 20s
Note that there are large unlit mooring buoys in NW of
   harbour.

Entrance

The harbour is entered between the head of the breakwater and Cliperau Rocks, marked with a red can bell buoy. The breakwater should be given at least 50m clearance. A small green buoy immediately within the harbour entrance should be left to starboard. Yachts must use the New Harbour, within the confines of the breakwater. Keep parallel to the breakwater until the small-craft moorings at the head of the harbour are sighted.

Moorings

Small-craft moorings are laid at the head of the inner harbour; these should be taken as directed by the sailing club boatman. Alternatively, a vacant mooring may be taken prior to reporting to the sailing club. There is a sailing club launch service. In the absence of a vacant mooring a yacht may anchor close to the moorings. Anchorage in the harbour entrance or approach is prohibited.

Charges

There are harbour charges.

VHF radio telephone

Call *Holyhead Harbour* Ch 16, work Ch 14.
Call *Holyhead Sailing Club* Ch 80.

Facilities

Fuel Holyhead Boatyard, on S side of the New
   Harbour. Yachts may come alongside the fuelling
   quay after half-tide.
Water By container from sailing club, or alongside
   from Holyhead Boatyard, as above.
Slip On S side of New Harbour.
Provisions Full provisions are available in the town.
   EC Tuesday.
Post office In town centre.
Yacht club Holyhead Sailing Club. Bar and showers.
Chandlery Holyhead Chandlery, on Lower Shore
   Road facing harbour.
Calor Gas and Camping Gaz Holyhead Chandlery.
Marine engineers Holyhead Marine.
Refuse disposal Skip in sailing club yard.

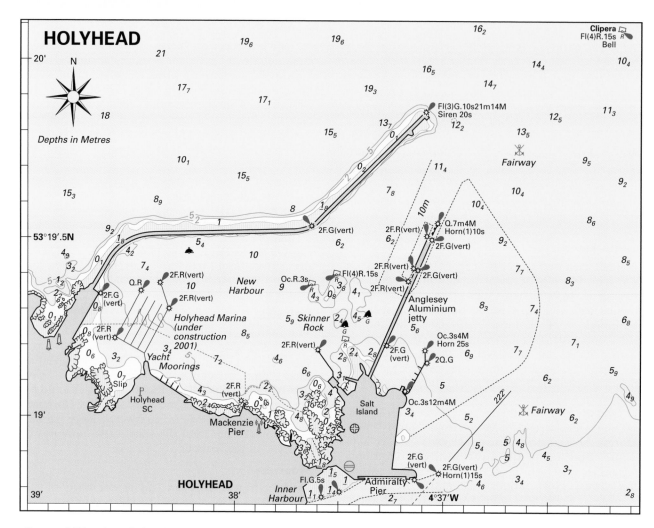

Carmel Head and the Skerries

Carmel Head is a bold headland situated 6M NE of North Stack at the N entrance to Holyhead Bay. To seaward of Carmel Head are numerous rocks and shoals, most prominent being the group of stacks known as the Skerries. The Skerries lighthouse (Fl(2)10s36m22M), a white round tower with a red band, stands on the highest part of the group of rocks. A fixed red light is shown below the main light over the sector of dangerous rocks to the ENE.

In the channel between the Skerries and Carmel Head the NE-going stream starts at +0500 Dover and the SW stream at −0100 Dover. At springs the stream can approach 6 knots. About one mile NW of the Skerries the NE-going stream starts at −0550 Dover and the SW-going stream at +0030 Dover.

Carmel Head can be passed close to at slack water to avoid the race between the headland and the Skerries. With even moderate contrary winds the tidal stream can cause confused seas in this area, and strong contrary winds can quickly build dangerous breaking seas. The rapid tidal stream causes heavy overfalls on East and West Platters, Middle Rock, Carmel Rocks and Passage Rock, and at all the inshore patches on this stretch of coast. At night or in unsettled conditions passage should be made at least one mile offshore of the Skerries.

There are traffic separation zones to the N and NW of the Skerries and Holyhead Bay.

To the E of the Skerries are numerous dangerous rocks, although the area is well buoyed and they should not cause any significant danger in settled conditions. A passage 2M offshore will avoid all dangers. West Mouse is an island ¾M NNE of Carmel Head, marked with a white pyramidal beacon. There is foul ground stretching one mile to the W and SW of the island, and heavy, dangerous overfalls occur in this area on the ebb.

Cemlyn Bay

The bay, 2·5M E of Carmel Head, affords shelter in winds from SE through S to W. It is particularly exposed to the NE. It is an isolated anchorage with a bird sanctuary on its W side and no facilities ashore. The E side of the bay is dominated by the Wylfa Power Station. Passage from the W should be outside the green conical Harry Furlong buoy, which must be left to starboard on the approach.

Cemaes Bay

Shelter may be found from NE through S to SW winds in the attractive anchorage at Cemaes. There is an inner harbour (which dries) protected by a stone breakwater, although this is crowded with local boats.

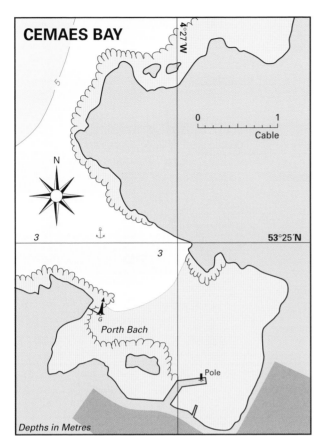

There is a shoal patch extending for 3 cables off Llanbadrig Head, and entrance should be made by proceeding to the centre of Cemaes Bay before turning to the SE when the anchorage at Cemaes is open. Anchor in 3m sand in the centre of the bay. When going ashore by dinghy, note that the small stone breakwater at Porth Bach is awash at HW.

Water is available at the root of the inner harbour breakwater. Provisions are available in the town. There is a post office in the town, and *Camping Gaz* is available at Mona's Stores.

Temporary anchorage may be found at Llanbadrig Cove, to the N of Cemaes, and off Lamb Island, on the W side of the bay, offering protection from W winds.

Amlwch

⊕ 53°25'·48N 4°19'·75W 5 cables N of breakwater head
Local High Water is –0030 Dover
Charts Admiralty *1977*; Imray *C52, C61*

General

Formerly an important commercial harbour exporting copper ore and building its own seagoing vessels. The harbour offers good shelter, although entrance is not possible in strong onshore winds. There are alongside floating moorings in the outer harbour and quayside moorings in the inner harbour, which dries.

Warning

The harbour can be entered at all states of the tide,

Almwch harbour

although a yacht should be aware of the tidal set when approaching the narrow entrance. Strong N or NE onshore winds will build up a big swell at the harbour entrance; no approach should be made in these conditions. The shelter inside the harbour is good, but winds from the N sector can set up a scend in the outer harbour. The inner harbour can only be entered for 2½ hours either side of HW.

Approach

By day There is a passage inshore of East Mouse to the W of the harbour entrance, although this is only recommended for use with local knowledge. The concrete wall forming the breakwater must be identified.

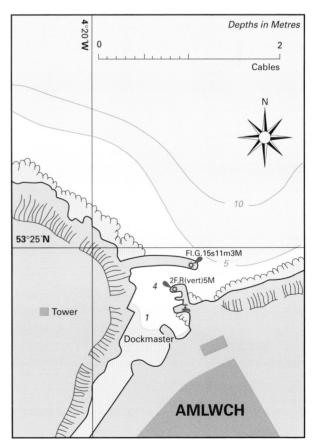

By night The 2F.R(vert) lights at the head of the breakwater must be identified. A night approach is not recommended without local knowledge.

The following lights will assist a night-time entrance:

Amlwch Harbour main breakwater Fl.G.15s11m3M
Inner breakwater 2F.R(vert)12m5M

Entrance

Enter the harbour round the head of the concrete breakwater, proceeding through the 50m-wide opening into the outer harbour.

Berthing

Alongside berths in the outer harbour (as directed by the harbourmaster).

Harbourmaster

Office on quay.

Charges

There are harbour charges.

Facilities

Water Tap on quay.
Provisions Provisions are available in the town.
Chandlery Pilot's Store, in town.

Moelfre

Shelter may be found from S through W to N winds in Moelfre Roads. Ynys Moelfre should be passed to seaward. Anchor to the south of the end of the lifeboat slip, in 3m mud. Anchorage is very exposed to NE. Similar shelter may be found in the cove of Traeth Bychan, to the S of Moelfre Roads.

Red Wharf Bay or Traeth Coch

Shelter from all directions except NE may be found in this attractive bay, which mostly dries to firm sand. Entrance must be made between 2 hours either side of HW. The 15m-high, steep-sided rocky mass of Castell Mawr is conspicuous at the harbour entrance and the channel is buoyed by the sailing club. Limited provisions are available ashore. Water and showers are available at the Traeth Coch Sailing Club, although the opening hours are limited.

Puffin Island

St Seriol's Tower is part of the ruins of a monastic settlement established on the island during the 6th century. The tower is conspicuous near the centre of

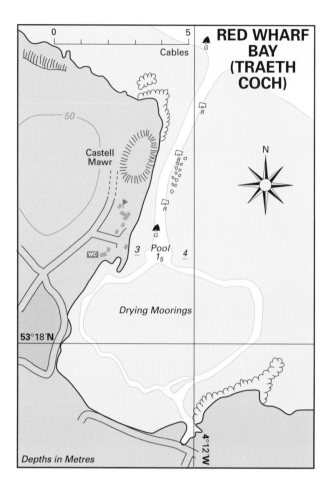

the island, as is the ruined semaphore station at the N end. The island is a private bird sanctuary and landing is strictly by permission.

Access to the N end of the Menai Strait should be obtained between the S of the island and Trwyn-du. Entrance to the Strait to the SE side of the island should not be attempted without local knowledge.

Puffin Sound can be approached at any angle, the only danger being a shoal with a least depth of 2m between the green conical buoy marking Dinmor Bank and Trwyn-du lighthouse. Trwyn-du lighthouse (Fl.5s19m12M) is situated at the end of a rocky shelf extending from Trwyn-du, and has a white circular tower with three black horizontal bands. Entrance to the Strait should be made between Trwyn-du lighthouse and the red Perch Rock beacon. The channel running in a SW direction to Beaumaris is buoyed, although only a few of the buoys are lit. A night entrance should only be attempted with care and preferably with local knowledge.

At the entrance to the Menai Strait, contrary wind and tide can quickly build up a steep sea. Strong onshore winds against the ebb should be avoided. The S-going stream begins at −0600 Dover and the N-going stream at −0115 Dover.

Approaching Red Wharf Bay

Beaumaris

⊕ 53°15'·6N 4°05'·18W B10 buoy
Local High Water is –0025 Dover
Charts Admiralty *1464*; Imray *C52, C61*

General

One of the main sailing centres on the Menai Strait; the laid moorings are fairly well sheltered. Beaumaris Castle is a moated fort built by Edward I.

Approach

By day Beaumaris is approached using the buoyed channel of the Menai Strait.

By night The channel buoys are not all lit, although there are a number of shore-based lights. A night approach should only be made with care and preferably with local knowledge.

Moorings

The moorings laid off Beaumaris are private, and whilst they are frequently made available to visitors, they must only be used by yachts with crew remaining on board or by prior consent. The yacht clubs may be able to allocate moorings to visitors. The moorings are well sheltered, although a NE

Yacht moorings, Beaumaris

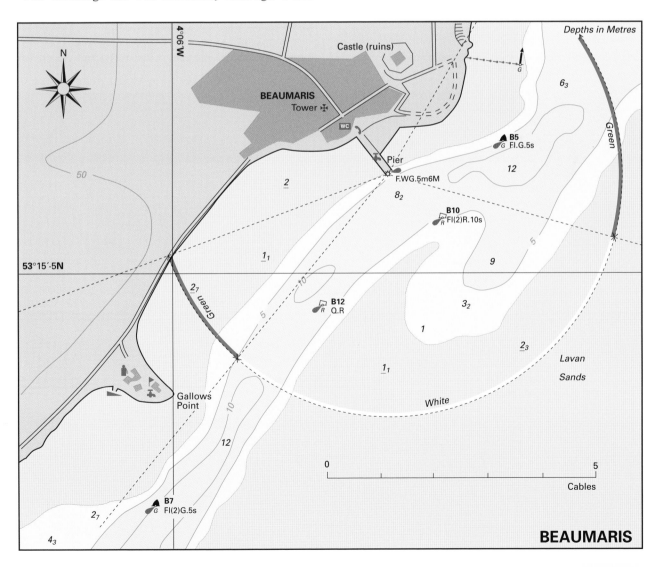

BEAUMARIS

Moorings at Beaumaris looking towards Gallows Point

wind can make them uncomfortable. Many of the moorings dry onto soft mud.

Berthing

Anchorage may be found in 2-3m in the pool to the SE of B10 buoy. Care should be taken to avoid the banks of the channel, which are steep-to. The pool is well sheltered to all wind directions except NE.

Facilities

Fuel By container from ABC (Anglesey Boat Co.) Boatyard, at Gallows Point.

Water Taps on Beaumaris Pier and on wall of yacht club on Gallows Point, and standpipe adjacent to the clubhouse.

Slip ABC Boatyard.

Provisions Full provisions are available in the town. EC Wednesday.

Yacht clubs Royal Anglesey Yacht Club, Beaumaris and North West Venturers Yacht Club, Gallows Point.

Chandlery ABC Boatyard.

Calor Gas and Camping Gaz ABC Boatyard.

Boat repairs and engineers ABC Boatyard.

The Swellies

The notorious narrow, rock-strewn reach begins 3M SW of Gallows Point and stretches for 9 cables between the Menai Suspension Bridge and Britannia Bridge. The complex nature of the tidal streams in the Strait can result in streams reaching 8 knots at springs.

The channel does, however, offer a perfectly safe passage to yachts arriving at or just before HW. Going against the last of a contrary tide will enable yachts without local knowledge to make a passage at a steady speed, in order to identify the necessary marks more easily. Making passage against the last of a foul tide can also assist a yacht further along the Strait as the tide becomes favourable.

It is possible to make the passage at LW slack on neaps. However, there is a least charted depth of

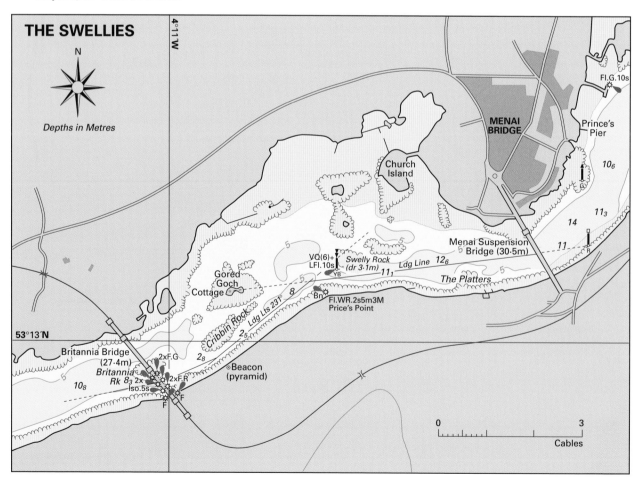

Heading from the NE at HW, a yacht should pass under the centre of the Menai Suspension Bridge and make to leave the S cardinal buoy, marking the Swelly Rock, close to starboard. The course should then be continued past the buoy towards the cottage on Gored Goch. This course is held until the metal pylon transit beacons on either side of Britannia Bridge are in line. The transit is followed until the white pyramidal beacon on the S shore is abeam, when the course is altered to pass under the centre of the south span of Britannia Bridge, leaving the centre pier of the bridge to starboard. These directions are reversed when heading from the SW.

Port Dinorwic

⊕ 53°11'·2N 4°12'·63W red buoy at harbour
entrance
Local High Water is −0105 Dover
Charts Admiralty *1464*; Imray *C52, C61*

General

The historic use of Port Dinorwic can be traced back to the 8th century, when the Vikings used this part of the Menai Strait as a secure anchorage. The harbour was developed in the 19th century to export slate from the quarries of Snowdonia. Total shelter can be found in the locked Yacht Harbour or the alternative tidal basin.

The Swellies

0·4m to the NE of Britannia Bridge, and whilst many rocks are exposed at LW, passage is easier at HW because there is then a depth of approximately 3m over the Platters; at this state of the tide these rocks can therefore safely be passed over. Passage should not be attempted at night. High water slack in the Swellies is −0150 Dover.

Britannia Bridge   *PRPA/Patrick Roach*

Warning

Access to the Yacht Harbour is via the lock gates, which are usually only opened (on request) between 2 hours before and 4 hours after HW. In an emergency, however, the gates can be opened at any time there is sufficient water. There is an average of 2m within the tidal basin at half-tide; berthing should be at the direction of the harbour office. Yachts using the tidal basin should be capable of taking the ground.

Approach

By day The harbour is approached following the buoyed channel of the Menai Strait.

By night Given the restrictions of the Swellies and Caernarfon Bar, it is unlikely that the harbour will be approached at night; however, the two red buoys at and to the N of the harbour entrance are lit, and a F.WR.5m2M is displayed from a pole on the N side of the entrance to the tidal basin.

Anchorage in the approach

Anchorage may be found in 4m soft mud close to and inshore of the moorings off the harbour entrance.

Entrance

The Yacht Harbour is entered from the red pillar buoy, keeping a minimum of 6m away from the quay between the entrance to the tidal basin and the lock gates. The tidal basin is entered between the stone quays; there is no sill.

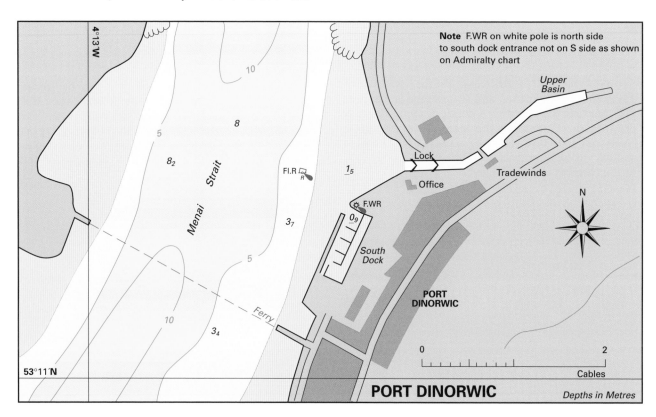

Approaching Port Dinorwic

Port Dinorwic harbour

Port Dinorwic, tidal dock   *PRPA/Patrick Roach*

Berthing

There are approximately 100 berths in the Yacht Harbour and a further 80 berths in the tidal basin. Berths can invariably be found for visitors. All berthing must be at the direction of the Yacht Harbour office.

Moorings

Deep-water moorings belonging to the Yacht Harbour are laid to the N of the harbour entrance. Private moorings are laid to the S of the entrance to the tidal basin.

Charges

There are harbour charges. Port Dinorwic Marina ☎ 01286 671500.

VHF radio telephone

Call *Dinorwic Marina* Ch 80.

Facilities

Port Dinorwic Yacht Harbour is a fully serviced yacht marina with water and electricity supplied to the berths. Fuel is available alongside the quay. There are toilets, showers and a restaurant.
Slip There is a slip in the tidal basin.
Provisions Limited provisions are available in the town. EC Wednesday.
Sailmaker J. Dawson (Sails).
Marine electronics M. J. Stallard.
Marine engineers P. D. Marine.

Bangor

Total shelter from all wind directions may be found alongside the quay in the drying harbours of

Approaching tidal dock, Port Dinorwic

Dickie's Boatyard, or in Penrhyn Dock. Approach should be made within 2 hours either side of HW. Water is available on the quay at Penrhyn Dock. Dickie's of Bangor is a fully equipped boatyard offering repair, servicing and ashore storage facilities. Water and diesel are available on the quay and *Calor Gas* from the shop. There is a comprehensive chandlery and yacht brokerage. Provisions are available in the town. EC Wednesday.

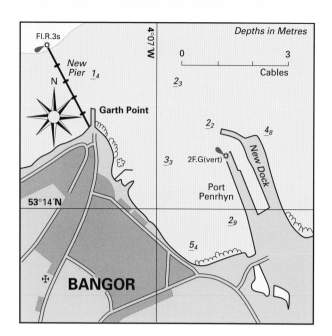

Conwy

⊕ 53°17'·96N 3°55'·49W Fairway buoy
Local High Water is –0015 Dover
Charts Admiralty *1977,1978*; Imray *C52, C61*

General

Conwy is probably the best-preserved medieval fortified town in Britain; the castle, its most dominant feature, was the most expensive of the chain built by Edward I. For decades the town has suffered from being the bottleneck through which all traffic along the North Wales coast must pass. The recently constructed tunnel under the river has alleviated this problem, and the casting basin for the tunnel sections has provided the setting for the construction of a new marina.

The new Conwy Marina provides excellent shelter in all conditions, and the moorings in the River Conwy itself are also well sheltered.

Warning

The bar has about 0·6m at MLWS. The Scabs is a gravel patch which dries at LWS, lying between port-hand buoys No.6 and No.8. The channel is subject to change and the buoys are moved accordingly. The channel can be entered for up to 4 hours either side of HW; shallow-draught craft will be able to enter at any time on a neap tide. First-time entry should be made between 2 hours before HW and HW. The tidal stream can run at over 7 knots in the narrowest part of the channel at springs,

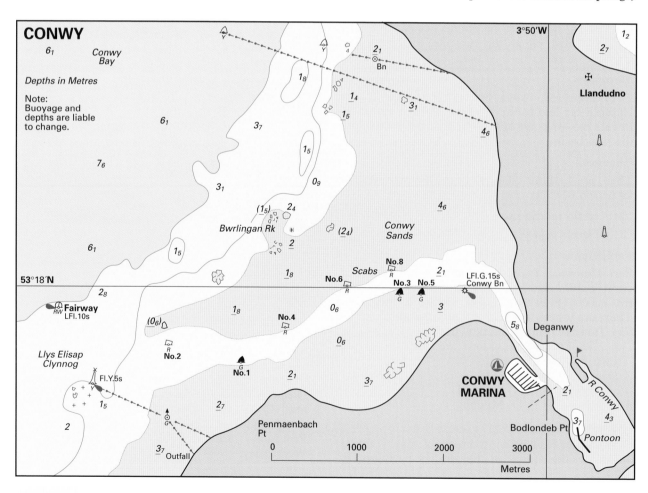

Approaching Conwy

tooth of rock halfway up the N side of Penmaenbach.

By night Only the perch beacon is lit in the channel, although the buoys have reflective topmarks. The marina entrance has fixed red and green lights. Entrance at night is not recommended without local knowledge.

Anchorage in the approach

Anchorage may be found off the entrance to the channel in settled conditions. Anchorage may be found between port-hand buoys No.4 and No.6 to wait for the tide, and at LW Conwy Sands will give some protection from NW winds.

Entrance

From the Fairway buoy, the channel is marked with lateral buoys which are repositioned as necessary. The inshore passage from the NW is unmarked and is not recommended. The perch beacon 3 cables N of Conwy Morfa should be left 30m to starboard. On rounding the perch beacon, Bonlondeb Point should be kept in line with the centre of the new road bridge. Conwy Marina is on the S bank of the river, to the NW of Bonlondeb Point.

Berthing

There are many private moorings laid throughout Conwy harbour, many of which dry. Visitors may be allocated a mooring by the harbourmaster. There is

and 2 hours after HW will be the latest practicable time to enter for most yachts. The channel can be entered in most conditions, although it is not advisable to do so in strong onshore winds, which will make the entrance difficult, especially on the ebb.

Approach

By day The Fairway light buoy should be located. On approach from Puffin Island, the buoy lies on a line between the centre of the island and a jagged

Conwy Marina   *PRPA/Patrick Roach*

also a floating pontoon where visitors may lie alongside as directed by the harbourmaster. The harbour is well sheltered, although strong NW winds can make the harbour uncomfortable, especially on the ebb. Visitors may only stay in Conwy harbour for a maximum of 7 days, except in an emergency; this does not apply to the marina.

Conwy Marina is a new yacht marina, opened in 1992, providing berths and services for around 450 yachts.

Harbourmaster

Office on quay near to road bridge.

Charges

There are harbour charges and charges in the marina.

VHF radio telephone

Call *Conwy Harbour* Ch 16, work Ch 14 or 12.
Call *Conwy Marina* Ch 37.

Facilities

Conwy Marina is a fully equipped yacht marina, with water and electricity to the pontoons ☎ 01492 593000. There is a fuelling quay and a sewage pump-out facility. There are toilets, showers and a laundry ashore. Dickie's at Conwy provide chandlery and a yacht brokerage. Provisions are available in Conwy, although the centre is over a mile from the marina by land.

Conwy Quay Harbour provides fuel and water, alongside a drying berth.

Yacht clubs Conwy Yacht Club, Deganwy: bar and showers. North Wales Cruising Club: bar and showers.

Boat repairs, engineers and marine electronics Conwy River Boatyard.

VIII. Great Ormes Head to Silloth

This stretch of coastline is predominantly exposed to the prevailing winds. Whilst good shelter is available in many harbours, the times of access are invariably restricted by conditions and by the state of the tide. There is no true harbour of refuge, and the coast should be cruised with a keen eye to the weather. Workington can be entered at any state of the tide, but it is a commercial harbour and its use by yachtsmen is not encouraged. The splendid scenery provided by Snowdonia and the Lake District is by way of compensation for the difficulties encountered.

Great Ormes Head

The headland is a prominent feature formed by a steep-sided mass of limestone rising to 203m. The lighthouse, a white square castellated tower (no longer lit), is on the N face of the headland. Temporary anchorage may be found in Ormes or Llandudno Bay, between Great Ormes Head and Little Ormes Head, in offshore winds or settled conditions.

Rhyl

⊕ 53°20'·0N 3°30'·3W 5 cables N of outer perch
Local High Water is +0005 Dover
Charts Admiralty *1978*; Imray *C52, C61*

General

A popular seaside resort. At the SW end of the seafront is Foryd harbour, at the mouth of the River Clwyd. It is a well sheltered, mostly drying harbour, although rather small.

Warning

The harbour can only be entered for 2 hours either

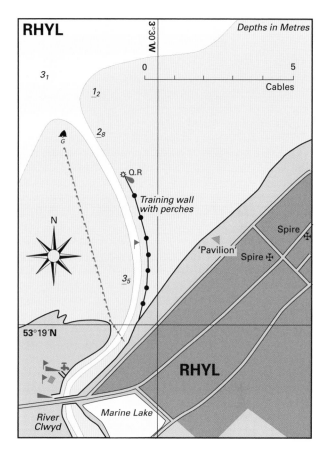

Approaching Rhyl

side of HW. First-time visitors are recommended to enter just before HW. Strong onshore winds make entrance impossible.

Approach

By day Rhyl Pavilion is a tall white tower with a domed top, conspicuous to the NE of the harbour. Rhyl Flats, to the N of the harbour entrance, have a least charted depth of 0·1m, and the harbour should not be approached near LW.

By night The outer perch is lit with a Q.R, but a night entrance is not recommended without local knowledge.

Entrance

The perches marking the line of the river training wall must all be left close to port. On entering the harbour follow the centre of the channel before favouring the NW side of the harbour towards the quay and yacht club.

Berthing

Yachts must be able to take the ground and space in

the harbour is limited. Visitors can invariably be found a mooring by a member of the yacht club, or they may tie alongside the yacht club quay. There is no harbourmaster and there are no harbour charges.

Facilities

Water Water tap on yacht club quay.
Slip Yacht club slip adjacent to the quay. Further slip by Foryd Bridge.
Provisions Full provisions are available in the town.
Yacht club Rhyl Yacht Club.

The Dee estuary

A large tidal estuary, mostly drying at LW. Reasonable shelter can be found in offshore winds, and the off-lying banks give shelter from onshore winds at most states of the tide except for HW. Access to the estuary is via the Welsh Channel or the Hilbre Swash. The Welsh Channel is entered from the W; it runs round the Point of Air inshore of the extensive drying sands of the West Hoyle Bank. The Hilbre Swash is entered from the N and runs between the drying banks of the West and East Hoyle Banks. Both channels are well buoyed, but although most buoys are lit a night entrance is not recommended without local knowledge. The channels are liable to change and the buoys are moved accordingly. The streams run strongly in the estuary, especially when the banks are exposed and the streams are confined to the channels.

Mostyn Docks, on the S side of the estuary, is a privately owned commercial port, and yachts are only allowed to use the harbour in an emergency. There is an anchorage to the SE of the harbour where shelter can be found from NW winds behind the mole forming the entrance to the harbour. Approach must be after half-tide.

There are drying moorings laid in sand off the foreshore at Hoylake, with access from the Hilbre Channel, although these are very exposed to onshore winds. Similar drying moorings are laid off West Kirby and further up the estuary off Caldy and Heswall, drying onto mud. These are a little better protected from onshore winds than Hoylake, being in the lee of Hilbre Island and the associated rocks.

There is plenty of space to anchor between the laid moorings in the sand off West Kirby and Hoylake. Hoylake Sailing Club has a slip at the N end of the town. West Kirby Sailing Club has good facilities and provisions are available ashore.

Liverpool

⊕ 53°31'·35N 3°15'·4W Queen's Channel Fairway buoy
Local High Water is +0015 Dover
Charts Admiralty *3490, 1951, 1978*; Imray *C52, C62*

General

The construction of the new yacht marina in the Brunswick and Coburg Docks has provided sheltered and well serviced moorings for yachts in the heart of this historic city. The restoration of the Albert Dock, with its Maritime Museum, quayside shops, bars and restaurants, and the arrival of the Tate Gallery have brought new life to the waterfront of what was one of the world's biggest and most prosperous ports.

Warning

The marina is accessed via lock gates, which are opened for approximately 2 hours either side of HW, the exact timing depending on the height of the tide. There is a waiting berth on the south side of the lock entrance, but this can be uncomfortable in other than settled conditions. Tides are strong, reaching 5 knots at springs, and strong onshore winds make the entrance to the channel dangerous, particularly against the ebb, when there are steep, breaking seas.

Approach

By day From the W or NW, there are no off-lying dangers to the approach to Queen's Channel.
By night Queen's Channel, Crosby Channel and the River Mersey are all well lit and a night approach does not present any difficulty. Contact the marina in advance if requiring access through the lock gates at night.

Entrance

The approach is via the buoyed Queen's Channel,

Drying moorings, Heswall, River Dee

Dukes buoy, Liver Building and entrance to Albert Dock

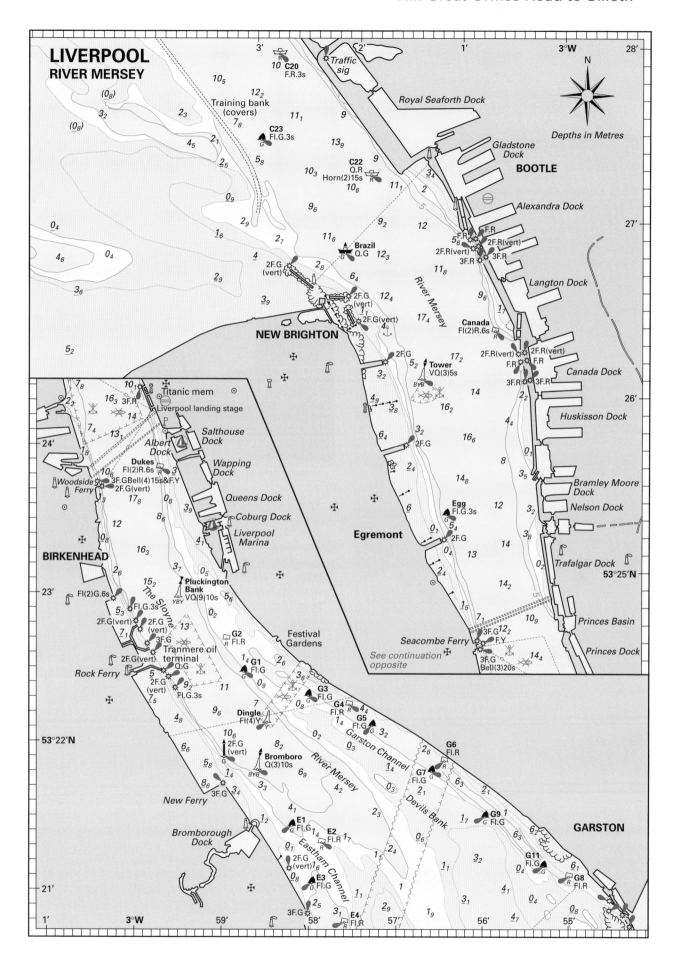

LIVERPOOL
RIVER MERSEY

Traffic sig

C20
F.R.3s

C23
Fl.G.3s

Training bank
(covers)

C22
Q.R
Horn(2)15s

Royal Seaforth Dock

Gladstone
Dock

BOOTLE

Depths in Metres

Alexandra Dock

F.R
F.R
2F.R(vert)
3F.R
2F.R(vert)
3F.R

Brazil
Q.G

River Mersey

Langton Dock

Canada
Fl(2)R.6s

2F.G
(vert)

2F.G
(vert)

2F.G(vert)

NEW BRIGHTON

2F.R(vert)
F.R
3F.R
3F.R

Canada Dock

2F.G

Tower
VQ(3)5s
BYB

Huskisson Dock

Egremont

26'

2F.G

Egg
Fl.G.3s

16₆

Bramley Moore
Dock

Nelson Dock

Titanic mem

Liverpool landing stage

Salthouse
Dock

3F.R

Albert
Dock

Wapping
Dock

Dukes
Fl(2)R.6s

3F.GBell(4)15s&F.Y
2F.G(vert)

Woodside
Ferry

Queens Dock

Coburg Dock

Liverpool Marina

2F.G

Trafalgar Dock

53°25'N

13

Princes Basin

BIRKENHEAD

Pluckington
Bank
VQ(9)10s
YBY

Seacombe Ferry

3F.G

F.Y

3F.G
Bell(3)20s

Princes Dock

Fl(2)G.6s

The Sloyne

Festival
Gardens

See continuation
opposite

Fl.G.3s

2F.G(vert)

2F.G
(vert)

3F.G

G2
Fl.R

G1
Fl.G

Tranmere oil
terminal
Q.G

G3
Fl.G

Rock Ferry

2F.G(vert)
2F.G
(vert)

Fl.G.3s

Dingle
Fl(4)Y

G4
Fl.R

G5
Fl.G

Garston Channel

G6
Fl.R

53°22'N

2F.G
(vert)

Bromboro
Q(3)10s
BYB

River Mersey

G7
Fl.G

Devils Bank

G9
Fl.G

GARSTON

New Ferry

3F.G

E1
Fl.G

E2
Fl.R

G11
Fl.G

G8
Fl.R

Bromborough
Dock

2F.G
(vert)

E3
Fl.G

3F.G

E4
Fl.R

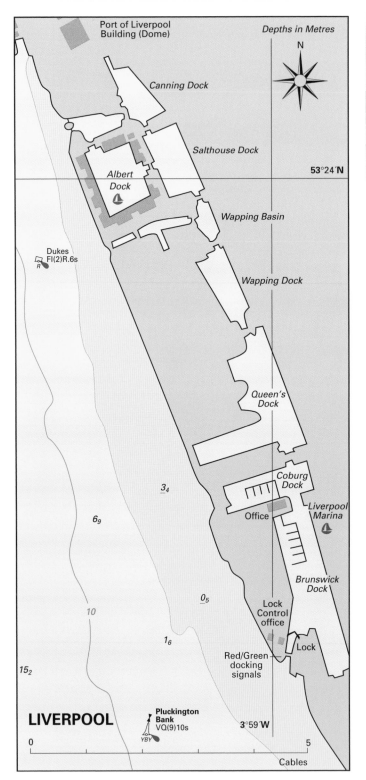

Depths in Metres

Port of Liverpool Building (Dome)

Canning Dock

Salthouse Dock

53°24′N

Albert Dock

Wapping Basin

Dukes
Fl(2)R.6s
R

Wapping Dock

Queen's Dock

3₄

6₉

Coburg Dock

Office

Liverpool Marina

10

0₅

Brunswick Dock

Lock Control office

1₆

Lock

Red/Green docking signals

15₂

LIVERPOOL

Pluckington Bank
VQ(9)10s
YBY

3°59′W

0 — 5

Cables

Approaching Liverpool Marina, entrance on right side of building with grey slate roof

Entering the lock, Liverpool Marina

lock gates are approximately one mile upstream of the Liver Building. The buoyed channel is followed as far as the W cardinal buoy marked 'PB', denoting Pluckington Bank, when the marina entrance will lie directly to port. Three vertical red/green docking signals indicate the availability of the lock; the lock control building is conspicuous, with a grey slate roof.

Anchorage

A drying anchorage offering good shelter is available to shallow-draught yachts on the River Alt. The access, from the Crosby Channel in the region of the C17 or C19 buoys, is subject to change and is marked each year by members of the Blundellsands Sailing Club. A further anchorage may be had in settled weather off New Brighton. Anchorage must be outside the fairway and yachts must be aware of the strength of the tidal stream.

Berthing

Liverpool Marina ☎ 0151 708 5228 has an ultimate capacity of around 450 berths. Berths can always be found for visiting yachts. Access to the Albert and Canning Docks is only by prior arrangement and must be during the 2 hours before HW. Access to the inland waterway system is via Eastham Channel and the Eastham Locks, on the SW side of the river.

VHF radio telephone

Call *Mersey Radio* Ch 12. Traffic movements, local navigational warnings and weather reports are

Crosby Channel and the River Mersey, which are navigable at all states of the tide. There are training walls on either side of the fairway, and yachts should take care not to pass beyond the lines of buoys. Rock Channel, to the N of New Brighton, is not buoyed and should not be attempted without local knowledge. Yachts should be aware of the strength of the ebb, and will have to time their approach according to the opening times for the lock gates when intending to pass into the marina. The marina

Liverpool Marina   *PRPA/Patrick Roach*

broadcast on Ch 09 at 3 and 2 hours before HW. Call *Liverpool Marina* Ch 37.

Facilities

Liverpool Marina is a fully serviced yacht marina with water and electricity supplied to the pontoons. There are showers, toilets, a restaurant, a bar and a chandlery ashore. *Calor Gas* is available adjacent to the marina entrance.
Marine electronics Robbins Marine, Coburg Dock.
Admiralty chart agents and chandlery Dubois Phillips and MacCallum.

Liverpool Marina, Coburg Dock

The Ribble estuary

Preston was once a prosperous port, but its trade declined over the years and it was closed to commercial traffic in 1981. The construction of the new Preston Marina, in the old Albert Edward Dock, and the associated Riversway Docklands commercial and residential developments have breathed new life into the port.

Additional facilities for yachts are to be found at Lytham and Freckleton, on the N bank of the estuary, and at the Douglas Boatyard at Hesketh Bank on the River Asland or Douglas, which enters the estuary on its S side.

Entrance

The original navigable channel of the River Ribble from the Gut buoy between the training walls has silted and the main channel now runs from a breach in the training wall through South Gut. From the Gut buoy (waypoint 53°41'·75N 3°08'·8W) an ESE course for 1·5M will lead to the entrance to the South Gut. Whilst the channel is accessible for 2 hours either side of HW, ideally a yacht should leave the Gut buoy at around 2 hours before HW. Local High Water is +0025 Dover. There is water in the South Gut at most states of the tide. The training wall is not covered before half-tide; early arrivals can find shelter from NW winds by anchoring to the S of the training wall. Anchorage is available at all times in the '11-mile hole'·

The channel of the South Gut is marked by local interests with unofficial buoys. The red and yellow

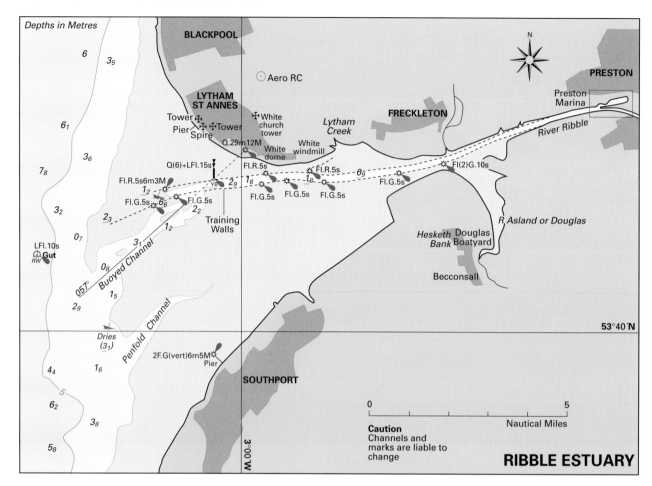

Depths in Metres

BLACKPOOL

Aero RC

LYTHAM
ST ANNES

FRECKLETON

PRESTON

Preston
Marina

Tower
Pier   Tower
        Spire

White
church
tower

Lytham
Creek

River Ribble

Q.29m12M

White
dome

White
windmill

Q(6)+LFl.15s

Fl.R.5s

Fl.R.5s

Fl.(2)G.10s

Fl.R.5s6m3M

YB

Fl.G.5s

Fl.G.5s

Fl.G.5s   Fl.G.5s   Fl.G.5s

Fl.G.5s

Training
Walls

R. Asland or Douglas

057°   Buoyed Channel

Hesketh   Douglas
Bank   Boatyard

LFl.10s
Gut
RW

Penfold Channel

Becconsall

Dries
(3₁)

2F.G(vert)6m5M
Pier

SOUTHPORT

53°40′N

0   5

Nautical Miles

Caution
Channels and
marks are liable to
change

RIBBLE ESTUARY

buoys should be left to port as the main channel is approached. The first two starboard-hand marks on the training wall of the original (now silted) channel are grey lattice towers. The third starboard-hand mark is a green-painted steel post. The fourth mark is again a lattice tower with a radar reflector, and the opening in the training wall is to the E of this tower. A bearing of 049° on the tower of the white church at Lytham St Anne's will lead directly from South Gut to this opening. The remainder of the channel is marked with perches on the training wall. Although a number of the buoys are lit, a night-time entrance without local knowledge is not recommended. Entrance should not be attempted in strong onshore winds.

Douglas Boatyard

The boatyard lies on the River Asland or Douglas and can be accessed for 2 hours either side of HW. The river is reached by means of the Ribble estuary channel, turning to starboard immediately before the 5-mile perch. There is a comprehensive chandlery and engineering and repair facilities. Visitors' berths are always available, as are winter storage facilities. Many berths dry, although there are pontoon berths with 1·8m at LW ☎ 01772 812462.

Douglas Boatyard, Hesketh Bank

Preston Marina

The new marina has been constructed at the entrance to the old Albert Edward Dock, one of the largest of its kind in Europe. There is an ultimate provision for around 350 berths, and spaces are always available for visitors. Entrance into the dock is through the new lock gates, which are open for approximately 1½ hours either side of HW Liverpool between 0700 and 2100 local time during the months of April to September. During the winter months the gates will be opened on any reasonable tide, given 24 hours' notice. There is a

Quayside moorings, River Ribble, Preston

Entrance Dock, Preston Marina

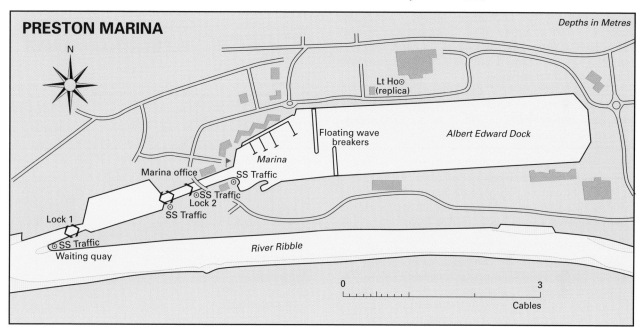

PRESTON MARINA

Depths in Metres

N

Lt Ho⊙
(replica)

Floating wave
breakers

Albert Edward Dock

Marina

Marina office

SS Traffic

⊙SS Traffic
Lock 2
⊙

SS Traffic

Lock 1

⊙SS Traffic
Waiting quay

River Ribble

0   3

Cables

waiting berth, in which yachts of moderate draught will lie afloat at LW, alongside the south quay of the entrance channel out of the tideway. Yachts should not be left unattended in the waiting berth.

Preston marina is a fully serviced yacht marina with electricity and water on the pontoons. There are toilets and showers ashore, a chandlery and yacht brokerage. *Calor Gas* is available at the marina. Fuel is available alongside during lock gate operation between the hours of 0900 and 1800. Winter storage facilities ashore are available. The Riversway Docklands development itself includes restaurants, cinemas and shopping areas. There are marina fees, but no charge is made for any lock-gate or docking activity. There are two VHF radio telephone stations covering marina activities. Call *Riversway* Ch 16, work Ch 14, between 2½ hours before and 1½ hours after HW for information regarding lock-gate operation, and call *Preston Marina* Ch 37 between 0900 and 1800 for information regarding berthing.

Lytham St Anne's and Freckleton

There are drying moorings in sand off the Ribble Cruising Club at Lytham St Anne's, although these are exposed to the S through W to the NW. Local

Freckleton Creek

boats find shelter in the drying Lytham Creek. Similar berths can be found at Freckleton Creek, where there is a boatyard. There is a slip, limited chandlery is available, and there are winter storage facilities.

Morecambe Bay

The bay is an extensive inlet, mainly drying to sand and mud, whose entrance stretches from Rossall Point in the south to the Isle of Walney. The bay is exposed to the prevailing SW and W winds. There are access channels into the bay, intersected by linking channels which are subject to change.

The Lune Deep is the principal channel into the bay. The River Wyre runs into the Lune Deep from the S and forms the entrance to the new marina at Fleetwood. Further anchorages on the River Wyre can be found at Knott End, Skippool Creek and Wardley's Creek. The marina at Glasson Dock is entered via the River Lune, which flows into the Lune Deep from the E.

The main channel of the Lune Deep runs to Heysham. This is a commercial harbour and yachts are only permitted to enter it in an emergency. There is no buoyage beyond Heysham; although yachts may reach Morecambe in settled conditions and on a rising tide, the drying anchorage is totally exposed to onshore winds.

At the N end of Morecambe Bay is the entrance channel to Barrow-in-Furness, which includes the anchorages off Piel Island and Roa Island.

Entrance to the Lune Deep

The Lune Deep S cardinal buoy (waypoint 53°55'·75N 3°10'·8W) must be located 4·5M WNW of Rossall Point. The channel is marked with lateral buoys and runs on a straight course to the Fairway No.1 N cardinal buoy (waypoint 53°57'·7N 3°02'·2W) at the entrance to the River Wyre. Yachts must keep to the marked channel, as the sides are steep-to, rising from depths of over 40m, and there are dangerous shoals extending 4M W of Rossall Point. The buoys are lit to allow for a night entrance. The stream can run at over 3 knots at springs, and onshore winds against the ebb can create short, steep seas.

Fleetwood Marina

The new yacht marina is part of the comprehensive development of the 70-acre area around the Wyre Dock at Fleetwood. The Fleetwood Harbour Village includes residential developments, shopping facilities and leisure amenities.

The channel to the Wyre Dock has been dredged and 210 berths of the projected total of 350 have been completed, with services provided ashore in Portacabins. The shelter within the marina is excellent, although the fishing boats passing through into the Fish Dock can create a wash ☎ 01253 872323.

Approach is via the buoyed channel of the River Wyre from the Fairway No.1 N cardinal buoy. The

disused Wyre Lighthouse is a steel structure on the W side of the river channel. Leading lights are displayed approaching Fleetwood on a course of 156° from a stone tower ashore and from a taller brick tower beyond. The channel should be followed past the ferry terminal on the W bank of the river. The channel, dredged 2m above chart datum, begins close to the end of the terminals and should be followed in a SSW direction until the lock entrance to the Wyre Dock is sighted. The channel is lit to allow for night access.

The locks are operated 2 hours either side of HW. Local High Water is +0015 Dover. Signals are displayed at the dock entrance; one black ball indicates that it is clear for inbound traffic and two black balls that it is clear for outward-bound vessels. There is a waiting quay at the entrance to the lock on the SE side of the channel. Yachts approaching

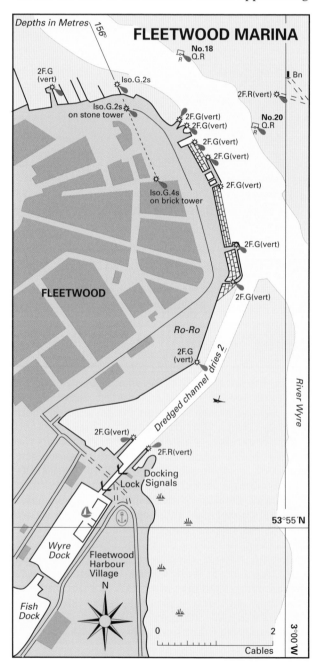

Fleetwood Marina   *PRPA/Patrick Roach*

the marina should use VHF radio telephone and call *Fleetwood Dock* Ch 16, work Ch 12.

Water and electricity are provided on the pontoons; showers, toilets, and laundry and waste disposal facilities are provided ashore. Provisions are available in the town (EC Wednesday).

River Wyre

There are laid yacht moorings and an anchorage off Knott End, out of the main channel to the E of No.20 and No.22 port-hand buoys. Many of the moorings dry, and yachts wishing to stay afloat should anchor in the pool to the S of No.22 buoy, away from the ferry manoeuvring area. The anchorage is well sheltered except to strong N winds. Limited provisions are available ashore, or the ferry may be taken to Fleetwood.

The channel of the River Wyre can be followed upstream to Wardleys Creek and Skippool Creek.

Wardleys Marina, river Wyre

First-time visitors should begin off Knott End 1 hour before HW and follow the channel midstream to the NW end of the ICI pier at Burn Naze, leaving the two green buoys to starboard. Wardleys Creek lies on the E bank of the river. There are drying moorings, belonging to Wardleys Marine; there is also a chandlery, and water is available. There is a slip and landing jetty.

Skippool, the home of the Blackpool and Fleetwood Yacht Club, is 5M above Fleetwood on the W bank of the river. Visitors may tie alongside the drying jetties on either side of the yacht club; there is no charge. There is a slip, and water is available on the jetties. There are toilets, showers and a bar at the yacht club. Private alongside moorings can be found in Skippool Creek.

Entrance to Wyre Dock, Fleetwood

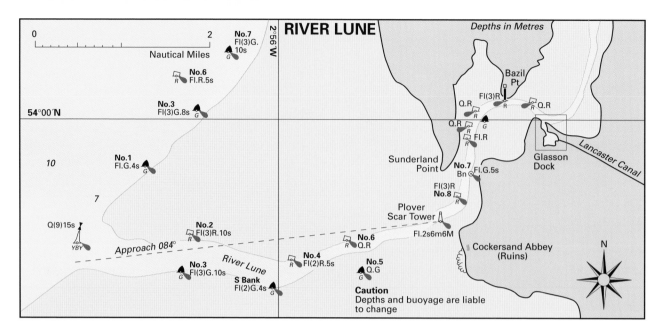

River Lune

The river flows into the Lune Deep 1½M NE of the Fleetwood Fairway No.1 cardinal buoy, and the confluence is marked by a W cardinal buoy. The channel to Plover Scar is marked with lateral buoys and is subject to change, the buoys being moved accordingly. An approach of 084° to the tower of Plover Scar (Fl.2s6m6M) will be approximate to the line of the channel, although it will not necessarily follow the deepest water. The channel then passes to the northwest of the tower. The lateral buoys themselves are lit as far as Glasson Dock to allow for night access. There are drying moorings to the E of Sunderland Point and N of No.10 buoy which are sheltered from all directions except S and SW, when a swell sets up the river. A pipeline crosses the river to the S of No.10 buoy; anchorage is not permitted in this locality.

It is possible for shallow-draught craft to reach Lancaster, 5M beyond Glasson Dock, approaching HW, although the unmarked channel is narrow and should only be attempted with local knowledge.

Glasson Dock

A well sheltered yacht marina with 260 berths, some of which are always available for visitors, offering good facilities for yachts. The entrance to the outer basin is via lock gates that are only opened for one hour before HW. Local High Water is +0030 Dover.

The approach is via the buoyed channel of the River Lune, leaving the Lune W cardinal buoy at up to 2 hours before HW to arrive at the lock gates at the appropriate time.

The outer dock is a commercial dock; yachts may lie alongside the quay of this dock as directed whilst waiting for entry through the lock gates into the inner basin containing the marina. The inner lock gates are only opened between sunrise and sunset. Yachts leaving the marina should present themselves at the upper lock gates 2 hours before HW. The dock connects with the British Waterways network of the Lancaster canal.

There are dock gate signals. By day a red flag and black ball and by night two red vertical lights indicate that the gates are open and that vessels in the dock are clear to leave. By day a red flag only and by night a red light over white indicates that the gates are open and that vessels are clear to enter the dock. Vessels must stand by and await the correct signal.

VHF radio telephone watch is kept from 2 hours before HW to 1 hour after HW; call *Glasson Dock* Ch 16, work Ch 08 for information regarding locking operations, call *Glasson Dock Marina* Ch 80 for information regarding berthing ☎ 01524 751491.

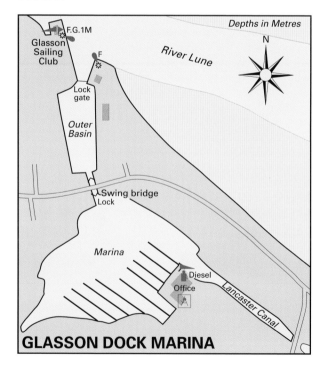

Glasson Dock   *PRPA/Patrick Roach*

Piel Island   *PRPA/Patrick Roach*

Glasson Dock Marina

Entrance to Glasson Dock

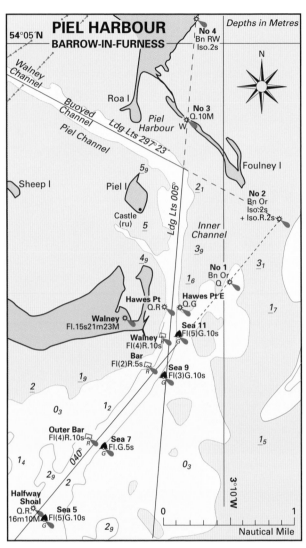

Yachts berth alongside the fixed marina pontoons. Water and electricity are available on the pontoons. There are toilets, a bathroom and showers ashore. Fuel is available alongside the quay, and a chandlery forms part of the marina complex. There is a boatyard, with boat, engineering and electronic repair facilities as well as winter storage. There are mooring charges, but no further fees for locking operations.

Glasson Sailing Club operates from premises close to the lock gates, where there is a slip. There is a post office, and provisions are available from the shops close to the outer basin, some 10 minutes' walk from the marina.

Piel Island and Barrow-in-Furness

The Walney Channel begins about one mile S of Hilpsford Point, at the S end of Walney Island. Walney Island lighthouse (Fl.15s23M) is a stone tower situated near the SE extremity of the island. Lightning Knoll Fairway Buoy (LFl.10s) is a RW spherical bell buoy (waypoint 53°59'·73N 3°14'·2W) 3·3M SSW of Hilpsford Point. A course from the buoy of 041° on the leading lights will leave the Halfway red buoy (Q.R) and Outer Bar red buoy (Fl(4)R.10s) to port. The leading lights are No.1 beacon (Q.10M), a black pile structure with a white daymark, and the rear No.2 beacon (Iso.2s10M), a red brick structure with a white face. The course indicated by the leading marks is followed until the Bar red buoy (Fl(2)R.5s) is abeam, when leading marks Nos 3 and 4 are followed on a course of 006°. The structures and light characteristics are the same for leading marks Nos 3 and 4 as for marks Nos 1 and 2. This course is followed until the Piel red buoy (F.R.5s) is abeam. The channel to Barrow is marked with lateral buoys.

Morecambe Bay itself should only be crossed by shallow-draught yachts with great care after half-tide. Allowance should be made for the strong tidal currents running into and out of the bay. The Walney Channel should be entered before the Bar buoy after crossing the bay.

The ruins of the castle on Piel Island are conspicuous, the only other buildings on the island being a public house and a row of pilots' cottages. There are moorings laid off the E side of Piel Island and a landing jetty ashore. Anchorage can be found clear of the moorings out of the main channel. Tidal streams can run at up to 2½ knots at springs, and care must be taken when using a tender between boat and shore. The anchorage is well sheltered from all directions except the SE, when a swell sets in across the bay.

The ruined castle, Piel Island

A similar anchorage and moorings can be found off Roa Island, which has the advantage of being connected to the mainland, so that provisions are more readily available. There is less room to stay afloat out of the channel than at Piel Island, but there are drying moorings and an anchorage for yachts that can take the ground between Roa Island and Foulney Island.

The commercial docks at Barrow are about a further 3M NW of Piel Island. There are moorings laid in the Walney channel beyond the commercial dock entrance and to the S of the bridge at Barrow. Shelter is excellent, although many of the moorings dry. Anchorage may be found clear of these moorings. Full provisions are available ashore.

Duddon Mouth

The estuary is exposed to onshore winds and mostly dries. The channel beyond the Duddon Bar is unmarked and constantly changing; it should only be used with the benefit of local knowledge. There is an anchorage off Haverigg. Yachts that can take the ground can anchor off Askam, where there is a pier, or off Hodbarrow, where there is a pier and a small drying harbour.

Ravenglass

⊕ 54°19'·7N 3°28'·8W 2M WSW of estuary mouth
Local High Water is +0020 Dover
Charts Admiralty *1346*; Imray *C62*

General

A large, well sheltered, mostly drying harbour formed by the estuaries of three rivers: the Irt, the Mite and the Esk. Formerly a Roman fortified harbour, it is a peaceful and unspoilt anchorage. The dunes at the mouth of the estuary are a bird sanctuary that can only be visited by prior appointment. Ashore, Ravenglass is the terminus for the Ravenglass and Eskdale Railway, a narrow-gauge steam railway originally built in 1875 to carry iron ore down the Eskdale Valley.

Warning

The harbour can only be entered between 2 hours either side of HW; first-time entry should preferably be made during the hour before HW. Strong onshore winds make entrance impossible.

Approach

By day The tall cooling towers of the Calder Hall reactors at Sellafield, 5M NW of the harbour, are

Ravenglass   *PRPA/Patrick Roach*

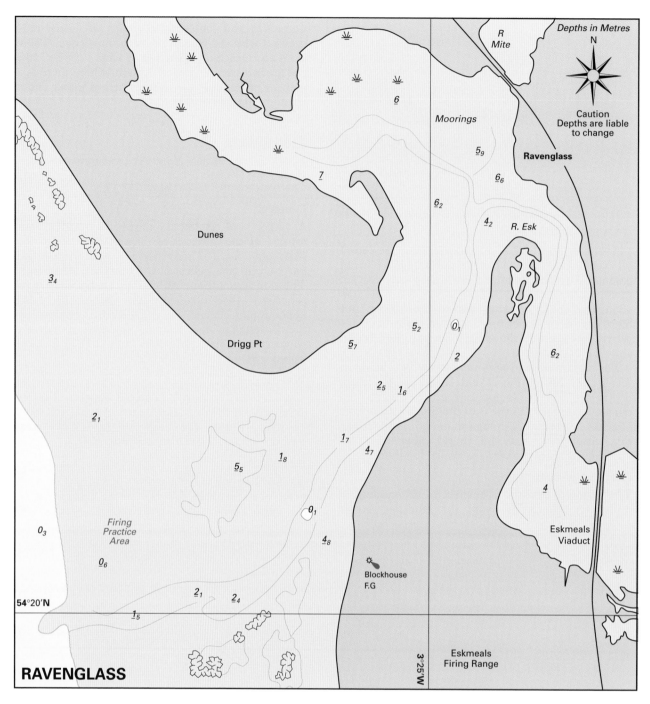

Depths in Metres

N

Caution
Depths are liable
to change

Moorings

Ravenglass

R. Esk

Dunes

Drigg Pt

R
Mite

Firing
Practice
Area

Blockhouse
F.G

Eskmeals
Viaduct

Eskmeals
Firing Range

54°20'N

3°25'W

RAVENGLASS

conspicuous. Approach must be made 2M offshore to avoid Drigg Rocks (awash at LW) to the N of the entrance, and Selker Rocks (which dry at MLWS) to the S. A green conical bell buoy (Fl(3)G.10s) is positioned to the W of Selker Rocks. The harbour entrance lies in a break in the coastal sandhills. To the S of the harbour entrance is Eskmeals Firing Range, where guns are occasionally fired up to 5M out to sea. Red flags are shown at either end of the range when firing is about to begin or in progress. Vessels have right of passage through the area when firing is taking place.

By night The harbour is unlit; night approach should not be attempted.

Anchorage in the approach

Anchor off the harbour entrance only in the most settled conditions.

Entrance

It is necessary to identify the small green hut with a white square shutter to the S of the harbour entrance. The hut lies above and to the E of a concrete blockhouse, painted with a white horizontal band, at the NW end of the firing range. To find the entrance channel, the hut should be aligned with Yoadcastle Peak (a conical peak, 490m high, 4½M to the E of the harbour) on a bearing of 083°. About 2 cables from the shore, turn on a bearing of 035° towards the village of Ravenglass.

Moorings

Private drying moorings are laid throughout the harbour.

Anchorage

Anchorage for yachts that can take the ground can be found close to the laid moorings in or between the channels of the rivers Irt and Mite. The banks of the River Esk are relatively steep-to and should be avoided.

Harbourmaster

No harbourmaster or harbour charges.

Facilities

Water Tap by butcher's shop on the main street, to the N of the Pennington Arms.
Slip At S end of main street.
Provisions Provisions are available in the village. EC Wednesday.
Post office On the main street.
Yacht club Ravenglass Boating Association.

St Bees Head

The headland is a perpendicular sandstone cliff 95m-high. The lighthouse (Fl(2)20s102m18M) has a white round tower.

Whitehaven

⊕ 54°33'·22N 3°36'·2W 2 cables WNW of head of W pier
Local High Water is +0020 Dover
Charts Admiralty *2013, 1346*; Imray *C62*

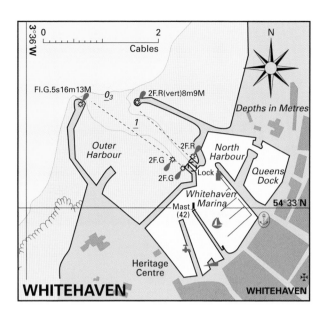

General

A large, well sheltered drying harbour which was developed during the 17th century as a port for shipbuilding and the exportation of local coal. By the early 18th century Whitehaven was one of the major ports in the country. Trade has dwindled since then, but Queen's Dock still handles cargo vessels of up to 3,000 tons. The newly completed sealock and marina have breathed new life into this historic harbour.

Whitehaven   *PRPA/Patrick Roach*

Whitehaven Marina

Warning

The outer harbour dries but the approach channel has been dredged to 1·0m above chart datum allowing access to the sealock 4 hours either side of HW. Entrance can be made in most conditions, only strong onshore winds against the ebb causing difficulty. Keep close to the W pier when entering with the flood, as a strong E tidal stream sets across the harbour mouth. At intermediate states of the tide it is prudent to give a wide berth to the W pier as a shoal patch extends from the pierhead.

Approach

By day The harbour is 2·6M NNE of the conspicuous St Bees Head, and is easily identified by the tall chimneys and towers to the S of the entrance. There are no off-lying dangers.

By night The harbour can be approached and entered using the following lights:

St Bees Head Fl(2)20s102m18M
Whitehaven West Pier Fl.G.5s16m13M
Whitehaven North Pier 2F.R(vert)8m9M
North Harbour Quay head 2F.R(vert)8m2M
Old Quay head 2F.G(vert)8m2M

Anchorage in the approach

Anchorage may be found off the harbour entrance in settled conditions.

Entrance

The harbour is entered between the stone-built West and North Piers. Both have lights at the head displayed from white round towers. Yachts should pass through the outer harbour, then through the sealock, into the new marina in the Inner Harbour. The sill of the sealock is at chart datum maintaining 5·5m in the Inner Harbour.

Moorings

There are private moorings laid in the South Harbour.

Berthing

Yachts are accommodated in the new secure marina in the Inner Harbour. The marina has full facilities with toilets, showers, sanitation recovery system and fuel quay ☎ 01946 692435.

Harbourmaster

Office overlooking Inner Harbour.

VHF radio telephone

Call *Whitehaven Harbour* Ch 16, work Ch 12.

Facilities

Fuel From fuel quay at western end of main marina pontoon.
Water From marina pontoons and on Old Tongue.
Slip Alongside New Tongue.
Provisions Full provisions in town. EC Wednesday.
Yacht club Whitehaven Sailing Club.

Harrington

⊕ 54°36'·75N 3°35'·2W 3 cables W of harbour entrance
Local High Water is +0025 Dover
Charts Admiralty *2013, 1346*; Imray *C62*

General

One of the smaller Cumbrian ports, Harrington reached its zenith at the turn of the last century. Many ships were built in the harbour; coal, iron and steel were the principal exports. Developments at Workington heralded the decline of the harbour. In 1932 the Harbour and Dock Board was wound up and in 1940 the harbour entrance was sealed with a concrete blockship. Local pressure resulted in the harbour being re-opened in 1966.

Warning

Both the inner and outer harbours dry to mud. Entrance is possible for 2 hours either side of HW for a yacht with 1·2m draught, although dredging is improving the situation. The inner harbour is well sheltered, although a swell is experienced in strong W or NW winds. Entrance should not be attempted in strong onshore winds.

Approach

By day The harbour lies 3·8M N of the conspicuous towers and chimneys at Whitehaven. There are no off-lying dangers.

By night Entry is only recommended with local knowledge.

Entrance to Harrington harbour

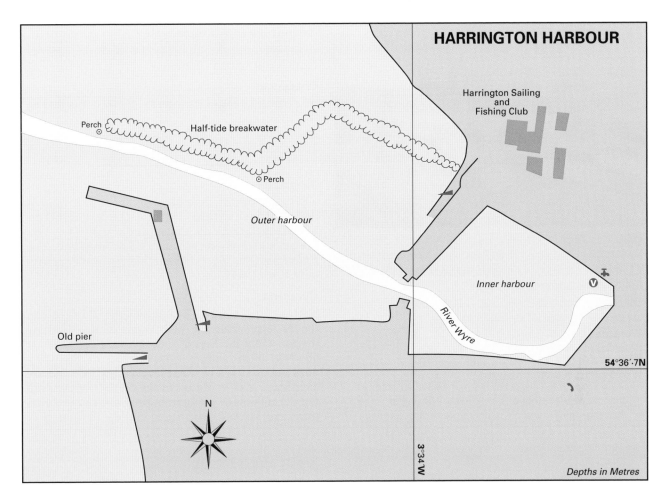

HARRINGTON HARBOUR

Harrington Sailing and Fishing Club

Outer harbour

Inner harbour

Perch

Half-tide breakwater

Perch

Old pier

River Wyre

54°36'·7N

3°34'W

N

Depths in Metres

Anchorage in the approach

Anchor off the harbour entrance only in settled conditions.

Entrance

Entrance is made between the stone S pier and the loose-rock N breakwater. The breakwater is covered at half-tide; its position is marked by two red perches. The deepest water is to be found close to the N breakwater. There is a concrete projection at the end of the stone breakwater; when this is awash there is 1·8m of water at the entrance to the inner harbour. Yachts should pass through into the inner harbour, the deepest water being found on the S side of the inner harbour entrance.

Moorings

There are private moorings laid in the inner harbour; these may be used by visitors as directed by the harbourmaster.

Berthing

The visitors' berth is clearly marked at the far end of the NE quay in the inner harbour. There are good ladders. Anchorage may be found in the outer harbour in suitable conditions. Do not anchor in the inner harbour.

Harbourmaster

Lives close to harbour.

Charges

There are no charges for visitors.

Facilities

Water Standpipe by visitors' berth.
Slip Slips on N and S sides of outer harbour.
Provisions Provisions are available in the town.
Yacht club Harrington Sailing and Fishing Club. Bar and showers.

Workington

⊕ 54°39'·45N 3°35'·2W 2 cables NW of harbour entrance
Local High Water is +0025 Dover
Charts Admiralty *2013, 1346*; Imray *C62*

General

A sheltered commercial port at the mouth of the River Derwent that can be entered at any state of the tide and in most conditions. Yachtsmen are not actively encouraged to use the harbour, although they will be assisted in an emergency.

Approach

By day There are no off-lying dangers for yachts when approaching from the S or W. Approach from the N should be at least one mile offshore to avoid drying rocky shoals. Strong winds with contrary tides can raise a difficult sea over Workington Bank, which can be avoided by using the inshore English

Outer Tidal Dock, Workington

Channel. There is a conspicuous chimney (68m) to the S of the harbour entrance.

By night The harbour can be approached and entered using the following lights:

Workington S Pier head Q.G
Workington S Pier Fl.5s11m8M Siren 20s
Bush perch Q.R
Workington N jetty 2F.R(vert)
Leading lights F.R.10m3M and F.R.12m3M indicating channel on a bearing of 131·5° with F.Bu lights marking the NE and SW extremities of the channel.

Anchorage in the approach

Anchorage may be found to the W of the harbour entrance in settled conditions.

Entrance

The entrance channel is dredged, and is marked by the conspicuous red and white leading marks on a bearing of 131·5°. The stream can run strongly across the harbour entrance and must be allowed for in the approach.

Moorings

There are private moorings, drying to soft mud at half-tide, in the tidal dock on the S side of the harbour before the inner harbour bridge. These are maintained by the local Vanguard Sailing Club. The bridge into the inner drying basin is now fixed, with only 1·8m clearance.

Berthing

Yachts which need to go alongside should tie up on the N jetty, with the permission of the berthing master. Only the E end of the N quay has water at all states of the tide, but the sheeting on the piling does not go down to water level at LW. Temporary anchorage may be found in the turning basin, with the permission of the berthing master, but the boat must not be left unattended during the hours of

Workington   *PRPA/Patrick Roach*

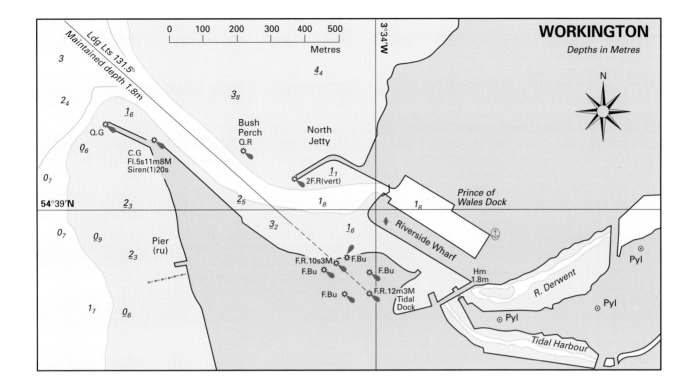

commercial movement. The lock gates to the Prince of Wales Dock operate between 2½ hours before and 2 hours after HW. VHF radio telephone watch is only maintained between these hours. Call *Workington Harbour Radio* Ch 16, work Ch 14 or 11. There are no facilities for yachtsmen.

Maryport

⊕ 54°43'·07N 3°31'·22W 2 cables W of harbour entrance
Local High Water is +0040 Dover
Charts Admiralty *2013, 1346*; Imray *C62*

General

The new marina in the Senhouse Dock has brought life back to this formerly bustling port at the mouth of the River Ellen. The docks were built by a local landowner, Humphrey Senhouse, to export the local coal. Iron and steel also became principal exports, and at one time over a million tons of cargo left the docks every year. The decline of trade saw the docks suffer from silting. The channel is now dredged to allow access to the new marina. There are currently 240 deep-water pontoon berths, with a number of berths reserved for visitors. There is also good shelter in the drying commercial Elizabeth Dock.

Warning

The channel is dredged to one metre above chart datum, allowing access to the entrance channel and holding basin for a yacht of 1·3m draught for 4 hours either side of MHWS and 5½ hours either side of MHWN, and for a yacht of 1·75m draught for 3½ hours either side of MHWS and 4½ hours either side of MHWN. The lock gates into the marina are open for a minimum of 2½ hours either

side of HW. The harbour can be entered in most conditions.

Approach

By day Approach from the S should be made at least one mile offshore to avoid drying rocky shoals. The pier is conspicuous when approaching from the S. When approaching from the Scottish coast, the sandbanks and strong tidal streams of the Solway Firth must be avoided by passing to the S of the Two Feet Bank W cardinal buoy. Allowance should be made for the tidal streams which run strongly off the harbour entrance.

By night A light (Fl.1·5s10m6M) is displayed from the head of the S pier, but given the absence of any further lights, night approach is only recommended with the benefit of local knowledge.

Anchorage in the approach

Anchor off the harbour entrance only in settled conditions.

Approaching Maryport

Entrance

The harbour is entered between the S pier (a concrete breakwater) and the stone-built N pier, which has timber piling at its W end. The dredged channel is approximately 25m wide. It can be found by using a transit of the N end of the Elizabeth Basin quay and the middle windows of a large, conspicuous cream-painted house at the bottom of the shipping brow. Turn towards the lock gates as they come abeam. There is a waiting berth to the E of the lock gates, although this will have less water than the entrance channel. Yachts waiting for the gates to open may anchor in the approach to the lock.

Marina facilities

Maryport Marina is a fully equipped yacht marina, with water on the pontoons and electricity supplied to most pontoons. Fuel is available from a fuelling berth, and there are showers, toilets and a launderette ashore. There is a chandlery on site, and *Calor Gas* is available. There are extensive boat and mechanical repair facilities and a yacht brokerage. VHF radio telephone watch is kept; call *Maryport Marina* Ch 37. There is a slip and hardstanding for winter storage. Provisions are available in the town. EC Wednesday ☎ 01900 814431.

Silloth

Yachts may use the outer harbour at Silloth, or, with the permission of the harbourmaster, be locked into the inner basin, although this is principally for commercial traffic and there are no facilities for yachts. The outer harbour dries to mud. The harbour maintains a listening VHF radio telephone watch from 2½ hours before HW to 1½ hours after HW; call *Silloth Harbour* Ch 16, work Ch 12. Approach must be made during the 2 hours before HW. The tidal streams run strongly, and off the harbour entrance can reach 7 knots at springs, when the channels narrow. The banks and channels are constantly shifting, and the buoys are laid for the use of the pilots and do not necessarily mark the navigable channel. Consequently, approach can only be recommended with the benefit of local knowledge. Provisions are available in the town.

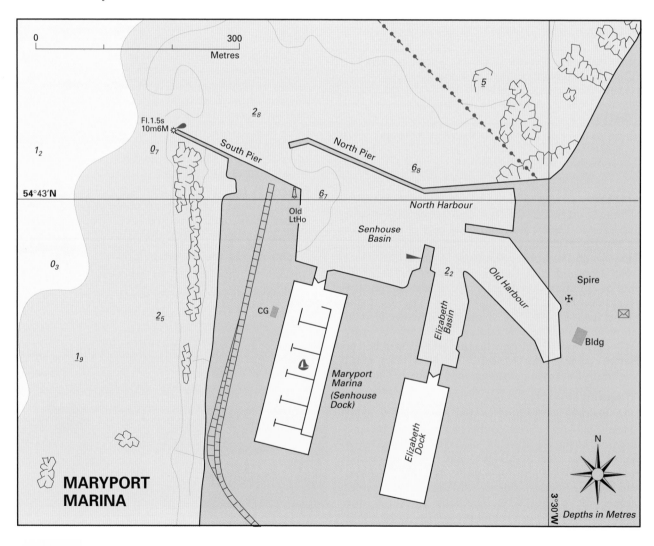

Maryport   *PRPA/Patrick Roach*

Silloth Outer harbour

IX. Solway Firth to Portpatrick

This chapter covers the Scottish coast from the shifting sandbanks of the Solway Firth, round the Mull of Galloway with its attendant races, to Portpatrick. All the harbours on the south coast of Scotland dry at low water; they are generally small, although there are anchorages in which a yacht may lie afloat. Portpatrick harbour may be entered at most states of the tide, and the outer harbour at Isle of Whithorn at any state of the tide, but not in adverse conditions. There are deep-water anchorages where limited shelter may be found in the Fleet estuary, the Dee estuary and Rough Firth.

Tides are of moderate strength, increasing round the headlands. In Luce Bay and Wigtown Bay there is a circular flow during the ebb and the flood, and there is often a slight counter-current close to the coast.

The Nith estuary

A navigable channel follows the course of the River Nith up to Kingholm Quay, one mile to the S of Dumfries. There is also a stone quay at Glencaple. Access is through the Dumfries Channel, where the banks and channels are constantly moving. The tidal streams are very strong, and the channel of the river itself is liable to change and is not buoyed. Navigation of the estuary can only be recommended with the benefit of local knowledge.

Kippford

⊕ 54°49'·65N 3°47'·9W 2 cables SE of Hestan Island lighthouse
Local High Water is +0035 Dover
Charts Admiralty *1346;* Imray *C62*

General

The popular sailing centre of Kippford lies on the E bank of Urr Water, 2½M from the entrance to the beautiful Rough Firth or Urr estuary. Wooded hills shelter this small, attractive resort. Yachts may use a rising tide to pass beyond Kippford to the former small commercial harbour at Palnackie, although the channel is not buoyed.

Warning

The estuary dries at LW, except for the river bed, which is not navigable until after half-tide. All the moorings and the new yacht club pontoon dry, so yachts must be capable of taking the ground. Tidal streams run quickly, in excess of 3 knots at springs.

Approach

By day Approach from the S or SE must be to seaward of the sandbanks of the Solway Firth, passing to the W of the Two Feet Bank W cardinal buoy. Approach from the SW will be through the Ministry of Defence firing range off Abbey Head, described below. There are no off-lying dangers except for Craig Roan, drying rocks to the S of Castle Point. Approaching from the S, Rough Island should be kept open of Castle Point to clear these rocks.

By night There is a light (Fl(2)10s42m9M) on Hestan Island, displayed from a white building. There are no other lights, and entrance should not be attempted at night.

Anchorage in the approach

Shelter may be found in the anchorages off Hestan Island whilst waiting for the tide. The anchorage close to the W of the island is exposed to winds from the S and SW. Anchorage to the NE of the island, sheltered from SW through W to N winds, should be found as close to the land as draught will allow in order to be out of the tidal stream. There is a very well sheltered anchorage, drying to soft mud, in Horse Isles Bay. A further anchorage can be found in Gibb's Hole, where shallow-draught yachts may stay afloat at LW, but the stream runs quickly and settled conditions are necessary.

Entrance

The estuary is entered to the S of Castle Point. There are stake nets off Horse Isles Bay, marked by withies, which can be cleared by keeping the lighthouse on Hestan Island open until the bay itself starts to open. Beyond Gibb's Hole to Kippford the

Kippford

126

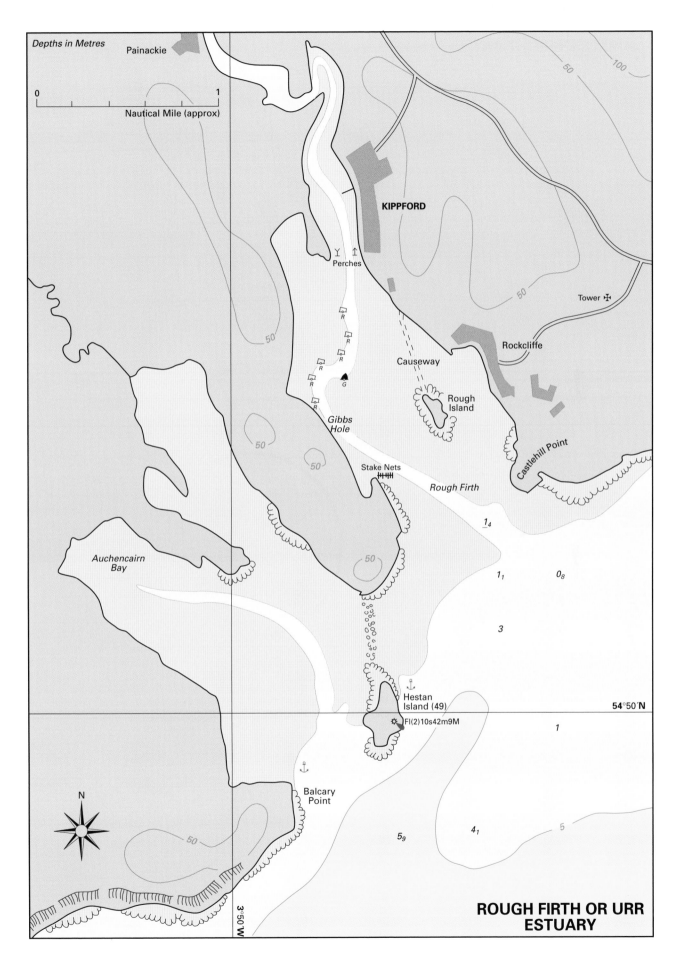

Depths in Metres

Painackie

0 ——————————————— 1

Nautical Mile (approx)

KIPPFORD

Perches

R

R

R

R

R

R

G

Gibbs
Hole

50

50

50

Stake Nets

Causeway

Rough
Island

Rockcliffe

Tower ⌖

Castlehill Point

Rough Firth

1_4

1_1 0_8

3

50

50

Auchencairn
Bay

Hestan
Island (49)

Fl(2)10s42m9M

54°50´N

1

N

Balcary
Point

5_9 4_1 5

50

3°50´W

**ROUGH FIRTH OR URR
ESTUARY**

KIRKCUDBRIGHT BAY

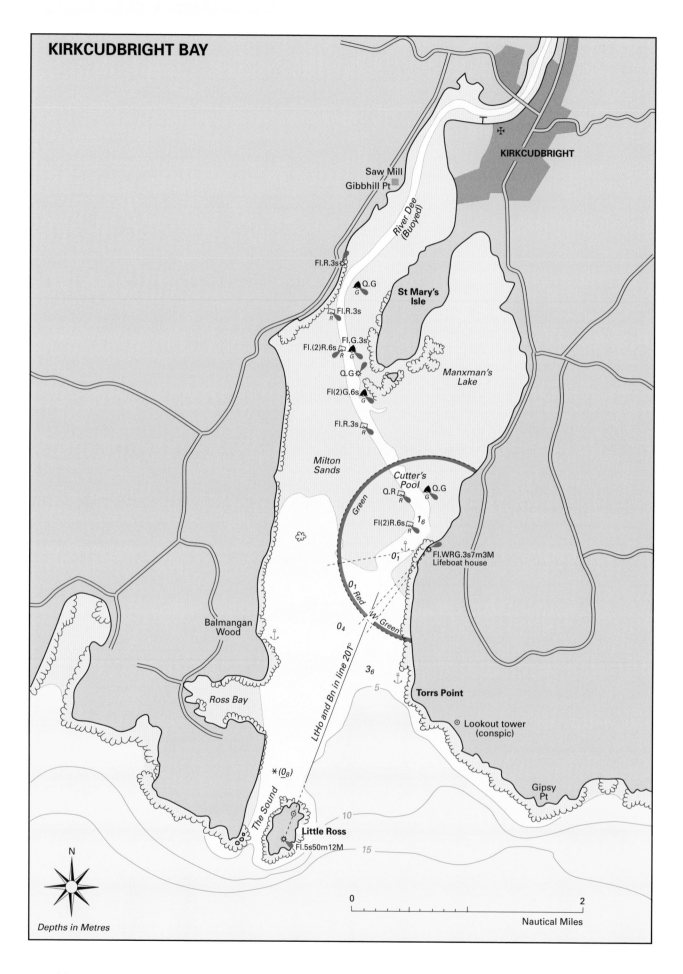

KIRKCUDBRIGHT

Saw Mill
Gibbhill Pt

River Dee
(Buoyed)

Fl.R.3s

Q.G
G

St Mary's
Isle

Fl.R.3s
R

Fl.G.3s
Fl.(2)R.6s *R* *G*

Q.G

Manxman's
Lake

Fl(2)G.6s
G

Fl.R.3s
R

Milton
Sands

Cutter's
Pool
Q.R *G* Q.G
R *G*

Green

Fl(2)R.6s 1₆
R

0₁

Fl.WRG.3s7m3M
Lifeboat house

0₁ Red W Green

Balmangan
Wood

0₄

3₆

Ross Bay

LtHo and Bn in line 201°

5

Torrs Point

⊙ Lookout tower
(conspic)

*(0₈)

Gipsy
Pt

The Sound

10

Little Ross
Fl.5s50m12M

15

N

Depths in Metres

0   2

Nautical Miles

channel is marked in the summer by buoys laid by the yacht club. The channel is subject to change and the buoys are moved accordingly. Keep to the centre of the channel on approaching the village.

Moorings

There are many private moorings laid off Kippford. A visitors' mooring may be allocated by the yacht club if required.

Berthing

Visitors should tie alongside the new yacht club pontoon. All moorings and the pontoon dry and a yacht must be capable of taking the ground.

Charges

There is a charge payable to the yacht club for the use of the pontoon.

Facilities

Fuel Marine diesel by cans from Kippford Slipway Ltd, on main street.
Water By yacht club slip.
Slip Slips by yacht club and by chandlery.
Provisions Limited provisions are available in the village.
Post office On main street.
Yacht club Solway Yacht Club. Open for toilets and showers every day throughout the season. Bar open every Saturday night throughout season.
Chandlery, boat and mechanical repairs Kippford Slipway Ltd.

Ministry of Defence firing range

A danger area extends 14 miles to the S from the four-mile-long firing range between Kirkcudbright and Abbey Head. Vessels wishing to pass through this area should liaise with the Range Safety Boat which will be on duty at firing times and then pass as close inshore as possible. Call *Kirkcudbright Range Control* Ch 16, work Ch 73.

Kirkcudbright

⊕ 54°45'·67N 4°04'·53W 4 cables SE of lighthouse on Little Ross Island
Local High Water is +0025 Dover
Charts Admiralty *1344, 1346, 2094;* Imray *C62*

General

Complete shelter can be found in the elegant county town of Kirkcudbright. Coasters and fishing boats use the town quay, although space is usually available for visiting yachts. The 16th-century McLellan's Castle, by the quay, has been partially restored and is open to the public.

Warning

The estuary dries at LW, except for the river channel, and should not be entered until after half-flood. Tidal streams can run strongly, and a favourable stream should be used when navigating the estuary. The estuary can be entered in most conditions.

Approach

By day The firing range to the E of the bay has been described above. There are no further off-lying dangers, although the tidal stream runs strongly along the coast. The sound to the W of Little Ross Island should only be used after half-tide. Richardson's Rock, on the W side of the sound, shows at HW.

By night Little Ross lighthouse shows Fl.5s50m12M from a white tower. The buoyed channel of the River Dee is well lit and entrance by night should not be a problem.

Anchorage in the approach

Anchorage whilst awaiting the tide may be found in Kirkcudbright Bay, although this is exposed to onshore winds. Anchoring in Ross Roads, close to the N end of Little Ross Island, will provide more shelter from winds from the S or SW. A well sheltered drying anchorage may be found in Ross Bay, sheltered from all winds except those from the E; the anchorage dries to sand and mud. At the entrance to the channel there is a depth of 0·1m over the bar. If there is sufficient water over the bar for a yacht to reach the lifeboat slip, then anchorage may be found in this area, away from the end of the slip itself.

Entrance

The white tower of the lighthouse on Little Ross Island and the pyramidal beacon on the N side of the island are leading marks which when in line astern on a bearing of 201° will lead to the bar. The channel passes close to the lifeboat house on the E bank of the bay. This is a light brown, rendered building which may be difficult to locate when approaching from the SW. There are two white flagstaffs attached to the S side of the building which should help identification. The remainder of the

Leading marks, Little Ross Island

Kirkcudbright   *PRPA/Patrick Roach*

channel to the town is marked with easily identified lateral buoys and perches.

Moorings

There are private and visitors' moorings, which mostly dry, laid in the channel off the town. Moorings may be allocated to visiting yachts by the harbourmaster if required.

Berthing

As directed by the harbourmaster. The town quay dries to soft mud, and visiting yachts can usually be accommodated alongside. There is 1m at LW at the floating pontoon which is only for landing and short stay use, whilst there is between 1m and 3m at LW at the pile moorings. The ebb may run strongly if excessive rainfall leads to the sluice gates of the upstream power station being opened.

Mooring pontoons were extended in 2001 to provide an additional 50 berths, 25 of which have been allocated for visitors. Toilets and showers are available ashore and water and electricity provided on the pontoons.

Harbourmaster

Office on quay ☎ 01557 331135.

Kirkcudbright

Charges

There are harbour charges.

VHF radio telephone

Call *Kirkcudbright Harbour* Ch 16, work Ch 12.

Facilities

Fuel Contact harbourmaster for supply.
Water Taps on town quay and on pontoons.
Slip At W end of town quay.
Provisions Full provisions are available in the town. EC Thursday.
Post office In square overlooking town quay.
Yacht club Kirkcudbright Sailing Club.

The Fleet estuary

There are attractive anchorages with limited shelter off the Islands of Fleet at the mouth of Fleet Bay. The islands are National Trust for Scotland property and are home to colonies of seabirds.

The anchorage to the NW of Ardwall Island, in 3m mud, is sheltered from all winds except those

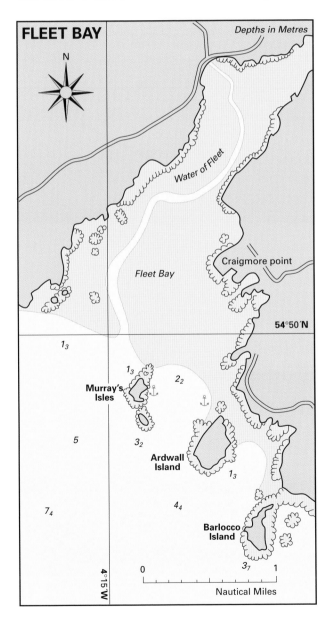

from the S to W. To the N of the island complete shelter can be found for yachts that can take the ground (the anchorage dries to soft mud).

The anchorage to the E of the main island of Murray's Isles, in the bay below the ruined cottages, is exposed to the S. There is good holding in the anchorages.

Garlieston

⊕ 54°47'·0N 4°20'·9W ½M SE of end of pier
Local High Water is +0035 Dover
Charts Admiralty *2094*; Imray *C62*

General

Garlieston is a neat, small town on the W side of Wigtown Bay, offering good shelter in the drying inner harbour. Some commercial vessels and a small fishing fleet operate from the harbour.

Warning

The approach bay to the harbour dries, and entrance should only be made between 2½ hours either side of HW. Approach is not recommended in strong SE winds.

Approach

By day The harbour lies at the head of a ½M-wide inlet to the W of Eggerness Point. The pole carrying the lights on the end of the concrete pier must be identified. There is a rocky reef to the S of Eggerness Point, and there are further rock outcrops on the W side of the bay. Approach should be made on a course of 295° from at least ½M out from the pierhead.

By night The lights (2F.R(vert)8m3M) on the end of the pier must be located when making a night entry. Approaching from the S, the lights of the town will not be visible until the harbour is open; this makes the pier lights easy to identify.

Anchorage in the approach

Anchorage may be found in moderate holding ground ½M SE of the pier light. The anchorage is exposed to winds from the S and SE.

Entrance

The harbour is entered by leaving the concrete pierhead to port after approaching on a course of 295°.

Moorings

There are a few private small-boat moorings.

Berthing

Yachts should tie up alongside the quay, where there are good ladders. On the N-facing quay to the E of the slip the river has cut steep-to banks some 6m away from the quay, and these banks continue 8m away from the W-facing quay. There are outfall pipes and isolated rock patches within the harbour, and yachts should not attempt to anchor.

Harbourmaster

Lives in town and will visit yachts.

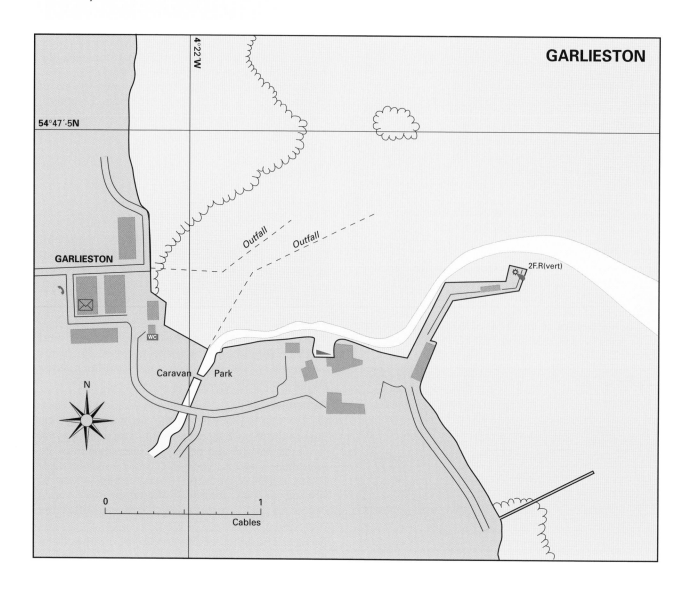

GARLIESTON

Charges

There are harbour charges.

Facilities

Water Tap on quay.

Slip On N-facing quay by warehouse.

Provisions Provisions are available in the town. EC Wednesday.

Post office In the town.

Calor Gas From caravan park on road into town.

The harbour, Garlieston

Isle of Whithorn

⊕ 54°41'·3N 4°21'·35W ½M SSE of St Ninian's
  Tower
Local High Water is +0035 Dover
Charts Admiralty *2094*; Imray *C62*

General

A popular and convenient port for yachtsmen, as the outer harbour can be entered at any time, although it is exposed to onshore winds. There is good shelter in the drying inner harbour.

Warning

The inner harbour dries, and can only be entered after half-tide. The outer harbour can be entered at any state of the tide, but is exposed to onshore winds, which will bring in an uncomfortable sea. Entrance can be made in most conditions, particularly at HW, but is inadvisable in strong onshore winds.

Approach

By day There is a radio mast that is conspicuous from all directions 2M to the W of the harbour. St Ninian's Tower is a white square tower on the promontory to the E of the harbour, close to the ruins of the 13th-century St Ninian's Chapel.

By night The leading lights are Oc.R.8s7m7M and Oc.R.8s9m7M on a bearing of 335°. The pierhead light is Q.G.4m5M.

Leading marks Isle of Whithorn

Entrance

The harbour is entered to the W of the promontory on which is situated St Ninian's Tower. Rocks extend a short distance W from this promontory, and there is a larger reef of rocks extending E from the mainland to the W of the entrance. This reef was formerly marked by an iron perch which is no longer in place. It is essential to identify the leading marks on a bearing of 335°; this course will avoid the off-lying dangers. The marks are conspicuous Dayglo orange diamonds on poles in a field on the W side of the harbour. The tidal stream sets strongly across the harbour entrance and must be allowed for, taking particular care not to be set on to the rocks at the harbour entrance.

Moorings

There are drying moorings in the inner harbour; these may be allocated to visitors by the harbourmaster.

Berthing

Visitors' alongside berths are marked on the quay at the root of the pier, where there are good ladders. Anchoring is not allowed in the inner harbour.

Harbourmaster

At McWilliam's Stores, in NE corner of harbour. There are harbour charges.

Facilities

Fuel By can from John's Petrol, in NE corner of harbour.
Water Tap on quay.
Slip In inner harbour.
Provisions Provisions are available in the village. EC Thursday.
Post office NW corner of harbour.
Yacht club Wigtown Bay Sailing Club. Showers.
Chandlery Rowley Marine, on road at N end of the harbour. Rowley Marine also have launderette facilities.

Conspicuous white tower to east of entrance, Isle of Whithorn

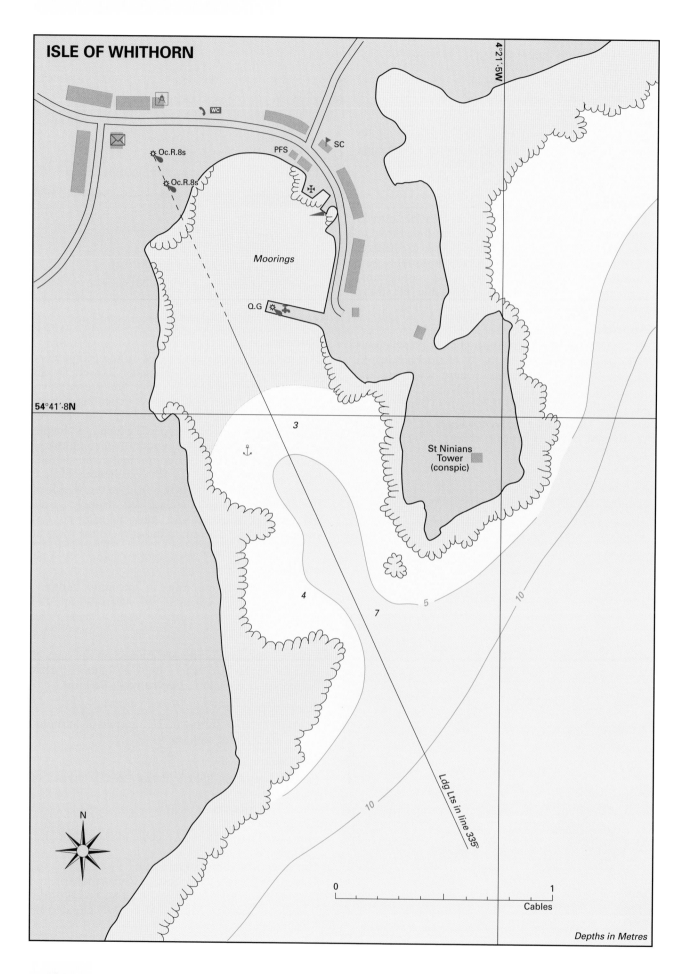

ISLE OF WHITHORN

4°21'·5W

Oc.R.8s

Oc.R.8s

WC

PFS

SC

Moorings

Q.G

54°41'·8N

3

4

7

St Ninians
Tower
(conspic)

5

10

10

Ldg Lts in line 335°

N

0   1
Cables

Depths in Metres

Burrow Head

The headland is a prominent steep cliff off which tidal streams run strongly. The E-going stream begins at +0430 Dover and the W-going stream at −0130 Dover. The spring rate is about 4 knots in both directions. A heavy race builds up off the headland, especially when the W-going stream is against a strong W wind. The race can be avoided by keeping well inshore, or well offshore into the Firth.

Port William

⊕ 54°45'·65N 4°35'·9W 4 cables W of harbour entrance
Local High Water is +0015 Dover
Charts Admiralty *2094;* Imray *C62*

General

A small drying harbour on the E side of Luce Bay where reasonable shelter may be found. The harbour is formed by a dog-leg quay which is protected by a stone causeway on its NW side.

Warning

The harbour dries, and can only be entered for 2½ hours either side of HW. There is more water in the outer harbour, and a further wait may be necessary before moving up into the inner harbour. The inner harbour is well sheltered, while a swell enters the outer harbour with strong onshore winds. Entrance to the harbour should not be attempted in strong onshore winds. Space is limited within the harbour.

Approach

By day The harbour is the only one on the E side of Luce Bay; the pier with its flagstaff is easily identified. There are rocks close inshore to the S of the entrance; approach, from about ½M offshore, should be in an E direction.

By night A night approach should not be attempted without local knowledge. The following lights will assist such an approach:
Ldg Lts 105° *Front* Pier head Fl.G.3s7m3M
Rear 130m from head F.G.10m2M

Anchorage in the approach

Anchorage may be found off the harbour entrance in 5m stones and mud, although this area is exposed from S through W to NW. Temporary anchorage may be found in Back Bay or Monreith Bay, to the S of the harbour entrance. These bays are also exposed to onshore winds.

Entrance

The harbour has a narrow entrance between the concrete pier and the stone causeway, the end of which is marked by a perch. Enter close to the pier, as a shingle bank tends to build up close to the perch.

Moorings

There are some private small-boat moorings in the NE part of the harbour.

Entrance to harbour, Port William

Berthing

Yachts should tie up alongside the quay of the inner harbour, which dries to soft mud. Anchoring is possible close to the slip on the NE side of the harbour, which dries to muddy clay, but space is limited.

Harbourmaster

Office on quay.

Charges

There are harbour charges.

Facilities

Fuel By arrangement with the harbourmaster.
Water Tap at toilets in the square.
Slip On NE and SE sides of harbour.
Provisions Provisions are available in the village. EC Thursday.
Post office On Main Street.
Calor Gas and Camping Gaz Dewar's, in main square.

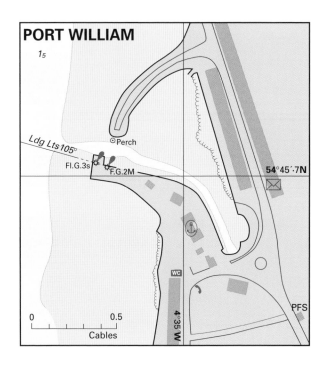

Drummore

⊕ 54°41'·5N 4°51'·6W one mile E of harbour entrance
Local High Water is +0015 Dover
Charts Admiralty *2094*; Imray *C62*

General

Scotland's southernmost village has a drying harbour, offering good shelter. It is a convenient spot in which to wait for the tide or suitable weather when planning to round the Mull of Galloway.

Warning

The harbour dries, and can only be entered for 2½ hours either side of HW. Levels of silting in the harbour can vary, and the harbour should not be used by deep-draught yachts.

Approach

By day The harbour lies 3½M to the N of the Mull of Galloway. The Scares are a group of unlit rocks 6½M to the ESE of the harbour; they are home to a colony of gannets. Luce Bay is used as a bombing range by the Royal Aircraft Establishment.

By night The harbour is unlit, and should not be approached at night.

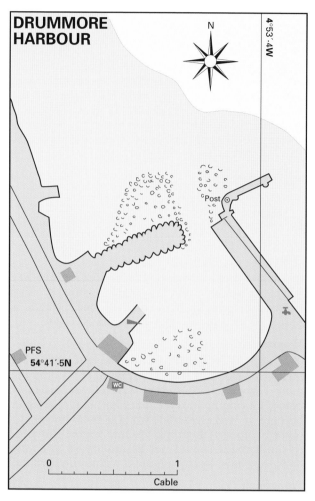

Anchorage in the approach

Anchorage may be found in 3m off the harbour entrance, although this area is exposed to winds from the N through E to S.

Entrance

The harbour is entered leaving the concrete pier to port and the loose stone breakwater to starboard; the deepest water is to be found close to the pier. There are shingle banks to the N of the stone causeway and from the end of the pier. Final approach should be made from the NW on a course of 140°.

Moorings

There are some private small-boat moorings close to the stone causeway.

Berthing

Visiting yachts may lie alongside the pier, although the ladders are poor. There is good shelter; the harbour dries to soft mud.

Harbourmaster

No harbourmaster, and no harbour charges.

Facilities

Water Tap at root of pier.
Slip On S side of harbour.

Drummore harbour   *PRPA/Patrick Roach*

1½ hours either side of HW, leaving the breakwater at least 50m to starboard to clear the loose rocks at its extremity. There are no facilities for yachts.

Drummore harbour

Provisions Available in the village. EC Thursday.
Yacht club Kirkmaiden Boating Club.

East Tarbet Bay

Anchorage may be found in the bay when waiting for the tide or suitable weather to round the Mull of Galloway. Anchor in 6m sand 8 cables WNW of the lighthouse, off the little jetty on the beach. Good shelter is to be found from the W or SW, although the race can extend for some distance to the NE of the Mull on the E-going stream and (especially in unsettled conditions) make the approach to the bay difficult.

Mull of Galloway

A bold headland rising to 82m that is steep-to on its S and W sides. The light (Fl.20s99m28M) is shown from a white tower near the SE extremity of the headland. A heavy race extends for 3M off the Mull, SW and W during the W-going stream and NNE during the E-going stream. The race can be dangerous to yachts, especially when there is a contrary wind.

To make passage round the Mull, a yacht must arrive at slack water and pass either close inshore or several miles offshore in order to avoid the race. Tidal streams can reach 4·5 knots at springs. The E-going stream begins at −0545 Dover and the W-going stream at +0020 Dover. There is a further race off Crammag Head, 3M to the NW of the Mull; this is at its worst on the flood when the wind is from the S. In these circumstances the race must be given a wide berth.

Port Logan

An attractive small village 4M N of Crammag Head that was abandoned as a port in the 19th century. There is a temporary anchorage off the breakwater in 6m, exposed to winds from the S and W. Additional shelter may be found, for yachts that can take the ground, behind the breakwater that extends for 180m from the S side of the bay. Enter between

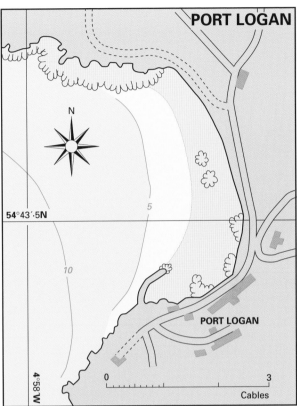

PORT LOGAN

54°43'·5N

4°58'W

PORT LOGAN

Cables

Portpatrick

⊕ 54°50'·0N 5°08'·0W 7 cables SW of the harbour entrance
Local High Water is +0030 Dover
Charts Admiralty *2198*; Imray *C62*

General

This popular cruising port was once the main ferry port for the short crossing to Northern Ireland, until a series of accidents resulted in the service being transferred to Stranraer in 1862. The harbour can be entered at most states of the tide, and good shelter can be found in the inner harbour.

Warning

The harbour can be entered at most states of the tide, but deep-keel yachts should not enter at LW if there is a swell running into the harbour. Strong tidal streams run across the entrance, and an approach should not be attempted in fresh to strong onshore winds.

Approach

By day The harbour is 2M S of the white tower of Kilantrigan lighthouse. There is a conspicuous radio mast to the E of the harbour. Approaching from the S or W, the large hotel above and to the N of the harbour is conspicuous.

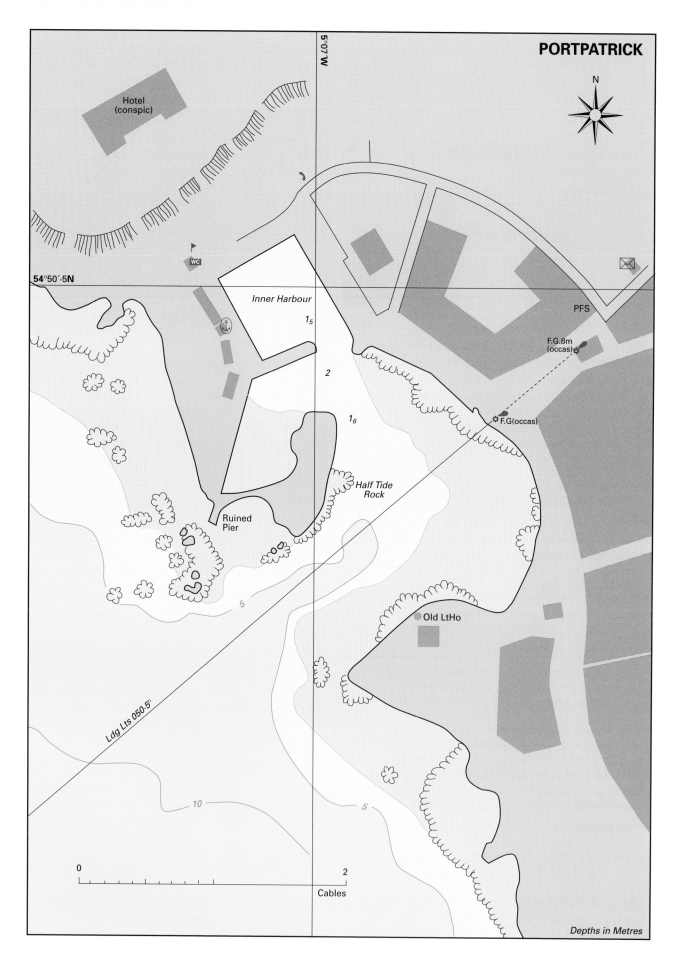

PORTPATRICK

N

Hotel
(conspic)

WC

54°50′·5N

5°07′W

Inner Harbour

1₅

2

1₆

PFS

F.G.8m
(occas)

F.G (occas)

Half Tide
Rock

Ruined
Pier

Old LtHo

5

Ldg Lts 050·5°

10

5

0   2

Cables

Depths in Metres

By night Kilantrigan lighthouse (Fl(2)15s49m25M) is 2M to the N of the harbour. There are leading lights on a bearing of 050·5°; the front light (F.G) is on the sea wall and the rear light (F.G.8m) on a building in the small square.

Entrance

Entrance is made between the ruined N and S piers. There is a disused lighthouse on the S quay. Rocks shoal from the S shore, and there are isolated rocks off the N shore. It is necessary to identify the leading marks on a bearing of 050·5°. The front mark is a painted orange stripe on the sea wall, below the orange pole carrying the front leading light; the rear mark is also an orange stripe, painted at eaves level on the left-hand side of the three-windowed gable of the building in the small square. Once inside the entrance, the barrel marking Half Tide Rock should be identified and left close to port. Turn for the inner harbour as soon as the entrance opens.

Moorings

There are private small-boat moorings in the shallow bay to the W of the inner harbour entrance.

Berthing

Visitors should moor alongside the N wall or the N part of the E wall in the inner harbour.

Harbourmaster

Office on the quay.

Portpatrick harbour and conspicuous hotel

Facilities

Fuel By can from Portpatrick Filling Station, off Main Street.

Water Tap on quay in inner harbour.

Slip From S side of bay onto shingle beach, for small craft only.

Provisions Provisions are available in the village. EC Thursday.

Post office On Main Street.

Calor Gas Portpatrick Filling Station.

Portpatrick harbour   *PRPA/Patrick Roach*

X. Isle of Man

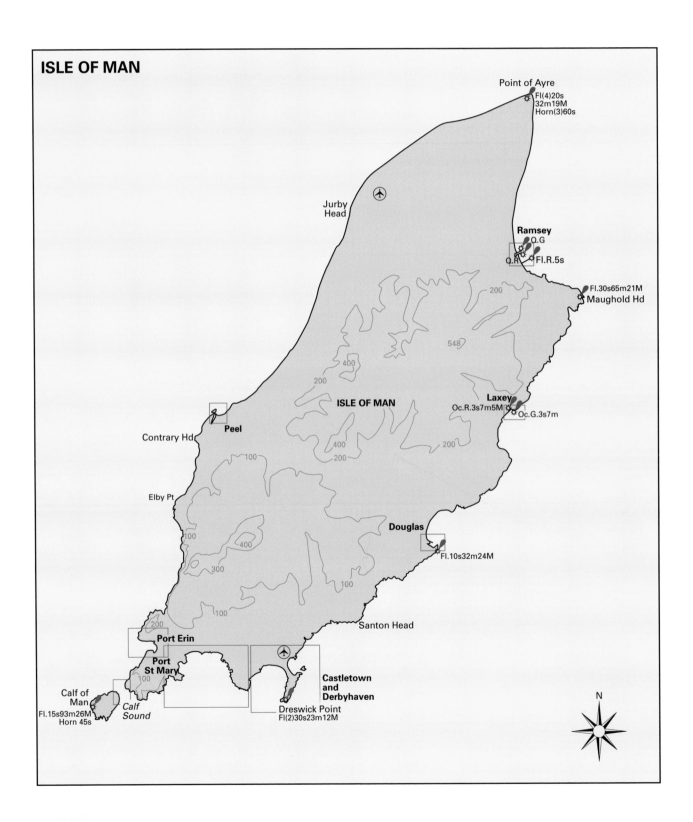

ISLE OF MAN

Point of Ayre
Fl(4)20s
32m19M
Horn(3)60s

Jurby
Head

Ramsey
Q.G
Q.R · Fl.R.5s

Fl.30s65m21M
Maughold Hd

200

548

ISLE OF MAN

Laxey
Oc.R.3s7m5M
Oc.G.3s7m

Peel

Contrary Hd

400

200

100

Elby Pt

100

400

Douglas

200

Fl.10s32m24M

400

300

100

Santon Head

100

200

Port Erin

Port
St Mary

100

Castletown
and
Derbyhaven

Calf of
Man
Fl.15s93m26M
Horn 45s

Calf
Sound

Dreswick Point
Fl(2)30s23m12M

N

By virtue of its position in the middle of the N Irish Sea, the Isle of Man not only provides an excellent cruising ground in its own right, but is also a useful resting point for yachtsmen crossing the Irish Sea, allowing full use to be made of the tidal streams.

The tidal streams around the island are complex. The streams to the W and NE of the island are controlled by the flow through the North Channel; on the flood the streams divide in NE and S directions at Contrary Head, to the S of Peel. The streams to the S and SE of the island are controlled by the flow through St George's Channel. The streams meet on the E side of the island at Maughold Head, to the S of Ramsey. The streams on the E side of the island are stronger than those on the W side, and run strongly round the headlands, particularly at the Point of Ayre, Langness Point and the Calf of Man.

There are ports of refuge at Douglas and Port St Mary which give fair shelter and can be entered in most conditions. The outer harbours at Peel and Port Erin can both be entered at any state of the tide, but provide only limited shelter.

The harbours are generally well maintained, and the harbourmasters are invariably accommodating to visiting yachtsmen.

Port St Mary

⊕ 54°03'·6N 4°43'·22W 8 cables SSE of head of outer breakwater
Local High Water is +0020 Dover
Charts Admiralty *2696, 2094*; Imray *Y70, C62*

General

A busy fishing port and popular yachting centre on the W side of Bay ny Carrickey. The drying inner harbour offers good shelter for yachts that can take the ground; the outer harbour and anchorage are subject to swell in strong E or SE winds.

Warning

The inner harbour dries to firm sand, and can only be entered for 3 hours either side of HW. Strong S winds make entrance difficult.

Approach

By day The harbour lies 2M ENE of Spanish Head and 4M WNW of Langness Point. There is a conspicuous TV mast (133m) above the town. The Carrick is a rock drying to 4·3m in the middle of Bay ny Carrickey, marked with an iron tripod beacon, and should be left to starboard on the approach. There are rocky ledges extending to the S of Kallow Point and the outer pier; these may be cleared by keeping at least 2 cables offshore when approaching from the SW. Tidal streams run strongly off the harbour and must be allowed for in the approach.

Port St Mary   *PRPA/Patrick Roach*

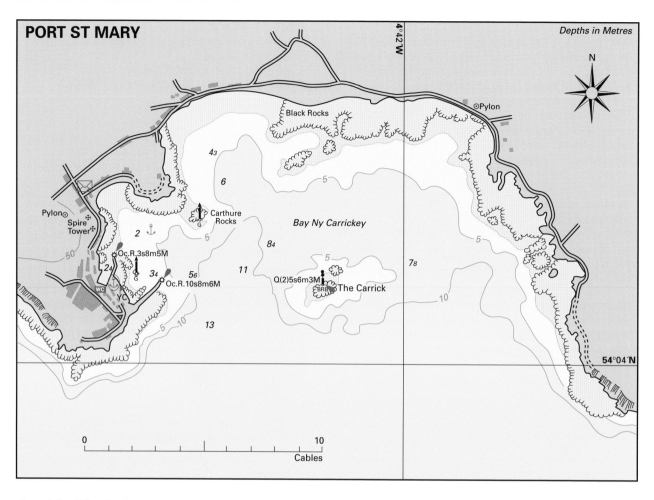

PORT ST MARY

Depths in Metres

Black Rocks

Pylon

⊙Pylon

43

6

5

Carthure Rocks

Bay Ny Carrickey

Pylon⊙

Spire Tower

2

5

84

Oc.R.3s8m5M

24

34

56

11

Oc.R.10s8m6M

Q(2)5s6m3M

The Carrick

78

YC

WG

5

10

13

5

10

10

54°04′N

0   10
Cables

By night The harbour can be approached and entered using the following lights:

Chicken Rock LtHo Fl.5s38m13M Horn 60s
Calf of Man LtHo Fl.15s93m26M Horn 45s
Dreswick Point Fl(2)30s23m12M
The Carrick Q(2)5s6m3M
Port St Mary outer pier Oc.R.10s8m6M
Port St Mary inner pier Oc.R.3s8m5M
The light on The Carrick can be difficult to identify.
Keeping the lights of the outer and inner piers in line
on a bearing of 301° leaves The Carrick to the NE.

Entrance

The harbour is entered between The Carrick and the outer pier. A drying rocky shoal extends from the shore within the outer harbour and close to the outer pier, marked at its seaward end with a green perch with a triangular topmark. This must be left to starboard when berthing at the root of the outer pier.

Moorings

There are private moorings laid in the inner harbour and off Gansey Point, and private drying moorings in the inner harbour. There are visitors' moorings laid off Gansey Point, the red buoys being capable of taking yachts of up to 5 tons and the white buoy of taking a yacht of up to 10 tons. These buoys should be used as directed by the harbourmaster. Yachts may anchor off Gansey Point close to the laid moorings, although the holding is indifferent

due to the number of stone patches and the quantity of kelp.

Berthing

Alongside berths may be found as directed by the harbourmaster. Yachts that wish to stay afloat may moor alongside the root of the outer pier; the remainder of the pier is used by the fishing fleet. Yachts that can take the ground can find complete shelter in the inner harbour, although space is limited.

Approaching Port St Mary

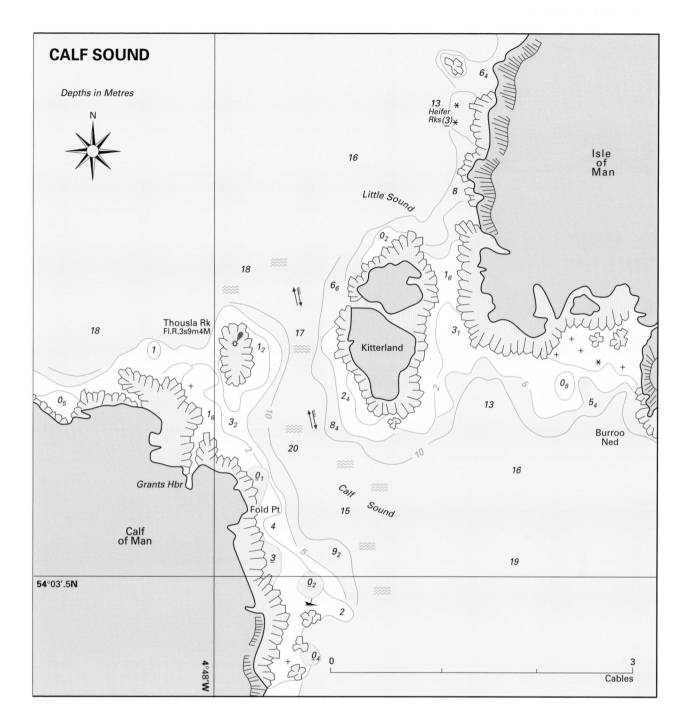

CALF SOUND

Depths in Metres

Harbourmaster

Office at root of inner pier.

Charges

There are harbour charges.

VHF radio telephone

Call *Port St Mary Harbour* Ch 16, work Ch 12 ☎ 01624 833205.

Facilities

Fuel Contact harbourmaster.
Water Taps on inner and outer piers.
Slip On W side of outer harbour.
Provisions Provisions are available in town. EC Thursday.

Post office On Bay View Road, on N side of town.
Yacht club Isle of Man Yacht Club. Bar and showers.
Calor Gas Manx Gas Service Centre or the Fishermen's Association.
Chandlery Limited chandlery from the Fishermen's Association.
Marine engineers Ballasalla Marine and Auto Engineers.

Calf Sound

Given the right weather conditions and a favourable tide, the sound provides a convenient daytime short cut round the SW corner of the island. In bad weather or at night, a yacht must pass well S of the Calf of Man and Chicken Rock to avoid the tidal

Calf Sound looking south

race. The passage between the Calf and Chicken Rock should only be used with settled weather and a favourable tide.

Calf Sound lies between Thoulsa Rock, clearly marked with a white round beacon, and Kitterland, a low, barren, grass-covered island. The other passages, Little Sound to the E of Kitterland and the passage to the W of Thoulsa Rock, should only be used with local knowledge.

The N-going tidal stream begins at −0130 Dover and the S-going stream at +0400 Dover. The stream runs strongly, at up to 4 knots at springs, and the sound should not be attempted with a strong contrary wind against the tide. There are overfalls to the N and S of the sound; the worst of these can be avoided by keeping to the E side of the disturbed water once clear of Kitterland.

Port Erin

⊕ 54°05'·3N 4°46'·92W 4 cables WNW of green buoy at head of ruined breakwater
Local High Water is +0020 Dover
Charts Admiralty *2696, 2094*; Imray *Y70, C62*

General

An attractive holiday resort at the head of a bay sheltered by two headlands. The outer breakwater protecting the harbour was destroyed by a storm in 1884, and as a consequence protection is limited in onshore winds.

Warning

The harbour is exposed to winds from SW to NW, although some additional shelter may be found in the small drying harbour to the E of Raglan Pier.

Approach

By day The approach from the S, through Calf Sound or to seaward of the Calf of Man, has been described above. Milner's Tower is a dark, square tower standing at an elevation of 131m on Bradda Head, to the N of the bay; it is conspicuous when approaching from the S or W.

Calf Sound   *PRPA/Patrick Roach*

Bradda Head

Approaching Port Erin

By night The harbour may be approached and entered using the following lights:

Chicken Rock LtHo Fl.5s38m13M Horn 60s
Calf of Man LtHo Fl.15s93m26M Horn 45s
Raglan Pier Oc.G.5s8m5M
Port Erin Ldg Lts 099·1° *Front* F.R.10m5M
   Rear F.R.19m5M
   The leading lights are in line on a bearing of 099·1°, which will clear the unlit green buoy marking the extremity of the ruined breakwater.

Entrance

The harbour is entered to the S of Bradda Head. The leading lights are displayed from a white, round light tower with a red band, situated above the beach in the centre of the bay, and a white pole with a red band on the promenade above. There is a white triangle painted on the cliff face below the rear mark. The leading marks are in line on a bearing of 099·1°. On a daytime approach the marks are not as important as they are at night, so long as the green

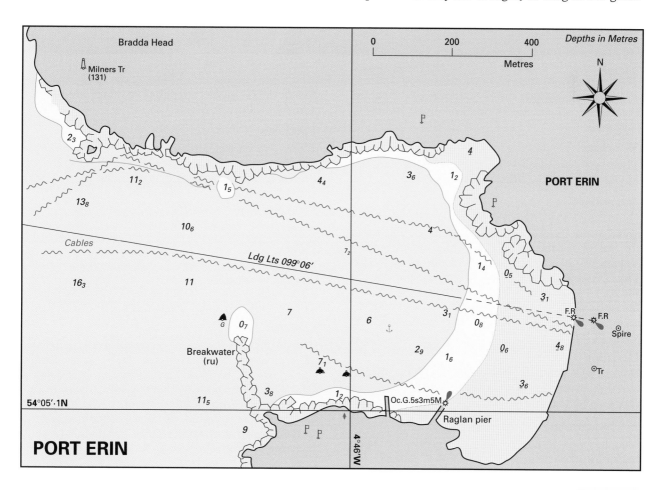

PORT ERIN

Port Erin   *PRPA/Patrick Roach*

conical buoy marking the N extremity of the ruined breakwater can be identified. This must be left to starboard.

Moorings

There are two black visitors' buoys lying between Raglan Pier and the lifeboat slipway.

Anchorage

Good anchorage may be found in 3m sand and gravel to the N of Raglan Pier, taking care to avoid the line of the telegraph cable which runs from the beacon on the shore, passing ½ cable N of Raglan Pier. Dinghies going ashore may use Raglan Pier or the jetty to the W of the pier. Note that the head of the jetty is covered at HW. Yachts that can take the ground can find additional shelter by anchoring to the E of Raglan Pier.

Berthing

Yachts that can take the ground may be able to berth alongside Raglan Pier, but this space is usually taken up by local fishing boats.

Harbourmaster

The harbour is controlled by the Port St Mary harbourmaster, who visits once a day. Charges are levied; VHF radio telephone contact should be made with Port St Mary.

Facilities

Water Tap on Raglan Pier.
Slip To the E of Raglan Pier.
Provisions Full provisions may be found in the town. EC Thursday.
Post office In town centre.

Peel

⊕ 54°13'·83N 4°42'·05W 3 cables NW of head of outer breakwater
Local High Water is +0010 Dover
Charts Admiralty *2696, 2094*; Imray *Y70, C62*

General

The harbour of this tourist resort and fishing port is at the mouth of the River Neb. Peel Castle dominates the harbour from its site on St Patrick's Isle. The castle, whose main walls date back to the 14th century, houses the ruins of the 13th-century St German's Cathedral. St Patrick's Isle is an island in name only; it is connected to the mainland, and provides the harbour with good shelter from the W.

Warning

The inner harbour mostly dries, and can only be entered for 2½ hours either side of HW. The outer harbour is exposed to winds from the NW to NE, when swell can also enter the inner harbour. Entrance to the harbour should not be attempted in strong NW to NE winds.

Approach

By day Corrin's Folly is a conspicuous square stone tower standing at an elevation of 150m at the summit of Contrary Head, 1M to the S of the harbour. Peel Castle, on St Patrick's Isle, is conspicuous on the approach. Rocks shoal for a short distance N of St Patrick's Isle, and must be cleared on the approach from the SW.

By night The harbour can be approached and entered at night using the following lights:

Peel outer breakwater head Oc.7s11m5M Bell(4)12s
The Groyne head Oc.R.2s4m
Castle Jetty Oc.G.7s5m4M
East Quay Oc.R.7s8m5M

Entrance

The harbour is entered to the N of the outer breakwater, which has a white light tower at its head. The inner harbour is entered between Castle Jetty and East Quay. Castle Jetty extends a short distance from the E side of St Patrick's Isle, and has a white light tower with green bands. East Quay has

Approaching Peel

a white light tower with a red band, over an office building at the N end of the quay. The Groyne runs 150m NE from near the outer end of East Quay, with its extremity marked by a black and white beacon; it must be left to port. There is deeper water along the bed of the River Neb, close to the W quay in the inner harbour.

Moorings

There are three red visitors' mooring buoys in line one cable NE of the Groyne; these are marked 'at your own risk'!

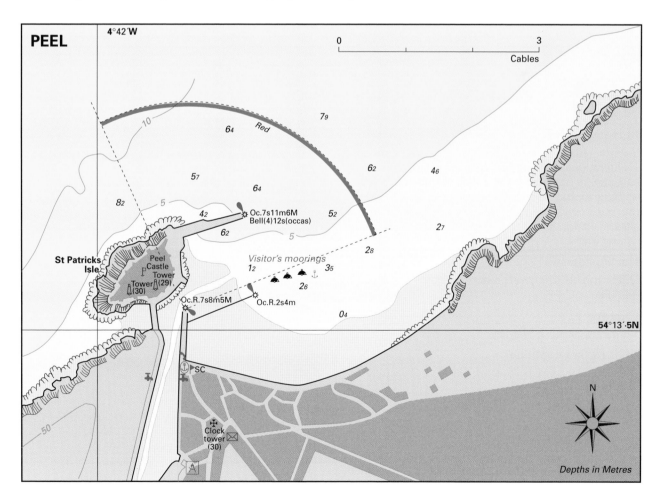

PEEL

4°42'W

0 ··· 3
Cables

10
79
64 Red
62
57 46
64
82 5
42 Oc.7s11m6M
52 Bell(4)12s(occas)
62 27
5
28
St Patricks
Isle
Visitor's moorings
Peel
Castle 12 35
Tower 26
Tower (29)
(30) Oc.R.2s4m
Oc.R.7s8m5M 04
54°13'·5N
SC
N
Clock
tower
(30)
Depths in Metres

Peel   *PRPA/Patrick Roach*

Anchorage

Anchor in 3m sand close to the visitors' moorings, keeping clear of the head of the outer breakwater.

Berthing

Yachts that can take the ground can be accommodated alongside the quays in the inner harbour, as directed by the harbourmaster. Yachts wishing to stay afloat may be able to lie alongside the outer end of the breakwater, where there is always water; however, priority is always given to fishing boats.

Harbourmaster

Office on E quay of inner harbour ☎ 01624 842338.

Charges

There are harbour charges.

VHF radio telephone

Call *Peel Harbour* Ch 16, work Ch 12, between 0830 and 1630.

Facilities

Fuel Contact harbourmaster to arrange supply.
Water Taps on quays of inner harbour.
Slip Cobbled slip on W quay of inner harbour. Slip on E quay only by arrangement with the harbourmaster.

Provisions Full provisions are available in the town. EC Thursday.
Post office In town centre.
Yacht club Peel Sailing and Cruising Club. Showers are available at the club; the key, for which there is a nominal charge, is obtained from the harbourmaster.
Calor Gas Manx Gas Service Centre.

Rounding Peel breakwater

Peel inner harbour at low water

Chandlery Fishermen's Association, Station Place.
Electricity Electricity is available on the quay if needed for repair or in an emergency; contact the Fishermen's Association.

Jurby Head

There is an active bombing range off Jurby Head. Yachts are advised to pass well to seaward of the yellow buoys and lights, or to pass inshore, keeping between ½M and 1M off the headland and passing close to Jurby Rock. There is 3·5m over Jurby Rock at MLWS.

Point of Ayre

The Point of Ayre is the N extremity of the island, and lies at the N end of a low-lying plain. The High Light (Fl(4)20s32m19M) is shown from a white tower with two red bands, situated ¼M SW of the point; the Low Light (Fl.3s10m8M) is shown from a tower with the upper part red and the lower part white, 2 cables NE of the High Light.

There are dangerous shoals off the point: to the NW the Strunakill Bank, with a least depth of 5·5m; to the E the Ballacash Bank, with a least depth of 2·4m, and the King William Bank, with a least depth of 3·7m; and to the SE the Whitestone Bank, with a least depth of 0·6m, and the Bahama Bank, with a least depth of 1·5m. The sea can break heavily over all the banks in bad weather.

Tidal streams around the point can reach 3·5 knots at springs. The E-going stream begins at +0600 Dover and the W-going stream at −0015 Dover. During the W-going stream an eddy forms W of the point, resulting in the tide running nearly continuously E between the point and Strunakill Bank. A race forms off the point when the eddy meets the W-going stream. To the SE of the point, the E-going stream forms an eddy which causes a race when the eddy stream meets the tidal stream.

Strong contrary winds can create heavy seas off the point and on the off-lying banks. Ideally, a yacht should try to round the point at slack water.

Ramsey

⊕ 54°19'·5N 4°21'·9W 3 cables ENE of harbour entrance
Local High Water is +0020 Dover
Charts Admiralty *2696, 2094*; Imray *Y70, C62*

General

Set in the centre of the long sweep of Ramsey Bay, the harbour of this popular yachting centre and commercial and fishing port is at the mouth of Sulby River. Queen's Pier, to the S of the harbour entrance, was originally built for excursion steamers, but has since been condemned. It offers no shelter, and is in the slow process of being demolished. There is a proposal for a half-tide 160-berth yacht marina to be located in the N basin above the swing bridge.

Warning

The harbour mostly dries, and can only be entered between 2½ hours before and 2 hours after HW. The inner harbour is well sheltered, although a swell comes in through the harbour entrance in strong onshore winds. Entrance should not be attempted in strong E winds.

Approach

By day The harbour lies at the transition point between the low-lying plain to the N and the cliffs which run S along the remainder of the E coast. The ten-storey block of flats immediately to the S of the harbour entrance is conspicuous. Approach from the N should be close inshore to avoid Whitestone Bank.

By night The harbour can be approached and entered using the following lights:

Maughold Head Fl(3)30s65m21M
Ramsey North Pier Q.G.9m10M
Ramsey South Pier Q.R.8m10M
Root 2F.R(vert)
Queen's Pier buoy Fl.R.5s
Dolphin Iso.G.4s
Swing bridge 2F.R(hor)

Approaching Ramsey harbour

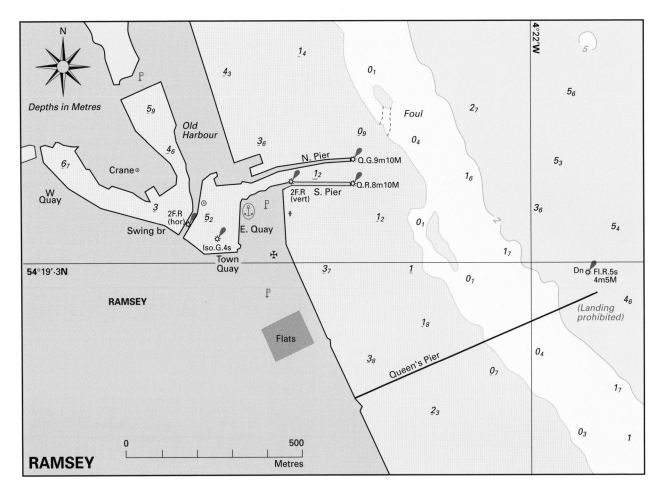

RAMSEY

Anchorage in the approach

Anchorage may be found in 4m sand to the N of the end of the derelict Queen's Pier in settled conditions or offshore winds. Landing on Queen's Pier is prohibited; dinghies should be taken to the steps inside the E end of the South Pier.

Entrance

The harbour is entered between the North and South Piers. Tidal streams can run quickly, invariably in a N direction, off the entrance, and must be allowed for in the approach. Both piers have white light towers on a black base; the South Pier light tower has a horizontal red band. Within the entrance the channel bears S, leaving the dolphin and the green perch with topmark to starboard.

Berthing

Berth as directed by the harbourmaster, usually alongside the SW quay below the swing bridge. Yachts that can take the ground may moor on the bank between the dolphin and the N quay, although this bank is subject to swell in onshore winds.

Harbourmaster

Office on East Quay ☎ 01624 812245.

Charges

There are harbour charges.

VHF radio telephone

Call *Ramsey Harbour* Ch 16, work Ch 12.

Facilities

Fuel Contact sailing club.
Water Tap on West Quay.
Provisions Full provisions are available in the town. EC Wednesday.
Post office Court Row, in town centre.
Yacht club Manx Sailing and Cruising Club, on West Quay. Bar and showers.
Calor Gas Manx Gas.

Laxey

⊕ 54°13'·2N 4°22'·6W 4 cables SE of harbour entrance
Local High Water is +0015 Dover
Charts Admiralty *2094*; Imray *Y70, C62*

General

A small drying harbour at the N end of Laxey Bay, at the mouth of the Laxey River. The Wheel of Laxey, above the main town, is one of the island's best-known sights. The mighty water wheel was constructed in 1854 to pump water out of the lead workings below Snaefell.

Warning

The harbour dries, and can only be entered for approximately 1½ hours either side of HW. There is

Ramsey inner harbour

a minimum of 2m in the harbour at MHWN, and 3·5m at MHWS. The harbour is only suitable for yachts that can take the ground. The inner harbour is well sheltered, but is full of local boats. The outer harbour is well sheltered from winds from SW through N to NE, but SE winds will bring an intolerable swell into this part of the harbour.

Approach

By day The harbour lies on the E side of Laxey Head, at the N end of Laxey Bay. Approach is straightforward, with no off-lying dangers. There is a conspicuous TV mast (142m) 3 cables W of the harbour.

By night It is necessary to identify the lights on either side of the entrance when making a night approach; the E jetty is lit Oc.G.3s7m5M and the W quay Oc.R.3s7m. The W quay light is obscured when bearing less than 318°.

Anchorage in the approach

Anchorage may be found in 3m sand to the S of the harbour entrance. There is a further anchorage in 3m sand in Garwick Bay, 1·2M to the S of the harbour. Both anchorages offer good holding in settled conditions or offshore winds.

Ramsey   *PRPA/Patrick Roach*

Approaching Laxey

Laxey outer harbour at high water

Laxey   *PRPA/Patrick Roach*

Entrance

Entrance is made between the E jetty, which has a white light tower with a green band, and the W quay, which has a white light tower with a red band. Keep close to the W quay on entering to avoid the patch of rocks extending S on the N side of the harbour entrance. Green perches mark the line of the river training wall; these must all be left to starboard.

Berthing

Berth alongside the W quay, which dries to a flat, firm bottom of sand and shingle. The inner harbour lies beyond this quay, but is likely to be crowded with local boats.

Harbourmaster

Office above inner harbour.

Charges

There are harbour charges.

VHF radio telephone

There is no VHF radio telephone at Laxey, although Douglas Harbour will advise the Laxey harbourmaster if a call is made to them.

Facilities

Water Tap on quay.

Slip On N side of inner harbour.

Provisions Limited provisions may be obtained close to the harbour. Full provisions are available in the main town, some 20 minutes' walk from the harbour. EC Thursday.

Post office There is a post office close to the harbour.

Yacht club Laxey Sailing Club, overlooking inner harbour.

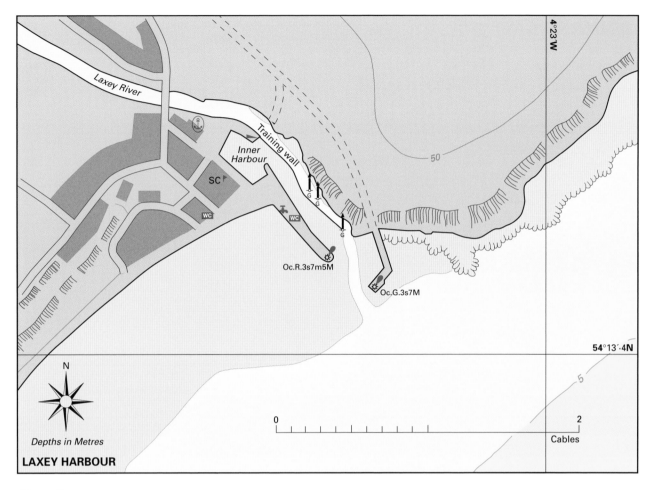

Oc.R.3s7m5M

Oc.G.3s7M

4°23'W

50

54°13'·4N

5

N

0   2

Cables

Depths in Metres

LAXEY HARBOUR

Laxey River

Training wall

Inner Harbour

SC

WC

WC

Douglas

⊕ 54°09'·03N 4°27'·53W 3 cables NE of harbour entrance
Local High Water is +0010 Dover
Charts Admiralty *2696, 2094*; Imray *Y70, C62*

General

The island's capital and chief port extends along the curve of Douglas Bay, with the harbour at its S end, at the mouth of the Douglas River. There is a considerable volume of ferry and commercial traffic. The outer harbour has water at all states of the tide, and is well sheltered, except that strong NE winds can send in a heavy swell. A new sill at the entrance has retained around 2m to 3m in the well sheltered inner harbour. There is a proposal for pontoons within this harbour to be available from spring 2001.

Warning

The volume of traffic using the harbour demands that a yacht should follow the displayed light signals and the directions of the harbourmaster at all times. The inner harbour is entered over a new flapgate allowing access 2½ hours either side of HW. The recently extended breakwater has improved shelter in the outer harbour, but strong NE winds will send in a heavy swell.

Approach

By day Douglas Head is seen as a bold headland when viewed from the NE or SW. The light is shown from a white tower near its extremity. The harbour entrance lies to the N of the headland. Conister or St Mary's Rock is a detached, drying ledge to the NNW of the harbour entrance; a castellated refuge tower stands on the highest part of the ledge. The approach to the harbour entrance is indicated by two leading marks to the W of the lifeboat house. The marks are white posts with red triangular topmarks, and are in line on a bearing of 229°. This course will leave the green conical buoys, Channel Markers Nos 1 and 2, to starboard.

There are International Port Traffic Signals shown by night or day as necessary from a mast at

Approaching Douglas from south

153

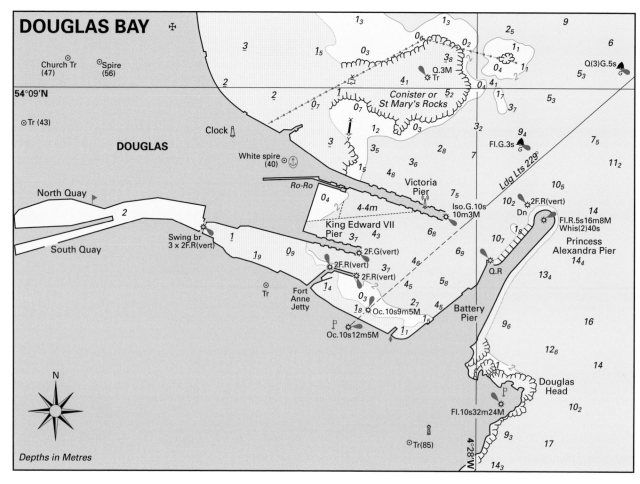

Douglas harbour entrance

the head of Victoria Pier. Three red vertical lights indicate that a vessel shall not proceed; two greens with a central white light shown vertically indicate that only specifically permitted vessels may proceed, and three green vertical lights indicate that vessels generally may proceed. Supplementary signals are shown below the lights, the panels having flashing amber lights on each top corner; a red cross indicates that vessels unless specified shall not proceed, and a white arrow indicates that vessels may proceed in the direction shown.

By night The harbour may be approached and entered using the following lights:

Douglas Head Fl.10s32m24M
Channel marker No.1 Q.G(3)5s4M
Channel marker No.2 Fl.G.3s5M
Dolphin 2F.R(vert)10m2M
Breakwater head Fl.R.5s16m8M Whis(2)40s
Battery Pier LtHo Q.R.12m1M
Victoria Pier Iso.G.10s10m3M
Ldg Lts 229·3° *Front* Oc.10s9m5M *Rear* Oc.10s12m5M

Entrance

The harbour is entered between the new breakwater and Victoria Pier. The dolphin at the end of the breakwater is left to port. The inner harbour is entered between King Edward VII Pier and Fort Anne Jetty.

Berthing

All berthing must be as directed by the harbourmaster. There is a black communal mooring buoy on the S side of the outer harbour; anchor off and take a stern line to the buoy. There is a landing pontoon at the inner end of Battery Pier where yachts may lie alongside. The proposed pontoon moorings should be available in the inner harbour from spring 2001.

Harbourmaster

In the Sea Terminal building, at the root of Victoria Pier ☎ 01624 686628.

Charges

There are harbour charges, which will be collected by the Harbour Patrol launch.

Douglas   *PRPA/Patrick Roach*

VHF radio telephone

Call *Douglas Harbour* Ch 16, work Ch 12.

Facilities

Fuel Contact harbourmaster to arrange supply.

Water Taps on Battery Pier and on the N quay of the inner harbour.

Slip Alongside Fort Anne Jetty.

Provisions Full provisions are available in the town. EC Thursday.

Post office Regent Street, in town centre.

Yacht club Douglas Motor Boat and Sailing Club. Bar and showers.

Calor Gas J. R. Riley Ltd.

Chandlery Manx Marine Ltd, on N side of inner harbour.

Derbyhaven

Good shelter may be found in winds from S through W to N in the anchorage between St Michael's Island and Ronaldsway Airport. There is a ruined fort on the NE end of the island, which is connected to the shore by a causeway. Rocky ledges shoal from the N side of St Michael's Island, which must be given a wide berth on the approach, as the tidal

stream (which is S-going for 9 hours) will invariably be setting a yacht in this direction. Anchorage should be in 3m sand and mud 2 or 3 cables E of the S end of the breakwater. The anchorage is untenable in E or NE winds, when a heavy swell sets into the bay. Some additional shelter may be found behind the detached breakwater for yachts that can take the ground. Entrance should be made round the S end of the breakwater, which has a white light tower with a green band (Iso.G.2s5m5M), leaving the perch marking the NE end of a rocky ledge to port. There is a depth of 3·5m at MHWN, and 5m at MHWS, at the entrance, gradually shoaling within. There are no facilities for yachts.

Langness Point

The promontory extends S along the E side of Castletown Bay. A light (Fl(2)30s23m12M) is shown from a white tower situated on Dreswick Point, the SE extremity of Langness. Tidal streams run strongly off the point, and overfalls develop with a contrary wind. With the E-going stream, a clockwise current develops in Castletown Bay and an anticlockwise current to the S of Santon Head. A race develops off Langness Point when these eddies meet the strength of the stream. With the W-going stream, there is a further eddy to the E side of Castletown Bay, causing a race as it meets the main stream to the S of the point.

Castletown

⊕ 54°02'·82N 4°38'·83W 1·5M S of harbour entrance
Local High Water is +0025 Dover
Charts Admiralty *2696, 2094*; Imray *Y70, C62*

General

Good shelter can be found in the drying harbour at Castletown, which was the capital of the island until 1874. The medieval fortress of Castle Rushen, formerly the home of the Viking kings of Man, dominates the harbour. The excellent Manx Nautical Museum is situated on the N side of the harbour.

Warning

The harbour dries, and should be entered between 2½ hours either side of HW. Strong SW winds will bring a swell into the outer harbour, reaching into the inner harbour above the bridge.

Approach

By day Castletown Bay is entered between Scarlett Point and Langness Point. The race and overfalls off Langness Point have been described above. The Skerranes are drying rocks extending SW from Langness Point. The Lheeah-rio Rocks are drying rocks on the W side of Castletown Bay; Boe Norris and Sandwick Boe are drying rocks on the N side of the bay. A red bell-buoy (Fl.R.3s) lies to the SE of the Lheeah-rio Rocks, and must be left to port. A straight course from this red buoy to the head of the breakwater will leave the other drying rocks to starboard.

By night The harbour can be approached and entered using the following lights:
Dreswick Point Fl(2)30s23m12M
Lheeah-rio Rocks buoy Fl.R.3s Bell
Outer breakwater Oc.R.15s8m5M
North side of entrance Oc.G.4s3m
Irish Quay Oc.R.4s5m5M
Swing bridge 2F.R(hor)

Anchorage in the approach

Anchorage may be found 2 cables SE of the harbour entrance, to the N of Lheeah-rio Rocks in 3m sand and gravel. The anchorage is exposed to SE to SW winds.

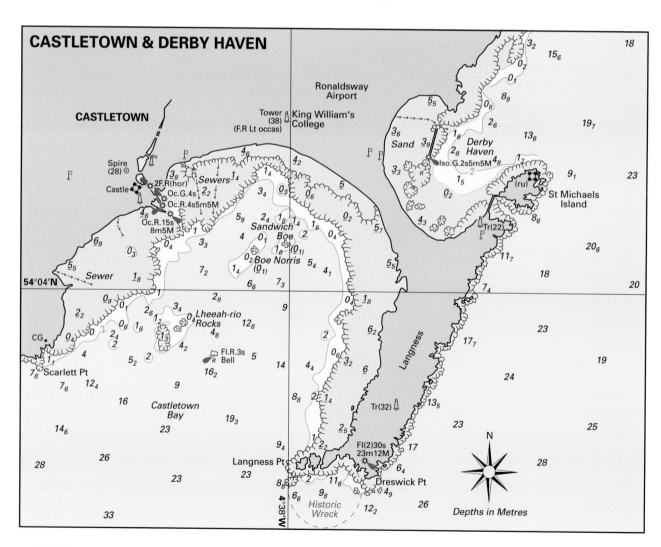

Approaching Castletown

Entrance

The harbour is entered leaving the outer breakwater, with a white light tower with a red band, to port. The outer harbour dries to firm sand and small stones. The inner harbour is entered between Irish Quay, which has a white light tower with a red stripe at its head, and the white perch with a green band marking the extremity of the rocks to the NE of the entrance, leaving the perch to starboard. The inner harbour is divided by the pedestrian swing bridge. Contact the harbourmaster to have the bridge opened.

Berthing

Berth as directed by the harbourmaster. Yachts can dry out alongside the quay of the outer harbour in suitable conditions. There are berths alongside Irish Quay and through the bridge in the inner harbour.

Harbourmaster

Office on Irish Quay.

Charges

There are harbour charges.

VHF radio telephone

Call *Castletown Harbour* Ch 16, work Ch 12, between the hours of 0830 and 1630. Port St Mary harbourmaster will reply to the call if the office at Castletown is not occupied.

Facilities

Fuel The harbourmaster can arrange to have fuel delivered from Port St Mary.
Water Taps on Irish Quay and by the Castle Arms, in inner harbour.

Castletown   *PRPA/Patrick Roach*

Castletown harbour entrance

Slip Outer harbour.
Provisions Full provisions are available in the town. EC Thursday.
Post office Parliament Square.
Showers Castletown Swimming Pool.
Calor Gas J. J. Clague Ltd, Arbory Street (near Town Hall).

Appendix

I. CHARTS
British Admiralty charts

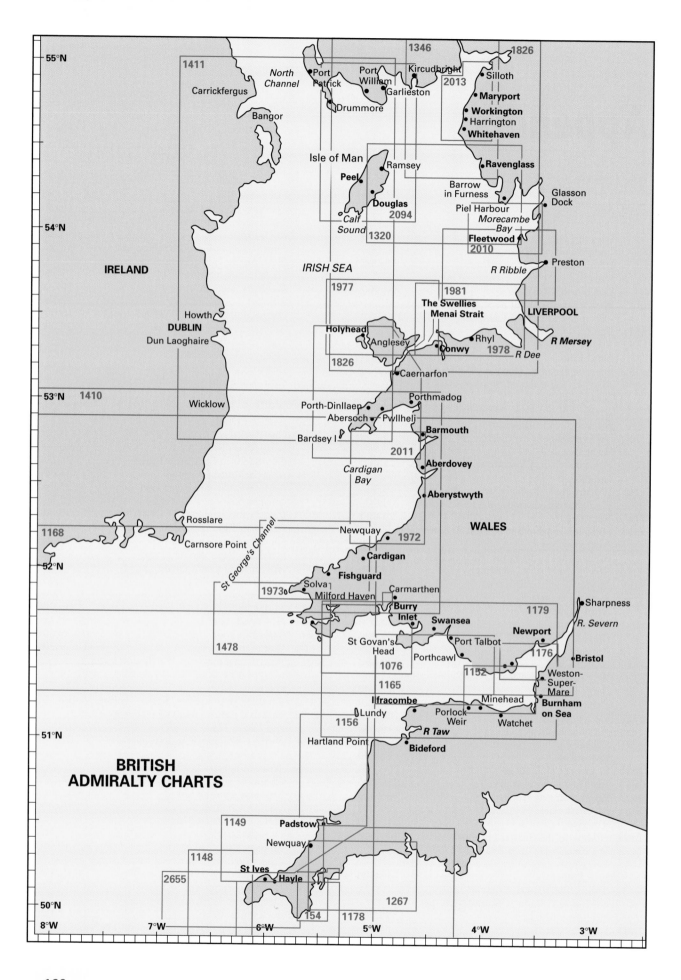

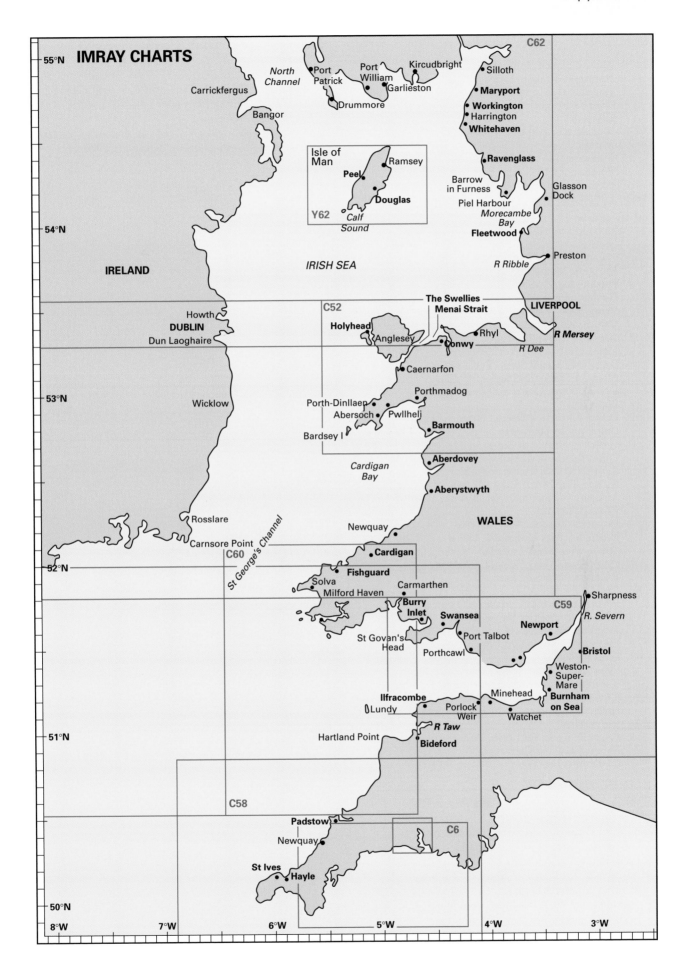

IMRAY CHARTS

55°N

North Channel
Carrickfergus
Bangor
Port Patrick
Port William
Garlieston
Drummore
Kircudbright
Silloth
Maryport
Workington
Harrington
Whitehaven
Ravenglass
Barrow in Furness
Piel Harbour
Morecambe Bay
Fleetwood
Glasson Dock
C62

Isle of Man
Peel
Ramsey
Douglas
Calf Sound
Y62

54°N

IRELAND
IRISH SEA
Preston
R Ribble

53°N

Howth
DUBLIN
Dun Laoghaire
The Swellies
Menai Strait
LIVERPOOL
C52
Holyhead
Anglesey
Rhyl
R Mersey
Conwy
R Dee
Caernarfon
Porthmadog
Wicklow
Porth-Dinllaen
Abersoch
Pwllheli
Barmouth
Bardsey I
Aberdovey
Cardigan Bay
Aberystwyth

Rosslare
Carnsore Point
Newquay
WALES
C60
St George's Channel
Cardigan

52°N

Fishguard
Solva
Milford Haven
Carmarthen
Sharpness
C59
Burry Inlet
R. Severn
Swansea
St Govan's Head
Port Talbot
Newport
Porthcawl
Bristol
Weston-Super-Mare
Ilfracombe
Minehead
Burnham on Sea
Lundy
Porlock Weir
Watchet
R Taw
Hartland Point
Bideford

51°N

C58
Padstow
Newquay
C6
St Ives
Hayle

50°N

8°W   7°W   6°W   5°W   4°W   3°W

Chart	Title	Scale
3275	Milford Haven: Milford dock to Picton Pt	12,500
	Pembroke Reach	5,000
	Continuation to River Cleddau	12,500
	Carew River; continuation of River Cleddau	50,000
3478	Manchester Ship Canal and upper Mersey	25,000
	Manchester docks: Runcorn and Western Point docks: Ellesmere Port and Stanlow oil docks: Partington basin	10,000
3490	Port of Liverpool	15,000

Imray charts

C7	Falmouth to Trevose Head and Isles of Scilly	100,000
	Plans: Newquay Bay, Penzance Harbour, Mousehold, Newlyn Harbour, Porthleven, St Mary's Road, Portreath	
C16	Western Approaches to the British Isles	612,800
	Plans: Brest, Falmouth, Milford Haven, Crosshaven, Crookhaven	
C52	Cardigan Bay to Liverpool	138,600
	Plans: Caernarfon, Port Dinorwic, Holyhead, Menai Strait, Porthmadog, Abersoch, Mochras Lagoon, Pwllheli, Conwy, Porth Dinllaen, The Swellies, Barmouth	
C59	Bristol Channel – Worms Head and Bull Point to Sharpness	114,500
C60	Gower Peninsula to Cardigan	127,700
	Plans: Jack Sound, Milford Haven, Ramsey Sound, Tenby and Caldy Islands, Fishguard, Solva	
C61	St George's Channel – Wales to the East Coast of Ireland	270,000
	Plans: Portmadoc, Aberystwyth, Tremadoc Bay, Barmouth, Menai Strait, Aberdovey, Cardigan, New Quay, Dublin Bay, Wexford, Arklow, Wicklow, Dunmore East	
C62	Irish Sea	280,000
	Plans: Entrance to Carlingford Lough, Portavogie, Skerries Bay, Kilkeel Harbour, Malahide Inlet, Ardglass, Entrance to Strangford Lough	
C63	Firth of Clyde	163,500
	Plans: Ayr, Troon, Irvine, East Loch Tarbert, Campbeltown, Ardrishaig, Crinan, Gourock, Rothesay, Rhu, Helensburgh, Largs, Lamlash, Millport	
Y70	Isle of Man	85,150
	Plans: Douglas, Port Erin, Peel, Ramsey, Bay Ny Carricky and Castletown Bay	

Cruising Anglesey, North West Venturers Yacht Club

Isle of Man Sailing Directions, Tidal Streams and Anchorages, Manx Sailing and Cruising Club

Solway Firth Sailing Directions and Anchorages, Solway SC, Kippford

The Yachtsman's Pilot - Clyde to Colonsay, Martin Lawrence, Imray, Laurie, Norie and Wilson

II. BIBLIOGRAPHY

West Coast of England and Wales Pilot NP37, Hydrographer of the Navy

Admiralty Tidal Stream Atlas Irish Sea NP256

The Cruising Almanac, Cruising Association, Imray. Biennial

Macmillan/Reeds Nautical Nautical Almanac. Annual. Nautical Data

Bristol Channel Yachting Conference Handbook, Bristol Channel Yachting Conference

Index